SUBVERSIVE SEQUELS
IN THE BIBLE

To Sonia,
It has been a pleasure
learning with you. I hope you
enjoy.
ג'ודי קליצנר

SUBVERSIVE SEQUELS IN THE BIBLE

How Biblical Stories Mine and Undermine Each Other

JUDY KLITSNER

2009 • 5770
The Jewish Publication Society
Philadelphia

JPS is a nonprofit educational association and the oldest and foremost publisher of Judaica in English in North America. The mission of JPS is to enhance Jewish culture by promoting the dissemination of religious and secular works, in the United States and abroad, to all individuals and institutions interested in past and contemporary Jewish life.

The Jewish Publication Society
2100 Arch Street, 2nd floor
Philadelphia, PA 19103
www.jewishpub.org

Design and composition by Desperate Hours Productions

Manufactured in the United States of America

09 10 11 12   10 9 8 7 6 5 4 3 2 1

Library of Congress Cataloging-in-Publication Data

Klitsner, G'udi.
 Subversive sequels in the Bible: how biblical stories mine and undermine each other / Judy Klitsner. -- 1st ed.
    p. cm.
 Includes bibliographical references and index.
 ISBN 978-0-8276-0888-7
 1. Bible. O.T. Pentateuch--Criticism, interpretation, etc. 2. Bible. O.T. Pentateuch--Feminist criticism. 3. Women in the Bible. I. Title.
 BS1225.52.K56 2009
 222'.1066082--dc22

2009006134

JPS books are available at discounts for bulk purchases for reading groups, special sales, and fundraising purchases. Custom editions, including personalized covers, can be created in larger quantities for special needs. For more information, please contact us at marketing@jewishpub.org or at this address: 2100 Arch Street, Philadelphia, PA 19103.

To my father, Israel Freistat, whose years, like those of the patriarch Jacob/Israel, were few and filled with struggle and with the giving and receiving of unbridled love.

And to my children: Akiva, Noam, Nechama, Yisrael, and Amitai; their spouses: Ariella, Eliad, and Laurie; and to my grandson, Mikey. Their lives are composing my father's most eloquent possible sequel.

לעשות רצונך אלהי חפצתי ותורתך בתוך מעי

To do what pleases you, my God, is my desire; Your Torah is in my innermost parts.

—Proverbs 40:9

Contents

Preface

A Note on Bible Translations and Abbreviations

Unless otherwise stated, my translations of the biblical text are taken from the New Jewish Publication Society TANAKH. In most cases, I deviate from the NJPS translation when I want to highlight word repetitions or to emphasize unusual or problematic language in the original Hebrew verse. What is lost in this approach is a certain degree of colloquial and syntactic smoothness. What is gained is an opportunity to access the many nuances of the original text, which often serve as a basis for deeper insight and creative exploration. In my translations, I have been particularly insistent on translating recurring words in a uniform way, rather than seeking synonyms to break up potential reader tedium. These repetitions form the basis of much of the work ahead. They serve as foundations in spotting patterns within passages and in locating parallels between texts.

Where I have differed from the NJPS translation, I have indicated as much, even if I have changed only a word or two. Thus, my frequent notes indicating "author's translation" are usually NJPS translations with slight modifications. In one case I have altered the NJPS translation without note. In my analysis of Genesis 1–3, I have substituted the word "humanity" for "man" in cases where I felt the strict sense of the text warranted the change. I did not note this change, as I felt it was consistent with the guiding principles of the NJPS literary style as seen in its many publications. I believe this decision is borne out in NJPS's *The Contemporary Torah,* a gender-sensitive translation of the Bible, in which, wherever necessary, masculine forms are replaced with more neutral terms.

With an awareness of sensitivities to the issue, I refer to God in this book in the traditional form, as "He," a translation of the Hebrew pronoun used in the Bible. I do this only in order to avoid stylistic awkwardness and not to attribute masculine gender to God.

All citations of classic Jewish commentaries are taken from the standard Rabbinic Bible (*Mikra'ot Gedolot*). Translations of Hebrew commentaries are the author's unless otherwise indicated.

The abbreviation "s.v." appears frequently in this volume. It stands for the Latin *sub verbo* ("under the word"), and is used to indicate the word or words in the biblical verse that the commentator is addressing.

In the coming chapters, I conduct close readings of biblical texts. Although I have provided English translations of all relevant passages, I strongly recommend reading this book together with an open Bible, and to whatever extent possible, consulting the original Hebrew.

Acknowledgments

In the long process of constructing this work about the Bible, I have frequently identified with the sentiment expressed by the biblical Jacob: *katonti mi-kol ha-hasadim*, I am unworthy of all the kindnesses. I have been on the receiving end of a great deal of generosity on the part of scholars, teachers, family, and friends; to all of them I am greatly indebted.

I am privileged to have studied with my generation's outstanding Bible scholar and pedagogue, Nehama Leibowitz, of blessed memory. Nehama's methodology—including careful attention to literary nuance and anomaly and close attention to fine distinctions in parallel texts—is all-pervasive in this work, as is her spirit of passion and respect for the written word. I am grateful to my very gifted teacher, David Silber, for opening my eyes to the wonderful surprises and deep insights to be culled from straightforward, unapologetic readings of the matriarchal and patriarchal narratives and to the expansive interpretive potential of intertextual readings.

When I list the educational influences in my life, I must include my students at the Pardes Institute of Jewish Studies, who, over the past two decades, have not ceased to inspire and challenge me. Unencumbered by, and often unimpressed with conventional or traditional interpretation, they have enabled me (and at times have left me no choice other than) to continue approaching oft-studied texts in fresh, new ways, seeing the text, as Rashi instructs, "as if it had been given today." With the help of their probing questions and creative suggestions, many of my ideas have undergone regular rethinking and revision. The results of this process permeate the six chapters of this book.

I am grateful to the administration and faculty of the Pardes Institute for fostering an environment of open inquiry in which new ideas are free to flourish.

I want to express my sincere thanks to my mentors and colleagues, whom I am fortunate to count as close friends. Daniel Schwartz and Martin Lockshin—two distinguished scholars, who are also active contributors to their communities—were somehow never too busy to read my manuscript in its various stages of lucidity, to offer insightful critique, constructive suggestions, and much-needed encouragement.

Aviva Zornberg—extraordinary teacher and author with an uncommon gift for revealing profound human truths in our ancient texts—has been a generous listener, a kind critic, and as always, a supportive friend.

In addition, the following colleagues and friends have offered greatly valued assistance: Ruth Lockshin, Baruch Feldstern, Cory Shulman Brody, Marc Brettler, Larry Krule, Susan Fader, Laya Silber, Eugene Korn, Tova Hartman, and Walter Herzberg. I am thankful to David Winick for calmly and graciously quelling my frequent computer crises.

I am grateful to the three wonderful editors who have helped me in different stages of this project. Ilana Kurshan, Ilene Prushure, and Benjamin Balint have been enthusiastic, intelligent, and understanding readers, and each has made a significant contribution to the coherence of the book.

I offer my sincere thanks to the very supportive and learned editors at JPS. It has been my pleasure and privilege to receive the guidance of Ellen Frankel and Rena Potok, and to benefit from the skilled direction of Carol Hupping, Janet Liss, Laurie Schlesinger, Anita Bihovsky, Julia Ostreich, and Robin Norman.

For inspiration in my chapters about the matriarchs, I have drawn on the remarkable living examples of my mother, Ruth Freistat, and my mother-in-law, Jane Klitsner. I am thankful to them and to their matriarchal models, Hannah Schectman and Anna Traxler, z"l.

My father-in-law, Marvin Klitsner, is sorely missed. The model of moral excellence and fearless integrity that he set during his life helped me to identify and to write about the crucial elements of outstanding leadership.

My deepest gratitude is to my husband, Shmuel (Steven) Klitsner, whose scholarly and practical contributions to this work are too great to enumerate. I have no doubt that the optimistic approach to gender equality that I have expressed in this book stems in large part from my own privileged position of living with an *ezer kenegdi*, a life partner who demonstrates a virtually endless capacity to both support and challenge me. Throughout the process of writing, he has fulfilled this dual role valiantly, acting as my greatest helper and most incisive critic. (In the latter role, he made sure to point out when some of my more outlandish textual parallels on the topic of women and fertility suffered from "stretchmarks.")

To my husband and children, I am thankful for the great patience and resourcefulness exhibited during the years of my preoccupation with this work. They gave me time when I needed it, good-humored distraction when I craved it, and moral support when I was depleted of it. But above all, I am thankful to them for the very dynamic paths our lives have taken. Their blessed nonconformity has helped me to understand that stories with unexpected turns and with ongoing revisions are the most fascinating stories of all.

• • •

I am grateful to Urim Publications for granting permission to print an expanded version of my article "From the Earth's Hollow Spaces to the Stars: Two Patriarchs and Their Non-Israelite Mentors" in chapter 3 of the present work. The original article appeared in *The Torah of the Mothers*, edited by Ora Wiskind Elper and Susan Handelman. Jerusalem: Urim Publications, 2000.

I am grateful to the Pardes Institute of Jewish Studies for their permission to print an expanded version of my article "The Spiritual Quest of the Matriarchy" in chapter 6 of this work. The original article appeared in *The Pardes Reader*, edited by Felice Kahn Zisken. Jerusalem: The Pardes Institute, 1997.

E

Introduction

Irrefutably, indestructibly, never wearied by time, the Bible wanders through the ages ...
It speaks in every language and in every age ... In fact, it is still at the very beginning of its
career, the full meaning of its content having hardly touched the threshold of our minds;
like an ocean at the bottom of which countless pearls lie, waiting to be discovered ...

—Abraham Joshua Heschel[1]

Heschel's words stand as a challenge to the modern reader. Indeed, for two thousand years we have kept our ancient text alive. We study it and revere it; we chant it weekly. But have we allowed it to "speak in every language in every age"? Do we trust that if we plunge deeply enough into its oceanic depths, we will reach the treasures that await us there?

Despite Heschel's claims as to the Bible's timeless relevance and accessibility, its words are frequently baffling. Sometimes the Bible's narrative voice is so expansive that its stories appear unnecessarily verbose and repetitive. At other times, the text's style is so terse that basic questions concerning the motives and actions of its characters are left unexplained. At times, the internal logic of a story breaks down; sometimes the information given in one story contradicts that of another. Rules of grammar and syntax are consistent, until we find that occasionally they are not. And most troubling of all, even if we manage to decode its language and familiarize ourselves with its style, we may find ourselves distanced and at times offended by its morality. How is a modern sensibility to relate to a text in which God responds to a sinful world by destroying it wholesale? What are we to make of a narrative— one that ostensibly speaks "in every language and in every age"—that exhibits a

---

1. Heschel, *God in Search of Man*, 242.

preference for male protagonists, prophets and leaders, and that has God and man marginalizing the female characters within its pages?

There are no simple or formulaic answers to these questions, but I will propose a particular type of textual analysis, literary in nature, that at the very least reframes the questions themselves.[2] As if aware of its own problematics, the Bible contains a lively interaction between its passages that allows for a widening of perspective and a sense of dynamic development throughout the canon. As we will see in the six chapters of this book, if certain gnawing theological or philosophical questions remain after studying one narrative, a later passage may revisit those questions, subjecting them to a complex process of inquiry, revision, and examination of alternative possibilities. I call these reworkings "subversive sequels." Like all sequels, they continue and complete earlier stories. But they do so in ways that often undermine the very assumptions upon which the earlier stories were built as well as the conclusions these stories have reached.

For example, the woman in Genesis 3 is portrayed in ways that may deeply affront a modern sensibility. God holds her largely to blame for man's downfall, telling Adam, "Because you *listened to the voice of your wife* and ate of the tree ... cursed is the ground ..." (Gen. 3:17).[3] As a result of her actions, woman is pronounced subservient and weak: "Your urge shall be for your husband and he shall rule over you" (v. 16). How are we to relate to a narrative that is so dissonant to our ears? Historically, readers have moved in two directions. They have either rejected the validity of such texts, dismissing them as anachronistic and irrelevant, or have accepted them as authoritative and unyielding—as some expression of eternal truths. In *Subversive Sequels*, I have suggested a third option, in which the Bible's words carry the gravitas of revered tradition, but are nonetheless subject to an internal process of radical revision that takes place throughout the canon. As we will see in chapter 5 of this volume, Genesis 21 will revisit Genesis 3 in order to recast it in a new light. While in Genesis 3, God faults man for "listening to the voice of his wife" (3:17), in Genesis 21 God actively instructs the male protagonist to "listen to the voice" of his wife in *all that she says* (21:12).[4] Such rescripting underscores the variety of biblical attitudes toward male-female interaction, as well as the Bible's affinity for movement and change. Although the initial tale of

---

2. For an expansion on a literary approach to Bible interpretation, see the next heading in this introduction.

3. Author's translation.

4. Ibid.

woman's subordination remains on record, it becomes part of a larger chronicle of woman's emerging inclusion and enablement.

While fundamental questions such as biblical attitudes in gender relations may continue to confound and disturb, they now belong to a chorus, at times harmonious and at times discordant, that comes from within the sequels of the canon. As careful readers of the text, we add our own interpretive voices to this multi-tonal concert that began in the pages of the Bible itself.

Close Readings: A Literary Approach

On the way to the subversive sequel, and as part of an ongoing effort to submerge ourselves in the text's infinite depths, we will embrace a literary approach to interpretation. In doing so, we will pay close attention to formal literary elements such as structure, context, grammar, syntax, tone, sound, convention, repetition, and imagery, as well as to aspects of content such as theme, motif, metaphor, character analysis, and much more. Although much of this literary focus is on minute detail, such an approach holds vast potential to afford deeper understanding of the text's messages. Literary readings of the Bible are not new; they were widely employed by the ancient midrash and in medieval commentary. Robert Alter, one of the foremost modern practitioners of this approach, elaborates on its significance:

> What we need to understand better is that the religious vision of the Bible is given depth and subtlety precisely by being conveyed through the most sophisticated resources of prose fiction ... The biblical tale, through the most rigorous economy of means, leads us again and again to ponder the complexities of motive and ambiguities of character, because these are essential aspects of its vision of man, created by God, enjoying or suffering all the consequences of human freedom ... Almost the whole range of biblical narrative ... embodies the basic perception that man must live before God, in the transforming medium of time, incessantly and perplexingly in relation with others; and a literary perspective on the operations of narrative may help us more than any other to see how this perception was translated into stories that have had such a powerful, enduring hold on the imagination.[5]

---

5. Alter, *The Art of Biblical Narrative*, 22.

In addition to demonstrating a keen sensitivity to textual nuance, both ancient and modern proponents of the literary method call our attention to a complex
network of literary connections—referred to by moderns as intertextual links—
among biblical passages. These connections contain vast interpretive potential, as
suggested by the following midrashic anecdote :

> When Ben Azzai sat and interpreted [the biblical text], fire surrounded him
> ... Rabbi Akiva went to him and said, "I heard that when you interpreted, fire
> flashed around you ... were you involved with the secrets of God's heavenly
> chariot?"[6] He said, "No, I was sitting and linking together the words of the
> Torah, and linking the words of the Torah with the words of the Prophets,
> and the words of the Prophets with the words of the Writings. The words
> were as joyous as the day they were given at Sinai, and they were as sweet as
> they were at their original pronouncement."[7]

In this view, the literary interconnections within the Bible have the power to
provide insights even more profound than those emanating from the most esoteric
religious compositions. While many interpretive methods yield deep insights into
the text, those who embrace the Bible's intertextuality may, according to Ben Azzai,
feel the scorching heat of God's fire lapping at their feet.

Application of a Literary Approach: Text and Intertext
in the Study of the Akeda

One of the most familiar, yet inscrutable narratives in the Bible is the story of
the *Akeda,* the Binding of Isaac (Genesis 22). If we were to use a literary approach to

---

6. The midrash refers to the rabbinic notion of studying the *ma'aseh merkavah,* a speculative inquiry into
the esoteric details of God's unknown domain. See *Hagiga* 2a.

7. *Song of Songs Rabbah,* I. 10. 2. We find other allusions to the centrality of an intertextual approach elsewhere
in the midrash, for instance, in the Jerusalem Talmud *Rosh Hashanah* 3:5, 58d: "The text is expansive in certain places and deficient in others." While the plain meaning of this statement is that information that is
missing in one passage is at times explicitly supplied in another, we might extend it to the midrashic practice
of learning about an inexplicit narrative from its clearer literary parallel. A later statement on the comple-
mentary nature of intertextual parallels may be found in the 32 hermeneutical principles attributed to R.
Eliezer son of R. Yossi Ha-Gelili (the principles are chiefly aggadic, and are generally considered to be post-
Talmudic). Principle 17 states, "A text is not fully expounded in its place, but is fully expounded in another."
Other midrashic concepts that call for intertextual readings are *hada hu dikhtiv,* "this is as is written [else-
where in the Bible]" and *middah keneged middah,* a poetic quid pro quo of crime and punishment.

interpret this narrative, we would note that one of its outstanding features is the repetitious presence of certain words that weave their way throughout the passage, gently guiding us toward central themes that the text wishes to highlight.[8]

For instance, the insistent recurrence throughout the chapter of the verb r-h, to see, marks Abraham's progress in understanding the divine will. At the chapter's opening, Abraham's vision is distant, as he "sees the place from afar" (Gen. 22:4). Yet by the end of the passage, his view is clear and immediate. He "sees" the ram, which he understands must be substituted for his son (22:13). Abraham's unfolding vision acts as a metaphor for his developing grasp of God's true intentions. Ultimately, he discovers that despite God's initial command to offer Isaac up on an altar, God does not, in fact, desire human sacrifice. It is at this point that Abraham names the place "the LORD will see," claiming that from this point forward divine-human visibility may be both clear and reciprocal: "And Abraham named that site 'the LORD will see,' whence the present saying, "On the mount of the LORD He will be seen"[9] (v. 14).[10]

But close readings with an emphasis on word repetition often prove inadequate, as they do not always address the most gnawing philosophical questions posed by the text. In the case of the *Akeda*, we are met with an ostensibly happy ending in which God and man are in visual and ideological harmony. Yet we remain troubled by the very premises on which the story is based: God's unethical demand for Abraham to slaughter his son and Abraham's seemingly unquestioning compliance with this dubious decree.

In search of responses to outstanding issues such as these, we reach beyond the scope of the passage itself and into to the realm of intertext, in which we seek out literary relationships between various passages within the canon. Perhaps by holding this enigmatic passage up against its literary parallel elsewhere in the Bible, we might draw closer to understanding its perplexing messages.

---

8. On the recurrence of such key "guiding words" as conduits to meaning, Buber has commented: "Such measured repetition, corresponding to the inner rhythm of the text—or rather issuing from it—is probably the strongest of all techniques available for making a meaning available without articulating it explicitly ... Those who listen will hear the higher meaning in the similarity of sound. A connection is established between one passage and another and thus between one stage of the story and another—a connection that articulates the deep motive of the narrative event more immediately than could a pinned-on moral." Buber, *Scripture and Translation*, 116. Throughout this volume on the Bible's subversive sequels, we will pay close attention to the text's use of the guiding word—*leitwort* in German—in an effort to heed its inherent messages.

9. Author's translation.

10. See Buber, *On the Bible*, 42. Buber elaborates on the function of the key word "to see" throughout the Abraham narrative.

Our search is guided by an anticlimactic epilogue to the *Akeda* story in Genesis, which provides a key to the intertextual link:

> Some time later, Abraham was told, "Milcah too has borne children to your brother Nahor: Uz the first-born, and Buz his brother and Kemuel the father of Aram; and Cesed, Hazo, Pildash, Jidlaph, and Bethuel"—Bethuel being the father of Rebekah. (Gen. 22:20–23)

If we look closely at these names, we note that they serve as a point of departure for another text, one that appears much later in the canon, and that will engage in a literary interpretive dialogue with the story of the binding of Isaac. Specifically, names of the characters in the Genesis story resurface, reconfigured as place names tied to key characters in the Book of Job. These similarities are especially noteworthy in that the names in question rarely appear elsewhere in the Bible.[11] Moreover, the sheer number of cross-references of such obscure names between these two biblical books renders them worthy of comparison.

The first such link takes the name of Nahor's first born, **Uz**, and recasts it in the Book of Job as the name of the title character's place of residence:[12] "There was a man in the land of **Uz** named Job" (Job 1:1).

Another character from the end of the Abraham narrative that finds his way into the Book of Job is **Buz**, brother of Uz. Buz is listed as the place of origin of one of Job's friends: "Then Elihu son of Barachel the **Buzite**, of the family of Ram, was angry—angry at Job because he thought himself right against God" (Job 32:2).

Still another brother, **Cesed** receives a literary nod: "This one was still speaking when another came and said, 'A Chaldean formation, *Casdim*[13] (plural of *Cesed*), of three columns made a raid on the camels and carried them off and put the boys to the sword; I alone have escaped to tell you'" (Job 1:17).

---

11. Aside from the *Akeda* story, Uz appears as a name in two other places in the Pentateuch; two of these names are then repeated in Chronicles. Uz is the name of a place in two verses outside of Job. Buz appears as a name in three places outside of the *Akeda* and Job narratives. As a name, Cesed appears only in the *Akeda* story; the nation Casdim appears many times.

12. In the Bible, it is common for names of people to reappear as names of places. For example, see Gen. 10:4,6, in which the names Javan, Mitzrayim, and Canaan refer to individuals. Later, they will all become well known as the names of nations.

13. The plural form of Cesed points to another Abraham-Job comparison: Abraham's birth place is *Ur Casdim* (plural of **Cesed**). Gen. 11:28.

These subtle echoes from one story to the next guide us toward a broader comparison of the two narratives. Upon closer examination, we note that the linguistic interconnections extend not only to names of people and places, but to basic concepts as well. For example, the climax of the story of the binding of Isaac comes when God bestows a rare accolade upon Abraham:[14] "Now I know that you are **God-fearing,** *yere Elohim*"[15] (Gen. 22:12). Similarly, at the beginning of the book that bears his name, Job is described as "blameless and upright; he was **God-fearing,** *yere Elohim,* and shunned evil" (1:2). Lest we miss the connection between Job and Abraham, at the book's end Job claims that he is but **dust and ashes,** *afar va-efer* (42:6), a self-reference employed by only one other biblical figure, Abraham. "Abraham spoke up saying, 'Here I venture to speak to my LORD, I who am but **dust and ashes,** *afar va-efer*'" (Gen. 18:27). Moreover, despite their suffering, both men find peace at the end of their lives. "And Abraham breathed his last, dying at a **good** ripe age, **old and contented,** *zaken ve-s-v-ʿ* (Gen. 25:8)." Similarly: "So Job died **old and contented,** *zaken u-s-v-ʿyamim*" (Job 42:17).[16]

If the number of linguistic similarities between the two stories is striking, the rare nature of the shared terms and concepts is yet more impressive. But what are we to make of all these connections? As we have seen, a central tenet of the literary school of interpretation is the notion that the Bible, in its constant replaying of its stories, invites comparison and interpretation of certain passages in the light of others. The language parallels we have seen point to more significant parallels of structure and theme.[17]

In the stories of Abraham and Job, some basic similarities are obvious, such as the featuring of God-fearing men who face a mortal threat by God to their offspring. But the two stories play upon each other in more complex ways as well. For example, while the *Akeda* ended with God's faithful servant receiving the title "God-fearing," the Book of Job *begins* by bestowing this distinction upon its hero. This sequencing suggests the presence of a sequel in that the Book of Job begins where the story of the *Akeda* ended.

---

14. Abraham and Job are the only two individual biblical characters to be defined either by the text's narrative voice or by God as *yere Elohim.*
15. Author's translation.
16. Abraham and Job are two of only four biblical characters for whom this formula is used.
17. Many, but not all of these connections have been noted and expounded by Yeshayahu Leibowitz in *Judaism, the Jewish Nation, and the State of Israel,* 393-94.

But the Book of Job is no ordinary sequel to the Abraham narrative. While the conventional sequel extends the original, bringing it to its logical conclusions, the biblical sequel, which is often subversive in nature, takes the original story back to its beginnings. It then challenges the very premises on which the story is built and reworks many of its conclusions. As we have seen, the *Akeda* left us with an uneasy equilibrium. Although God threatened to overturn the divine system of justice by demanding the death of an innocent youth, in the end, God restores order as His angel instructs Abraham to spare Isaac. The subversive sequel refuses to accept this unnaturally sanguine conclusion, instead demanding further analysis. This type of sequel poses a series of "what if" questions: What if—as is frequently the case in the real world—the evil decree is not miraculously repealed at the last moment and the innocent actually suffer? We wonder what the God-fearing human hero might say, were his mouth to be unsealed and he could protest the injustice. Would God tolerate his objections? Might God reverse, or even apologize for, undeserved human anguish?

The Book of Job takes up these questions by placing its hero in circumstances that are similar to those of Abraham, but exacerbated. As we have seen, both stories feature the suffering of righteous men as their children are imperiled by God. But the story quickly spins in a radically new direction when, in the Book of Job, God actually allows the blameless children to die. Moreover, ratcheting up the injustice, the hero loses not one, but ten children.

These differences lead to the most striking point of contrast between the two stories, which is Abraham's silent compliance with God's plan to kill the innocent as opposed to Job's outspoken objections to God's injustice. Abraham proved his ability to call God to task in Sodom when he boldly insisted that a just God must act justly (Gen. 18:25). But at the *Akeda*, Abraham's assertive stance gives way to an unquestioning compliance with God's morally perplexing decree.[18] In the end, God is pleased with Abraham's willingness to obey Him (22:12) and seemingly with Abraham's silence as well. In contrast, as Job's life is unjustly shattered, the hero rejects all attempts to accept God's actions as justified and

---

18. Abraham's compliance may be detected in the string of action verbs (in Gen. 22:3), unaccompanied by questions or objections, that constitute his response to God's command. "Abraham *arose* early in the morning and he *saddled* his ass and he *took* his two lads with him as well as his son Isaac and he *split* the wood for the burnt offering and he *arose* and he *went* to the place of which God had told him" (22:3).

instead demands answers from God with ever-increasing audacity. Yet despite his contentious words, so antithetical to the wordless obedience of the God-fearing Abraham, God upholds Job's responses over those of his friends, God's apologists. God instructs Job's friends to bring sacrifices and to have Job pray for them, "since you have not spoken to Me correctly as did My servant Job" (42:8). In this, the subversive sequel to the binding of Isaac narrative, to be God's beloved servant no longer requires voiceless acceptance of all God's actions and decrees. Rather it is to protest God's injustice and to demand a quality of life commensurate with one's deeds.

The subversive sequel adds a dimension of exegesis that is inaccessible through close readings and ordinary intertextual comparisons alone. By focusing not only on similarities between texts, but on the ongoing revisions of the Bible's stories, the subversive sequel measures the dynamic movement that takes place between one story and another. In the example of Abraham and Job, this type of analysis tracks the hero as he evolves from God's stalwart soldier into an unrelenting critic of the divine right to wreak injustice upon the world.

God and the Subversive Sequel

The subversive sequel reveals the development not only of its human protagonists, but of God as well. From the *Akeda* to the Book of Job, God's responses to the tormented hero have dramatically changed. While God congratulates Abraham for his unquestioning acceptance of the divine will, He commends Job for his insistent challenging of God's actions.

For many readers, the notion of the dynamic nature of humanity may be far more palatable than ascribing an evolutionary nature to God. But the concept of God's development is not new in Jewish tradition. It is evident in numerous Kabbalistic[19] and midrashic[20] texts, and modern scholars have found ample evidence of it throughout

---

19. See Idel, *Kabbalah, New Perspectives*, 159. Idel defines the notion of theurgy as God being literally affected—He is diminished or empowered—by human actions. Thus God is constantly changing.

20. In the midrashic view, God's development is expressed in different aspects of God that are manifest in different situations. For example, the following appears in Gen. Rabbah 12:15 (quoted by Rashi, Gen. 1:1, s.v. *bara Elohim*) and in the anonymous *Midrash Aggadah* (referred to in *Torah Shelema*, vol. 1 p. 33, footnote 209, referring to Gen. 1:1, s.v. *bereishit bara*): "God initially considered creating the world with the quality of justice alone; when He saw that the world could not survive, He combined it with the quality of mercy."

the Bible's pages.[21] By viewing God as a literary character and by monitoring His development between one biblical story and the next, we are privy to one of the central and most consistent messages of the canon as a whole, namely, the ideal of constant movement and growth.

God, who is to be distinguished from the omniscient narrative voice of the text, is complex as a literary character. At times He is transcendent and infallible. He instructs His followers to be holy "for I the LORD your God am holy" (Lev. 19:2). This God figure is worthy of direct emulation. As the Talmud states: "Just as He is gracious and compassionate, so should you be gracious and compassionate."[22]

Yet in other instances, God is described in imperfect, shockingly human terms: God is "sad" (Gen. 6:6), and "jealous" (Exod. 20:5). God may even "regret" His ways (Gen. 6:6) and learn from prior experience—as seen in God's decision never to repeat the type of wholesale destruction enacted in the Great Flood (Gen. 9:21), and as seen later in our analysis of Noah and Jonah. How are we to reconcile these divergent images of the biblical God?

Perhaps these conflicting views are both presented to humanity for emulation. The first is an ideal: a distant, largely unattainable goal for human striving. The second, found primarily in the narratives of the Pentateuch, is translated into terms that human beings can more easily relate to and comprehend.[23] The attributes ascribed to God in these passages do not delimit and define the transcendent. They are meant to call to mind our own emotions, reactions, and even our

---

21. For example, Muffs, *The Personhood of God*, 4, claims the following: "God was a king who in His youth behaved one way and in His older age, poetically speaking, yet another. Having learned from His mistakes, He now allowed His mercy ... to overcome His anger. God could be worshipped by man since He was so much like Him. He constantly appeared in many and ever-changing roles lest He be frozen and converted into the dumb idols He himself despised. God was a polyvalent personality who, by mirroring to man His many faces, provided the models that man so needed to survive and flourish." I am grateful to David Hartman for directing me to Muffs' book.

22. *Shabbat* 133b.

23. The idea that the Bible translates statements about the divine into language that is comprehensible to human beings is in line with the rabbinic statement that originates in the Talmud (*Berakhot* 31b): *Dibbera Torah kileshon benei adam*, the Bible speaks in language that is understandable and recognizable to its human readers. The entire structure of the Kabbalistic and Hassidic conceptions that distinguish between the infinite (*ein sof*) and God's emanations is geared to allow for a static abstract God to coexist with the dynamic, immanent God found in the Bible and in the religious experience of historical circumstance.

growth patterns.[24] God may be seen as furious and destructive in one situation. He may then "correct" that behavior by reacting with equanimity and patience in a similar instance. By His very changeability, this God models a dynamic response to circumstance. Extending the midrashic dictum on emulating God, "Just as He is gracious and compassionate, so should you be gracious and compassionate," we might say, "Just as He is dynamic so should you be dynamic."

Subversive Sequels: How Biblical Stories Mine and Undermine Each Other

Throughout the coming pages, we will follow the process described above, reading individual passages closely, and then presenting parallel texts that serve as their subversive sequels. To illustrate this method, I have chosen two basic themes. The first three chapters of the book address questions related to the self. These include the struggle for individuality and the relationship between the individual and community, between Israelite and non-Israelite, and between the individual and God. The final three chapters are concerned with gender relations, highlighting God's role in the evolution of those relations.

In chapter 1, we will compare two stories that share the themes of hazardous waters, the threat of wholesale destruction and the transformative potential of the human being. The first of the pair, the story of Noah, is the more straightforward narrative; through our close reading we will reveal new insights into Noah's psyche. The second of the two stories, the Book of Jonah, is much more cryptic, given that the motives and attitudes of its protagonist are quite elusive. We will analyze the more difficult story of Jonah by identifying it as a subversive reworking of the earlier story, noting the many ways in which it questions and overturns the assumptions and conclusions of the Noah narrative. In these two stories, God acts as a model for change, while humanity remains uncertain of its ability to transform itself.

In chapter 2, an unlikely pair of stories is compared, both of which feature the building of massive structures, and both of which highlight a fear of wide-scale human proliferation. The enigmatic story of the Tower of Babel will find elucidation in

---

24. Muffs expands on the idea of the Bible's portrayal of God reflecting human perspectives and emotions. Muffs claims that the Bible purposely presents a diverse array of prophets, each of whom "sees what he can of the infinite spectrum of the divine self. In the last analysis, we are only capable of knowing that which is akin to ourselves. This is why it was necessary to send many prophets, of different emotional makeups: together, they enable us to fathom the Divine from many points of view." Muffs, *Personhood*, 87.

the chronicle of the Israelite enslavement in Egypt (Exod. 1). Both stories include the erasure of names, which suggests subjection through the suppression of the individual. Both stories culminate in the resurgence of individuals—Abraham in the Babel narrative and the Hebrew midwives in the Exodus story. These figures will restore names to the narrative by defying conventional ideologies. We will see, then, how the Exodus story serves as subversive sequel to the Tower of Babel narrative, for in the second story, instead of succumbing to the forces of conformity (as in the story of Babel), humanity finds the courage to rescue itself, asserting individuality in the face of totalitarian repression. This chapter will shift the focus from God to humankind as the primary instrument of change, since it highlights the role of individuality in humanity's search for godliness.

Chapter 3 will examine the limits of individuality, tracing the fortunes of two iconoclastic patriarchs, Abraham and Moses. This chapter emphasizes the role of the non-Israelite[25] outsider, noting how both patriarchs receive guidance in moments of crisis by mysterious priests: Melchizedek, Priest to God Most High and Jethro, Priest of Midian. By comparing and then contrasting these episodes, a nexus is disclosed between individual vision and communal leadership in the life of the Israelite leader.

Chapters 4–6 examine the ever-evolving role of women in the Bible. While most readers recognize the Bible's presentation of human beings as complex and multifaceted, when the spotlight falls on the half of humanity that is female, there is a tendency to seek a more circumscribed and uniform biblical attitude. On one level, this inclination can be challenged when it is shown that biblical women are every bit as diverse as biblical men. Their stories contain elements of majesty and subjugation, of harmony and strife, of godliness and rebellion. As her many layers are peeled away, we will find that woman, like man, defies easy categorization and constricting definition.

Yet on another plane, there is some support in the Bible for a uniform standard of woman. In the Garden of Eden, her character is often called "the woman," suggesting that she is prototypical of all women. Moreover, there is a profoundly foundational quality to the Eden story, which evokes a feeling that all other stories of women must somehow relate back to this one.

In order to do justice to these paradoxical qualities the chapters on biblical women will differ from the others in this volume. To begin with, an entire chapter is

---

25. For want of an alternative that is not too cumbersome, I am using this anachronistic term in relation to Melchizedek and Jethro.

devoted to an analysis of a single text, the Garden of Eden narrative, instead of immediately pairing it with another. This focus is warranted by the unusually complex nature of the Bible's first woman and by her uniquely archetypical role in relation to other biblical women. As we will discover, many other women-centered narratives refer back to the Garden and its fundamental messages about woman.

Once we understand the Bible's first woman more fully, we will begin to question the finality of her narrative's details and conclusions. Must her foundational role dictate the nature of subsequent texts involving biblical women? Or are there hints from the very outset that some corrective is called for? Chapter 5 will uncover literary hints at repair, as it pairs the story of the first woman with that of the matriarch Sarah. Sarah's story of infertility and persistent struggle plays in unexpected ways on the tropes of Eve, "the mother of all the living," as well as on the other facets of primordial woman. Although the two stories will have much in common, Sarah's chronicle will in many ways serve as subversive sequel to the earlier narrative.

Chapter 6 will, in one sense, continue the paradigm of the subversive sequel and will in other ways broaden its scope. First, two narratives are compared that share a great deal in language and in theme: the stories of Sarah and Rebekah. Then, because of the fundamental centrality of the Bible's first woman, Rebekah's chronicle will be compared to the Eden story as well. This will enable us to see how Rebekah advances and retreats not only in relation to Sarah, but in relation to the Bible's original woman.

Next, this chapter will venture beyond the doubling of narratives we have seen until now, toward tripling, and ultimately toward a chain of narrative sequences. Each story will manipulate the one before it; it will then be reworked by the one after it; the next will revise its predecessor yet again. This type of ongoing sequencing suggests that biblical stories are much longer and far more intricate than they first appear. Multiple sequels indicate a canon comprised of many layers; the more layers we uncover, the greater the potential for broadening and deepening our grasp of biblical messages. In our study of the women of the Bible, we will come to view each woman's story as links in a chain of a larger "woman's story" that weaves its way through the canon. The combinations of texts expose a dynamic process engaged in by God, man, and woman as they revisit and often reverse their early actions and reactions. Woman's story, while frequently linked to that of the original biblical woman, will ultimately prove to be as wide-ranging and dynamic as the chronicle of humanity itself.

Reading Biblical Women

In our close readings of women-centered texts, we will re-examine some long-standing assumptions, avoiding as much as possible apologetics and agenda-driven interpretations that may interfere with close readings. There are potential pitfalls on all sides. At times, traditional readings overlook the plain sense of the text when the behavior of a female character seems to run counter to prevailing norms of religious etiquette. On the other end of the spectrum, feminist readers may tend to find signs of patriarchal oppression even when the plain sense of the text does not indicate it. Contemporary feminist Bible scholar Phyllis Trible comments on this latter type of encumbered interpretation:

> The women's movement errs when it dismisses the Bible as inconsequential or condemns it as enslaving. In rejecting Scripture women ironically accept male chauvinistic interpretations and thereby capitulate to the very view they are protesting. But there is another way: to reread (not rewrite) the Bible without the blinders ... The hermeneutical challenge is to translate biblical faith without sexism.[26]

Ideologically driven readings can lead to conclusions that unnecessarily rankle the sensibilities of modern readers and cause them to render the entire Bible irrelevant. The alternative is to sidestep these interpretations and return to the text itself, in a search for messages that are more enduring and truer to the text's language and context. As Trible contends, "Depatriarchalizing is not an operation which the exegete performs on the text. It is a hermeneutic operating within Scripture itself. We expose it; we do not impose it."[27]

Subversive Sequels in the Bible exposes layers of the text that are frequently overlooked as we reread several of the Bible's most well-studied passages and as we note the development from one story to the next. As we do so, some basic assumptions about biblical attitudes toward women will be called into question. At the same time, alternative models will emerge within individual passages and from the dynamic interaction among texts.

---

26. Phyllis Trible, "Depatriarchalizing," 218.
27. Ibid., 235.

Methodological Questions and Categories

The thorniest methodological question raised by this work is that of historical sequence. If there were many hands in the writing and editing of the Bible over
the course of many centuries, how can I claim that one section purposefully plays
upon another? More troubling, how can I base the method of sequeling on the order
in which passages appear in the Bible? What if we have evidence that a work that
appears later in the canon was actually written at an earlier date?

Unfortunately, it is hard to address such questions dispassionately, as they
are often closely tied to ardently-held ideological positions. Those who assume unified divine authorship find the claims of historical Bible critics blasphemous, while
those who are certain of the inviolable truth of the documentary hypothesis have
contempt for the naïveté of the faithful.

I would like to transcend this ideological debate by again adhering to the literary school of interpretation. With a literary approach, we redirect our attention
from "excavative"[28] methods: that is, the historical placement of biblical texts and
sociological contextualization of particular passages, helpful though these methods might be. Instead, we move toward an appreciation of the canonized Bible as it
appears before us. Here again is Robert Alter:

> I have no quarrel with the courage of conjecture of those engaged in what Sir
> Edmund Leach has shrewdly called "unscrambling the omelet," but the es-
> sential point for the validity of the literary perspective is that we have in the
> Bible, with far fewer exceptions that the historical critics would allow, a very
> well-made omelet indeed.[29]

Who concocted this omelet in the first place? Alter considers this question to
be somewhat beside the point:

> If in general the literary imagination exhibits ... a faculty for molding dispa-
> rate elements into an expressively unified whole not achieved outside of art,
> this power is abundantly evident in the work of the so-called redactors, so
> that often the dividing line between redactor and author is hard to draw, or
> if it is drawn, does not necessarily demarcate an essential difference.[30]

---

28. Alter, *The Art of Biblical Narrative*, 13.
29. Alter, *The Literary Guide*, 25.
30. Ibid.

My hope is that the literary connections I draw in this book will be equally compelling to those who view the Bible as the work of one divine author and to those who see it as an artfully crafted composite work woven together by very gifted redactors. In the latter case, the time of historical writing of any given passage is less significant than its literary positioning in the biblical canon. It is thus legitimate to speak of "earlier" and "later" narratives, irrespective of the time of their authorship.

Ultimately, questions of historical authorship notwithstanding, the coherent literary structure that is the Bible stands on its own, and it is with a profound sense of awe and respect for its majestic standing that I ask not *when* or *how* the Bible was written, but *what* are the meanings contained in its pages.

Those who are accustomed to traditional Jewish Bible study may wonder whether the type of reading I have outlined purports to be the *"peshat"* of the text: that is, does it claim to convey the plain meaning of the text, based on its grammar, syntax and context? Or perhaps it is *"derash,"* an applied, often homiletic reading-in, which adds to the text's plain meaning in order to educate the reader in some way, and which often aims to present a more comprehensive understanding of whole passages.

Thankfully, in recent years, these constricting categories have begun to break down, as a new approach, termed "Bible at eye level," has taken hold. Martin Lockshin describes this phenomenon as a balance between "under-reading" and "over-reading." In this approach, one does not fail to comment when the text, including whole stories, requires the interpretive filling of narrative gaps. Yet neither does one read in references that go far beyond the plain implications of the written word.[31]

In the coming pages, I aim to strike this balance. Like the strict *peshatist,* I will engage in careful data gathering, paying close attention to literary nuance. Yet, so as not to fall into the minimalist trap of under-reading, I will not shrink from adding a speculative layer to my findings, drawing connections and positing theories about the motives and actions of biblical characters. This layer is not technically *derash,* as it has its foundations in close reading, and will not contradict the plain sense of the text in order to make a point. My offerings do not presume to be sole or definitive readings of passages, but rather possible interpretations that rest on strong literary foundations. If I must confine myself to familiar labels, I have sought to develop a *peshat* that is infused with the expansive and creative ethos of *derash* in the hope of

---

31. Martin Lockshin, "A Bible Commentary for the 21ˢᵗ Century?" 9.

deepening a conventional understanding of the dynamics of the Bible's main focus, its characters.

An additional methodological concern lies in setting limits in the hunt for the parallel passage. On what basis might one identify a passage as parallel, or as a sequel to another? The lines are admittedly undefined. I have tried to restrict my choices to convincing and compelling thematic and linguistic parallels, while basing my analysis on words and phrases that are relatively rare or that are unusually insistent in parallel stories. I am fully cognizant of the dangerous pull toward over-indulgence in flimsily based parallels, or "parallelomania," a warning sounded by a master of the biblical parallel, Yair Zakovich.[32] I have tried to resist this temptation; my readers will judge how successfully I have done so.

Another question that arises from my methods is this: am I suggesting that subversive sequels measure only forward motion in the actions and attitudes of biblical characters? Although I have chosen to examine stories that illustrate a positive progression, the opposite can most certainly be true as well. One example that comes to mind is a comparison of the story of Judah and Tamar with that of David and Bathsheba. Parallels in word and theme abound as the second story dismantles and replays the first—all in shockingly negative ways. Undoubtedly, there is intentionality behind this ordering. But that, perhaps, is a subject for another volume.

Bible vs. Torah

My aim in the six chapters of this book is to illustrate how close readings and the study of sequels reveal the Bible as a book of surprisingly enduring relevance to humanity, a book about which we can wholeheartedly echo Heschel's sense that it is "never wearied by time." As we delve into the Bible's narratives, we find characters, God included, who in the different versions of their stories are seen to struggle, err, and approach familiar challenges in courageous new ways. With the model of the subversive sequel, we readers may come to see the Bible as an inspiring blueprint for humanity, which challenges us to emulate God's dynamic example.

---

32. Zakovich has done a great deal of pioneering work on parallels in the Bible, most notably in his small volume, *Through the Looking Glass: Reflection Stories in the Bible.* Zakovich's parallels focus mainly on literary justice: he demonstrates how later stories deliver apt punishments for misdeeds committed in earlier, parallel narratives.

One final remark: The proliferation of Bible study in the late 20th and early 21st centuries is a fact to be welcomed and celebrated. But in many settings our foundational text has been reduced to a dry, academic pursuit rather than a living, breathing vehicle to religious and moral meaning. The English word for the canon, "Bible"—literally "book"—does not begin to capture its uniqueness. A book is read and studied, its background and context researched. Much more encompassing of its essence is the book's own term for itself, "Torah," the Hebrew word for "teaching," which suggests an educational relationship from book to reader. In this volume I have attempted to convey my relationship with the Bible as "Torah," a book that is in many ways studied like all other books, but whose ultimate purpose is to guide and inspire, to be deeply affecting in the human search for a godly existence.

Chapter 1

The Wings of the Dove:
Noah and Jonah in Flight from Self

They are ill discoverers that think there is no land, when they can see nothing but sea.
—Francis Bacon

N oah and Jonah: two prophets[1] navigate perilous waters aboard their boats, apart from the doomed populations they might have saved. Names, words, and themes are shared freely by their narratives. In both, rampant injustice, *hamas*,[2] threatens to seal the people's fate; both speak of a forty-day period preceding a planned annihilation. Each story prominently features a *"yonah"*—Jonah's Hebrew name is identical to that of the winged messenger sent by Noah, the dove. Both stories highlight such rare locations as Tarshish and Nineveh. Both narratives focus on the personal chronicles of the prophets themselves, while presenting the barest minimum in the way of the actual prophecy they deliver. And both prophets, as we will soon see, judge themselves and others very harshly. As a result, each sinks into a state of self-induced oblivion: Noah through alcohol, Jonah through a coma-like slumber.

These parallels, once explored, compellingly demonstrate how each story unlocks the other's mysteries. But there is even more to be mined from the comparison.

---

1. Neither Noah nor Jonah is ever called "prophet" in the text. Yet because both receive God's word and, in different ways, convey it to others, I apply this label to them.

2. *Hamas* has a wide range of connotations: violence, as in Gen. 49:5; a personal wrong, as in Gen. 16:5; injustice, as in Jon. 3:8; wickedness and ruthlessness, as in Mic. 6:12. I am translating it as "injustice" throughout this work, despite the fact that it will not always be the precise translation in context. I have done this in order to retain the deliberate cross-referencing that is evoked by its repeated use.

The stories are not merely parallel; as we move in more closely, we note that they are sharply contrasting as well. For example, while both errant populations, Noah's generation and the wicked people of Nineveh, engage in widespread *hamas*, the former *continues* on its path until its fate is sealed, while the latter *renounces* injustice and is spared. And while both stories speak of a forty-day period surrounding the coming disaster, in the first story this time period is used to *bring on* destruction, while in the second it serves as an opportunity to *avert* it.

As we will see, the Book of Jonah serves as a subversive sequel to the story of Noah. The Jonah narrative adopts much of the Noah story's language and many of its themes in order to invite comparison. But then the second story begins to dismantle and revise the first, questioning many of its basic assumptions about the prophet, about God, and about the doomed population. To begin with, the Book of Jonah will ask whether Jonah, with all his similarities to Noah, will be able to rewrite his story. Perhaps this time, the prophet could adopt a more generous view toward others, and by extension, toward himself. In addition, the sequel will question God's behavior, asking whether God might eschew the strict justice of Noah's Flood in favor of a more forgiving attitude toward humanity. Finally, the Book of Jonah will revisit the role of the wayward population, exploring its potential to repent and to repair its actions, thereby achieving its own salvation.

Taken together, the two stories will chronicle a remarkable potential for change within several fundamental relationships. In the divine-human bond, we will note God's emerging desire for human survival as He offers second chances to those who have erred. In the inter-human relationship, we will trace the prophet's struggles in facing his responsibility toward those around him. And in the sphere of intra-human relations, we will observe the hero's progress as he is called upon to begin healing his connection with himself. As he begrudgingly accedes to God's demand to help save others, Jonah will face opportunities to rescue himself as well.

Noah: Failed Hope

Before we can reap the rewards of the Noah-Jonah comparison, we must first probe the depths of Noah's personal narrative. Noah's story begins with great promise. Of all the people in his generation, God deems him alone to be worthy of survival:

> The earth became corrupt before God; the earth was filled with injustice.
> When God saw how corrupt the earth was, for all flesh had corrupted its
> ways on earth, God said to Noah, "I have decided to put an end to all flesh

for the earth is filled with injustice because of them: I am about to destroy
them with the earth. Make yourself an ark of gopher wood ... For My part, I
am about to bring the Flood—waters upon the earth—to destroy all flesh under the sky in which there is breath of life; everything on earth shall perish ...
(Gen.6: 11–14,17)

>   Then the Lord said to Noah, "Go into the ark, with all your household,
>   for you alone have I found righteous before Me in this generation ..." And
>   Noah did just as the Lord commanded him. (7:1,5)

Noah is God's faithful servant, who follows His chilling instructions without hesitation. But is this is a clear sign of impeccable character? Moving back
several verses, we note the text's indeterminate stance on this question in its
testimonial to Noah:

>   This is the line of Noah—Noah was a righteous man; he was blameless in
>   his age; Noah walked with God. (Gen. 6:9)

The verse's effusive praise is quickly diminished by a hint of disappointment.
Drawing from the Talmud (*Sanhedrin* 108a), Rashi, the preeminent 11th-century
French exegete, makes the following oft-cited comment:

>   There are those among our rabbis who interpret the term "in his age" as
>   praise (to Noah): all the more so, had he lived in a generation of righteous
>   people, he would have been even more righteous. And there are others who
>   interpret it (the term "in his age") to his discredit: in his age he was righ-
>   teous, but had he been in the age of Abraham, he would have been consid-
>   ered as nothing. (Rashi, Gen. 6:9, s.v.[3] *be-dorotav*)

Troubled by the text's inclusion of the qualifier "in his age," Rashi offers two
interpretations, one more generous to Noah than the other. But even the first, which
seeks Noah's "praise," conveys the sense that he was not all he might have been.
Had he lived in a more positive environment, he would have developed more of his
potential. In Rashi's view, either way one looks at the verse, it is reticent in its portrayal of Noah's righteousness.

---

3. As stated in the preface, the abbreviation "s.v." stands for the Latin *sub verbo*, meaning "under the
   word." This term indicates the word in the biblical verse that the commentator is addressing.

In fact, the suggestion that Noah was good but not quite good enough finds its origins even earlier in the biblical record of his birth. Noah's arrival is heralded by the prayer of his father Lemekh:

> May this one comfort us [*yenahamenu*] from our work and from the toil of our hands, out of the very soil which the Lord cursed."[4] (Gen. 5:29)

With his words, Noah's father prays that his son will bring comfort, from the Hebrew root *n-h-m.* He hopes that the world, which has been suffering since humanity's expulsion from the Garden of Eden, will at long last find some relief from its pain.[5] But nine verses later, the *n-h-m* verb, which was used to describe the hopes for Noah's effect on humanity, returns to present an ironic end to that hope. The same Hebrew root *n-h-m*, which contains Noah's full name, can mean both to comfort and to regret. Shortly after Noah's birth, the text reports:

> And the Lord regretted [*n-h-m*] that He had made humanity on earth and His heart was saddened. The Lord said, "I will blot out from the earth the humanity I created—human beings together with beasts, creeping things, and birds of the sky; for I regret [*n-h-m*] that I made them." (Gen. 6:6–7)

Not only does Noah's birth fail to bring comfort to the world; it does not even prevent God's regret at having created it. Despite Lemekh's hopes for his son, Noah's righteousness proves to be self-contained.

The disappointment of Noah is further reflected in a new play on his name, which, while still complimentary to him, mitigates the optimism expressed at his birth: "And Noah found favor, *ve-Noah matza hen*, in God's eyes" (Gen. 6:8). The Hebrew palindrome—נח is reversed to חן (*n-h* becomes *h-n*)—hints that the hoped-for impact Noah was to have on the world is replaced by the much more limited, personal impression he makes on God. In fact he will never bring consolation to others. The favor Noah finds in God's eyes will be enough to save only himself and his immediate family.[6] Thus, already at the beginning of Noah's narrative, the text signals that ultimately he will be a worthy individual, but a failed leader.

---

4. Author's translation.

5. This notion is reinforced by the text's use of the word *itzavon*, pain, which sends us back to the admonishments in Eden to both the woman (Gen. 3:16) and the man (Gen. 3:17). See Cassuto, *Genesis*, 198.

6. It seems from Gen. 7:1 that Noah's family is spared because of Noah's merit: "Then the Lord said to Noah, 'Go into the ark with all your household, for you alone have I found righteous before Me in this generation.'"

Noah and Abraham

The view of Noah as failed leader might be enriched by a brief intertextual digression, one that Rashi himself encourages when he contrasts Noah with Abraham. Both figures, after all, confront God's plan of large-scale destruction. Yet their responses reveal significant differences in their leadership efforts.

After Abraham receives warning of God's intention to annihilate the cities of Sodom and Gomorrah, he launches into a prolonged and impassioned plea to God to try to save the people (Gen. 18: 23–33). "Far be it from You!" he declares. "Will not the Judge of the earth deal justly?" (18:25). Abraham bargains with God, suggesting six times that **perhaps**, *ulay*, the situation in Sodom is not as dire as it seems (18:24–32); **perhaps** there are enough righteous people whose merits could mitigate God's harsh ruling and save the entire city. **Perhaps**, *ulay*, there are fifty. If not fifty, then forty, or thirty, or twenty; or **perhaps** ten (18:21–32). By his emphatic repetition of the word "perhaps," *ulay*, Abraham questions the all-too apparent reality that lies before him. He beseeches God to join him in considering an alternative vision—unlikely but still possible—of a smattering of worthy individuals whose combined virtue could turn the tide from the evil decree toward collective survival. Perhaps the innocent few were hidden or dormant; the rampant wickedness around them may have rendered them virtually invisible. In his monumental efforts to save others, Abraham desperately grasps at any possibility, no matter how improbable, and asks God to do the same.

Abraham's extraordinary exertions attest to his faith in the abundant human potential for change. In addition, they convey his belief that human beings bear responsibility toward one another. Though his own survival is never in question, he refuses to submit to a complacent acceptance of God's decree to kill others. Instead he risks bringing God's wrath upon himself as he tirelessly pleads on behalf of the citizens of Sodom (Gen. 18:30,32).

In the end, God accepts Abraham's proposition that if only ten righteous people are to be found, the entire city would be spared. Yet even by these generous standards, the city proves unworthy, and, as a result, God "**rained** [*m-t-r*] upon Sodom and Gomorrah brimstone and fire ... from the heavens" (Gen. 19:24).

We now return to Noah. In his narrative, the verb *m-t-r* is one of several terms that link the destruction of Sodom to Noah's Flood. Both stories also contain the verb *sh-h-t*, to destroy; Noah uses *gofer* wood to build the ark (6:14), while God rains down the phonetically similar *gofrit vamelah*, sulphurous fire,

upon Sodom (19: 24). Moreover, in both stories, God gives advance warning of
His intentions to His chosen leader.

Yet, despite the linguistic and thematic similarities between the two tales,
Noah's response to impending catastrophe contrasts dramatically with Abraham's.
This reversal hints at the presence of a subversive sequel. Even *before* we consider the
larger Noah-Jonah comparison, we note than in a significant way, Abraham's actions invert those of his predecessor, Noah. While Abraham had vigorously pro-
tested God's plans for destruction, the text relates the following about Noah:

> Then the Lord said to Noah ... "For in seven days' time I will make it rain
> [*m-t-r*] upon the earth, forty days and forty nights, and I will blot out from
> the earth all existence that I created." And Noah did just as that the Lord
> commanded him. (Gen. 7: 1, 4–5)

In Sodom, Abraham beseeches God to consider a potentially wider range of human behavior, and to view individuals as interlocking links in a firmly melded chain.
Noah, in contrast, wordlessly accepts God's judgment of his generation as absolute. He
neither challenges God's conclusion nor asks for mercy within its framework. The question of an alternative reality, of Abraham's "perhaps," *ulay*, does not cross Noah's lips; he
accepts the finality of humanity's guilt and the inevitability of its destruction. Nor does
Noah ask God to apply his merits to help save others. Such efforts were likely to fail, yet
in subtle ways the text hints that God might be swayed by human intervention.[7] To return to Abraham in Sodom as an example: before God actually destroys the evil city and

---

7. One might argue that God's comments before destroying Sodom are designed to elicit Abraham's intervention. First, God speaks (apparently to Himself) of including Abraham because "I have singled him out
   that he may instruct his children and his posterity to keep the way of the LORD by doing what is just and
   right ..." (Gen. 18:19). It seems that God wants Abraham to exhibit his ability to purvey justice by speaking out on behalf of the sinners of Sodom. Next, God tells Abraham that the sins of Sodom and Gomorrah
   have reached Him and that dire consequences are likely to follow. Unlike Noah, Abraham does not need to
   make arrangements for his own safety. Why then does he need advance warning? This may be another
   invitation for Abraham's intercession on the people's behalf, in which God informs Abraham of His plans
   so that Abraham might try and prevent them. For a similar phenomenon, see Exod. 32:10. Before Moses
   prays on behalf of the errant people for the sin of the Golden Calf, God warns, "Now, *let me be,* that my
   anger may blaze forth against them and that I may destroy them ..." Rashi comments (Exod. 32:10, s.v.
   haniha li): "... Here God created an opening and informed him that the matter rested on him; if he would
   pray, God would not destroy them." By commanding Moses, "Let me be," God hints that Moses has the
   power to dissuade Him from destroying the people. He hints further that Moses should make use of that
   power by petitioning God to save them.

its surroundings, He announces His intentions to Abraham in a way that seems less than final (Gen. 18:20–21). In what may be a subtle rejection of Noah's silent compliance, God signals to Abraham the possibility of appeal and reversal of the evil decree.

Viewed in isolation, Noah's behavior seems impeccable, and Rashi's evaluation unduly severe. But comparing Noah's behavior at the Flood to Abraham's actions in Sodom confirms Rashi's views. Though irreproachable as an individual, Noah as a leader was a tragic failure. If he had only acted more like Abraham, Noah might have gone on record as a righteous man, not only "in his age," but for all times.

Breakdown of the Prophet

Soon enough, the devastation that was announced to Noah arrives. Aside from Noah and his family and the animals in the ark, every living thing—"all in whose nostrils was the merest breath of life, all that was on dry land ... man, cattle, creeping things, and birds of the sky" (Gen. 7:22–23)—was obliterated.

What is the prophet's frame of mind in the wake of such wholesale destruction? Does he maintain his belief in absolute justice while all of creation perishes? A comparison of Noah's entry into the ark at the Flood's beginning with his exit at its end offers a small window into the prophet's psychological state. Just prior to the Flood, God instructs Noah:

> And I will uphold my covenant with you; and you will come into the ark, *you and your sons and your wife and your sons' wives with you.* (Gen. 6:18)[8]

Instead of the expected order of man and wife, the verse speaks of man and sons, and then wife and daughters-in-law. This anomaly prompts Rashi to comment:

> Men and women separately, because sexual relations were forbidden—since the world was steeped in suffering. (Rashi 7:7 s.v. *Noah u-vanav.*)

By inverting the expected syntax, God informs humanity that they are to remain celibate while the world was being destroyed. A later verse, which records the family's entry into the ark, echoes the unusual word order of Noah, his sons, his wife, and his sons' wives (Gen. 7:7). The repetition suggests that the family entered as instructed, with men separate from women.

---

8. Author's translation and emphasis.

After the Flood, however, God's instructions change:

"Leave the ark, *you and your wife, and your sons and your sons' wives* with you."
(Gen. 8:16)[9]

In line with his earlier observation, Rashi comments:

Man and wife. Here God permitted them sexual relations. (Rashi 8:16, s.v.
atta ve-ishtekha.)

By reverting to the more expected formula of men and wives God suggests that
the time for abstinence is over, and that it is now time to resume living full lives.

But curiously, instead of following God's wishes, the family exits the ark in
the same order in which it entered:

And *Noah* exited, *and his sons and his wife and his sons' wives* with him.
(Gen. 8:18)[10]

If Rashi is right and the verse's word order signifies the condition of marital
unity, Noah and his family are surprisingly unwilling to resume sexual relations. A
further hint of this reluctance appears later in the text, when God twice exhorts
Noah to "be fruitful and multiply" (Gen. 9:1,7), though this command was given
only once to humanity's first couple. God's insistence points to Noah's unspoken
hesitation. Perhaps the trauma of witnessing destruction has led to deep reserva-
tions about beginning life anew.[11] Although he had expected to stand safely aside as
"all existence on earth was blotted out" (7:23), perhaps now Noah feels a belated pull
toward his fellow human beings, along with a sense of deep loss at their demise. In
this frame of mind, the act of procreation, with the physical pleasure and optimism
for the future that it represents, seems impossible.

---

9. Author's translation and emphasis.
10. Ibid.
11. This reading is based on Nehama Leibowitz's analysis of Rashi (although she claimed that Rashi's
    initial difficulty was sparked not by the anomalous word order of Gen. 7:7, but by the text's *changing*
    that order in 8:16). Leibowitz brings support for this reading from Genesis Rabbah 34:6: "So God
    said to Noah, 'Leave the ark,' but he did not agree to leave. He (Noah) said, 'Will I leave and procreate
    for cursed purposes?' (He held this position) until God swore to him that He would not bring an-
    other Flood upon the earth, as it says (Isa. 54:9) 'For this to Me is like the waters of Noah: As I swore
    that the waters of Noah would never again Flood the earth.'" See Reiner, *Mo'adei Nehama,* 612.

In addition to his unexpected pain, perhaps Noah feels guilt at his own survival, compounded by the knowledge that as God's prophet and confidante, he had held the potential to avert the wholesale suffering. It is possible that in failing to defend his guilty generation, Noah now shares with it a bond of guilt. If Noah is to be consistent in his harsh view of the unchangeable nature of the human psyche, he might feel that he, like his sinful generation, is now irredeemable. As a result, like them, he must die.

The idea that Noah is resigned to his own death finds support in his behavior following the Flood. In an act of escapism that leads directly to the biblical account of his demise, Noah plants a vineyard, drinks from its produce, and gets drunk:[12]

> Noah, the man of the earth, began to plant a vineyard. He drank of the wine and became drunk, and he uncovered himself within his tent. Ham, the father of Canaan, saw his father's nakedness and told his two brothers outside.[13] (Gen. 9:20–22)

There is irony in the "man of the earth" planting something as inessential as grapes in the aftermath of the world's destruction, instead of a more basic crop such as wheat. But his actions highlight his desperation to escape his unbearable reality, to simulate death by living in self-induced unconsciousness. The next logical step, his actual death, is recorded immediately afterwards,[14] despite the fact that it occurs many years later:

> Noah lived after the Flood 350 years. And all the days of Noah came to 950 years; then he died. (Gen. 9:28–29)

God had wanted to spare the prophet from the Flood, but in a sense Noah, like all those around him, drowns. It is not God, but Noah who extinguishes his own breath of life by inundating his body with liquid. Noah may have been spared initially because of his relative righteousness, but he ultimately meets a fate very similar to the rest of his generation.

---

12. I am grateful to Shmuel Klitsner for connecting Nehama Leibowitz's analysis of Rashi (see note 11) with God's repeated charge to procreate and with Noah's subsequent drunkenness.

13. Author's translation.

14. The account includes Noah's reactions to his children's handling of his drunkenness and the ensuing blessings and curses (Gen. 9:25–27) he bestows upon them.

The Book of Jonah: Subversive Sequel to the Story of Noah

Unable to imagine forgiveness for the sinful people, Noah remains unforgiving toward himself. Although his personal narrative ends tragically, many volumes later, the Book of Jonah presents his story anew. The new story, which contains different names and an often inverted format, will offer a divergent direction, and the hope of a nobler conclusion.

We have noted some of the obvious parallels between the stories of Noah and Jonah: water, boats, and the threat of impending destruction. We have alluded, as well, to some of the striking *differences* between them.

These differences suggest an inverse relationship between the stories, in which the second story serves as a subversive sequel to the first. If, in stories that are initially parallel, the language and details of one narrative invert those of another, we may argue that one story seeks a more sweeping reversal of the other by overturning its attitudes and outcomes as well.

In general, Noah's story reverses that of Jonah in its approach to destruction. In the Noah narrative, humanity's annihilation was neither negotiable nor avoidable; God and His prophet were united in viewing death as inevitable. The inverted details of the Book of Jonah will lead us away from destruction as a narrative necessity. They will point instead toward a more generous view of humanity adopted by God and by humanity itself.

Before we arrive at the broader thematic contrasts between the two narratives, we must first look closely at the specific details that lead us there. To begin with, we note the opposing uses of the verb *n-h-m*, to regret. In the Flood story, as we have seen, God's decision to *destroy* the world is expressed with this word: [15]

> The Lord said, "I will blot out from the earth the human beings whom I have created—human beings together with beasts, creeping things, and birds of the sky; for I regret [*n-h-m*] that I made them." (Gen. 6:7)

In the Book of Jonah, God's intention to *spare* humanity its destruction is expressed with the same word:

---

15. At a conference some years ago, I delivered a paper based on this chapter. I was then approached by David Arnow, who directed me to his article "Reflections on Jonah and Yom Kippur," which appeared in *Conservative Judaism*, pp. 33–48. I was gratified to see that in his essay, Arnow points out many of the same literary and thematic similarities—and some of the contrasts—between the stories of Noah and Jonah that I have listed above. In addition, he notes as central themes in the book God's move toward greater mercy, the interconnectedness of all living beings, and the human capacity for change.

God saw what they did, how they were turning back from their evil ways.
And God regretted [n-h-m] the evil He had planned to bring upon them, and
did not carry it out.[16] (Jon. 3:10)

Playing on the tropes of the Noah story, then, the Jonah story reverses its outcome,
demonstrating a newly forgiving attitude on the part of God. God's greatest regret is no
longer the living presence of sinners, but the death of His human creations.

Hamas is another term that weaves its way in a contrasting manner throughout both stories. In Noah's narrative, the fate of the people is *sealed* because of the
injustice, *hamas,* that people inflict upon each other:

God said to Noah, "I have decided to put an end to all flesh, for the earth is
filled with injustice[17] [*hamas*] because of them: I am about to destroy them
with the earth." (Gen. 6:13)

In the Book of Jonah, the evil decree is *reversed* because the people turn back
from the *hamas* that they were practicing:

By decree of the king and his nobles ... Let everyone turn back from his evil
ways and from the injustice [*hamas*] of which he is guilty ... God saw what
they did, how they were turning back from their evil ways. And God regretted the evil He had planned to bring upon them, and did not carry it out.[18]
(Jon. 3:7,8,10)

Here again, the same term is used to achieve opposite effects, this time in
presenting the attitude of humanity at large. The Book of Jonah will revisit humanity's ability to assume responsibility for its own future. As opposed to the story of
Noah, this time the doomed population is able to conceive of and carry out a reversal of its behavior and consequently to overturn its fate.

In yet another inverse parallel, both stories highlight a forty-day period, but
to opposite ends. The destruction in Noah's Flood *lasts* for forty days:

The Flood continued forty days on the earth ... all existence on earth was
blotted out. (Gen. 7:17,23)

---

16. Author's translation.
17. Ibid. See note 2 for the different connotations of the word *hamas.*
18. Author's translation.

In contrast, the destruction in the Book of Jonah is *averted* by a forty-day warning period:

> Jonah started out and made his way into the city the distance of one day's walk and proclaimed: "Forty days more, and Nineveh will be overturned!"[19]
> (Jon. 3:4)

Taken together, these literary contrasts are central to the relationship between the stories. In the first, humanity, steeped in injustice, will assuredly meet their destruction within the space of forty days. God, the prophet, and it seems the population itself, accept this as unalterable fact. In the second story, these details unite for antithetical purposes. This time, with a new attitude by God toward humanity and by humanity toward itself, there is great potential for survival.

Another inverse parallel centers on plants that appear with seeming suddenness. The story of Noah features a fast-growing vineyard (Gen. 9:20,21),[20] which leads Noah to drunkenness and to the biblical account of his *death*. In contrast, Jonah encounters a spontaneously-sprouting gourd (Jon. 4:6), which will symbolize his renewed chance at *life*.

Furthermore, both stories highlight the importance of beasts, *behemah*. In the Noah narrative, beasts blend with humanity in meeting their common doom:

> And all flesh that stirred on earth perished—birds, cattle, beasts [*behemah*]—and all the things that swarmed upon the earth and all humankind. (Gen. 7:21)

The Book of Jonah has beasts and humanity cooperating to *escape* their shared fate, as in the following peculiar, almost comic description:

> By decree of the king and his nobles: No man or beast [*behemah*]—or flock or herd—shall taste anything! They shall not graze, and they shall not drink water! They shall be covered with sackcloth—man and beast [*behemah*]—and shall cry mightily to God. (Jon. 3:7–8)

Both stories link the destiny of humanity with that of the world's other living creatures. This linkage highlights the interconnected nature of all of God's creation,

---

19. Ibid.
20. The text presents a curious account of Noah planting a vineyard in which Noah drinks wine immediately following his act of planting. Thus the text skips over the intervening years.

a relationship that both Noah and Jonah are reluctant to recognize. At the end of Jonah's narrative, God emphatically draws this connection:

> And should I not care about Nineveh, that great city, in which there are more than a hundred and twenty thousand persons who do not know their right hand from their left, and many beasts [*behemah rabba*] as well! (Jon. 4: 11)

As we study Jonah's story more closely, we will look for signs that Jonah is able to see himself as an integral part of God's world. If he could, perhaps he would be ready to reverse Noah's sense of detachment from his surroundings, thereby enacting a subversive sequel to Noah's unfortunate end.

God's Heart

In order to reach a more expansive appreciation of Jonah's story as subversive sequel to Noah's, we take a close look at the first chapter of the Book of Jonah:

> The word of the Lord came to Jonah son of Amittai: "Get up and go to Nineveh the great city, and call before it that their evil has risen up before Me. (Jon. 1:1)[21]

The first verses of the book already point to a significant difference between the stories of Noah and Jonah. Instead of merely informing the prophet of the world's doom as He did with Noah, here God commands the prophet to take definitive action on humanity's behalf. God expresses His wishes with three brisk verbs: get up, *kum;* go, *lekh;* and call, *kera.*[22] Unlike the generation of the Flood, the people of Nineveh must receive a warning that they are in danger of annihilation, along with a chance to appeal. What accounts for this divine about-face?

A brief return to the Flood narrative reveals the first signs of change. In the verses leading up to the Flood, God takes stock of the hopelessly wicked state of the human heart:

---

21. Author's translation.
22. How does one "call upon" a city? *Targum Yonatan* (Jon. 1:2) translates *"kera aleha"* as "prophesy against it," a reading that is supported by several other verses, including Deut. 15:9. If one refuses to assist the needy in the year approaching the Sabbatical *shemittah* year, the needy kinsman will "cry out against you," *ve-kara alekha,* and you will incur guilt." The implication here is that Jonah must inform the city of its guilt, so that it will be forewarned about the impending consequences. This reading is borne out by the ensuing events of Jonah 3. Jonah finally "calls" to the city about God's intentions to destroy them. The people interpret the proclamation as a warning, and as an opportunity to reverse the decree.

The Lord saw how great was humanity's wickedness on earth, and how every plan devised by their heart was nothing but evil all the time. And the
Lord regretted having made humanity on the earth, and His heart was saddened. The Lord said: "I will blot out from the earth the people whom I
created—people together with beasts, creeping things, and the birds of the
sky; for I regret that I made them."[23] (Gen. 6:5–7)

The link made between the human heart and God's heart is absolute and
deadly. Humanity's evil heart saddens God's heart, and the treatment for God's
ailing heart is the obliteration of the world.

After the destruction, however, God draws a new parallel between the hearts
of humanity and the heart of God:

And the Lord said to His heart: "Never again will I doom the earth because of
humanity, since the devisings of the human heart are evil from his youth; nor
will I ever again destroy every living being, as I have done."[24] (Gen. 8:21)

Here, instead of succumbing to a "saddened heart," God speaks to His heart,
resolving never to repeat the Flood's ravages. Mass annihilation is no longer a necessary response to widespread human evil. Although the wicked nature of humanity remains largely unchanged, destruction has reshaped God's response to it. Strict
justice and death now give way to mercy and life.

To appreciate the full significance of the heart metaphor, we turn to the Book
of Ezekiel, which appears in the canon after the story of Noah and before the Book
of Jonah. Ezekiel takes the heart metaphor to a new level as the prophet heralds
further divine movement toward the rehabilitation and survival of humanity:

Cast away all the transgressions by which you have offended, and get your-
selves a new heart and a new spirit, that you may not die, O House of Israel.
For it is not my desire that anyone shall die—declares the Lord God. Repent,
therefore, and live! (Ezek. 18:31–32)

In this optimistic passage, the human heart is no longer a stumbling block,
inevitably leading humanity toward evil and requiring God's mercy. Now it is an
instrument of change. Although it tends toward evil, if humanity so decides, the

---

23. Author's translation.
24. Ibid.

heart can be refashioned.

In the story of Noah, God's attitude to humanity is at first dispassionate and judgmental: "I will blot out from the earth the people I have created." Then it is merciful: "Never again will I doom the earth because of humanity." Later, in Ezekiel, God expresses an unmitigated partiality toward life: "It is not my desire that anyone shall die ... repent, therefore and live!" This preference underlies God's actions in the Book of Jonah, beginning with His very first words to the prophet. In this story, unlike the Flood narrative, there will be no destruction without warning and without the opportunity for repentance and salvation.

Messengers

We turn back to the Book of Jonah to see if the prophet's attitudes toward the world's errant people have changed along with God's, and if Jonah will find the resolve that Noah lacked to help spare them.

The early signs are not encouraging. Despite God's more forgiving relationship with His world, the prophet is decidedly *less* inclined toward compassion, as seen in the following verses from Jonah 1. These verses follow immediately upon God's command to Jonah to get up, go, and call upon the offending city of Nineveh:

> And Jonah got up to flee to Tarshish from before the Lord. He went down to Jaffa and he found a ship going to Tarshish. He paid its fare and went down into it to come with them to Tarshish, from before the Lord. But the Lord cast a great wind upon the sea and there was a great tempest in the sea, and the ship was in danger of breaking up. The sailors feared, and they cried out, each to his own god; and they flung the ship's cargo overboard to make it lighter for them. And Jonah had gone down into the hold of the vessel where he lay down and fell into a deep sleep. The captain went over to him and cried out, "How can you be sleeping so soundly! Get up and call to your god! Perhaps he will be kind to us and we will not perish."[25] (Jon. 1:2–5)

Like Noah, Jonah refrains from warning the people of the coming catastrophe. In this version of the story, however, the prophet is not simply inactive; he is *actively opposed* to intervening on the people's behalf. God wants Jonah to "get up," seemingly to meet eye to eye the evil that has "risen up" before Him (Jon. 1:1). In response to

25. Ibid.

God's order to "get up," Jonah gets up. But instead of getting up to "go to Nineveh and call before it," Jonah gets up *to flee* God by going as far as he can in the opposite direction, to Tarshish.[26] Moreover, in contrast to God's order to "get up," Jonah "goes down, *y-r-d*," three times. First, he "goes down" to Jaffa. Next, he "goes down" into the ship. Finally, he "goes down" into the lower hold of the ship, where he "fell into a deep sleep" (v. 5)[27] The Hebrew word *va-yeradam,* he fell deeply asleep, plays phonetically on the word *va-yered,* he went down.[28] Jonah seeks to escape God's merciful command by sinking into a deep slumber, an extreme psychological manifestation of the flight he began in verse 3.[29]

The Book of Jonah has begun to revise the story of Noah, presenting a more compassionate attitude by God toward His world, combined with a less charitable perspective by God's prophet. The result is Jonah's desperate attempt to avoid the divine charge, as he seeks to escape from God in any way possible.

But the Book of Jonah recasts the story of Noah in another way: by taking a new look at the emotional toll exacted on the prophet as a result of his refusal to help humanity. While Noah *ended* his career in a state of self-induced unconsciousness soon followed by his death, Jonah *begins* by putting himself to sleep. This is the first expression of an ongoing death-wish, further exhibited in Jonah's request that the sailors cast him overboard (Jon. 1:12), and in the final chapter of the book, by his cry, "Please LORD, take my life, for I would rather die than live" (4: 3).[30]

---

26. Ibn Ezra brings an opinion that Tarshish is Tunis, the most distant corner of the Mediterranean, which was the farthest known western part of the world (Jon. 1:3 s.v. *Tarshish*). God had said to go in the opposite direction, eastward to Nineveh in what is now Iraq. With his chosen destination, Jonah makes the utmost geographic effort to "flee from before the LORD."

27. Further evidence of Jonah's active resistance to God's desires can be found later in the verse. Instead of complying with God's wishes to denounce the evil that had risen *"before Me [lefanai]"* (Jon. 1:2), Jonah repeatedly flees "from *before the LORD [mi-lifnei Adonai]*," a detail that is mentioned twice in v. 3, and again in v. 10. How can one flee from before God? Uriel Simon suggests that although his flight takes a physical form, what Jonah really seeks is emotional and psychological distance from God. His physical motion symbolizes his psychic condition, much as Abraham's "here I am *[hinneni]*" (Gen. 22:2) signifies his emotional readiness to do God's will. See Simon, *Mikra le-Yisrael,* 41. Support for the notion that "fleeing God" reflects an internal distancing from the divine can be found in Gen. 4:16, in which Cain, in his estrangement from God following the murder of his brother, goes out "from before the LORD."

28. I heard this suggestion in a lecture by Nehama Leibowitz on the Book of Jonah.

29. Reiner, *Mo'adei Nehama,* 365.

30. For further expressions of Jonah's death wish, see Jon. 4:8–9.

The Book of Jonah questions the inevitability of Noah's end. It asks not only if a failed society can be rehabilitated, but if a failed prophet can be reformed as well. This time God refuses to let the prophet ignore his responsibility to the world, to wallow in his own self-destructive feelings, and to die. Instead, God sends messengers to pursue Jonah into his exile. Their task is to shake Jonah out of his slumber, to urge other choices upon him, and consequently, to return him to life. If God's messengers can help Jonah to acknowledge his oneness with the world, he might act to save it. And by striking a more compassionate stance toward the rest of humanity, this time the prophet might find forgiveness within himself as well, thereby avoiding the tragic fate of Noah.

We turn back to the story's beginning, to Jonah's role as defiant messenger. Jonah's refusal to do God's bidding is laden with irony. As we have seen, Jonah shares his name with Noah's dove, both *Yonah* in Hebrew. The dove is the Bible's prototypically faithful messenger, appropriately chosen by Noah to bring some sign of the earth's condition following the Flood (Gen. 8:8–12).[31] From the title of Jonah's book, we might expect it to feature a prophet who delivers messages. Instead, the story unfolds as a series of messages delivered *by others to the prophet*. God dispatches His many messengers: human beings, animals, and forces of nature, to wear away at Jonah's resistance.

God's opening speech introduces certain key terms, which lay the literary groundwork for the agents He will send to Jonah. God orders Jonah to "*get up* and go to Nineveh the *great* city and *call* before it," (Jon. 1:2) words that soon find their echoes in unexpected ways. Jonah will not *get up* to go to the *great* city, nor will he *call* upon it. Instead, these terms will be ironically assigned to God's messengers, who will apply subtle pressure on Jonah to do God's bidding. First, God casts a "*great* wind" upon the sea, followed by a "*great* storm," reminders of the "*great* city" that awaits him. Next, the ship's captain serves as God's mouthpiece, reiterating two of the three verbs in God's order to Jonah. God had said, "*Get up*, go, and *call* [to the people of Nineveh]" (v.2); now the captain says, "*Get up* and *call* [to your god]" (v. 6).[32] From the very beginning of the story, there are literary hints that while Jonah will not deliver God's messages, others will deliver messages to *him*.

---

31. Noah first chose the inappropriate raven, which did not complete its mission (Gen. 8:7).
32. Although twice ordered to "call" in Jonah 1—once to save the people of Nineveh and then again to save the people on the boat—Jonah never does. In the first chapter of his book, he steadfastly refuses to save Nineveh by calling to them, or to save the ship by calling out to God. Significantly, the only people who actually do call in this chapter are the sailors: "Then they *called* out to the LORD: O please, LORD, do not let us perish on account of this man's life" (v. 14).

Of all the book's messengers, it is the sailors who are the most compelling and surprising. We return to the text of Jonah 1 in order to closely examine their behavior.

> The sailors feared, and they cried out, each to his own god; and they flung the ship's cargo overboard to make it lighter for them. And Jonah had gone down into the hold of the vessel where he lay down and fell into a deep sleep. The captain went over to him and cried out, "How can you be sleeping so soundly! Get up and call to your god! Perhaps he will be kind to us and we will not perish."
>
> The men said to one another, "Let us cast lots and find out on whose account this evil thing has come upon us." They cast lots and the lot fell on Jonah. They said to him, "Tell us, regarding whom has this evil thing befallen us? What is your business? Where have you come from? What is your country, and of what people are you?" "I am a Hebrew," he replied. "I fear the LORD, the God of Heaven, who made both the sea and the land." The men felt a great fear, and they asked him, "What have you done!" because the men knew he was fleeing from the LORD—for so he had told them. They said to him, "What must we do to you to make the sea calm around us?" For the sea was growing more and more stormy. He said to them, "Lift me up and cast me overboard, and the sea will calm down for you; for I know [yode'a ani] that this great storm came upon you on my account."
>
> And the men rowed hard to return to the shore, but they could not, for the sea was growing more and more stormy about them. They called out to the Lord: "Oh, please Lord, do not let us perish on account of this man's life. Do not hold us guilty of killing an innocent person! For you, O Lord, by Your will You have brought this about." And they lifted Jonah and cast him overboard, and the sea stopped raging. The men feared the Lord greatly; they offered a sacrifice to the Lord and they made vows.[33] (Jon. 1:5–16)

These unusual men first appear as "sailors" (Jon. 1:5), people defined solely by their profession. Gradually, they evolve into "men" (vv. 10,16) who are capable of remarkable personal development.[34] Their progress is evident in the different types of fear they experience. At first, as simple sailors, they fear nature's might (v. 5) and

---

33. Author's translation.
34. Reiner, *Mo'adei Nehama*, p. 368.

call out to their various gods for salvation. Then, when Jonah informs them of the all-powerful God he worships, "the God of Heaven, who made both sea and land" (v. 9), they fear again, this time as men. As a result of Jonah's words they are moved to consider the possibility of one God, more powerful than any they had imagined. Finally, they achieve a "great fear of the LORD" (v. 16), bringing sacrifices and making vows to Him.[35]

The sailors' development, both religious and moral, is extraordinary. At first, when the stormy sea threatens their lives, they pray to their gods and heave overboard, t-v-l, all excess weight. They also draw lots, hoping to find the person responsible for their peril. They will presumably cast off the offender with the other jetsam that endangers their ship. But when the lots implicate Jonah, they instead ask him a string of questions, including, "What must we do to you to make the sea calm around us?" Jonah instructs them to "lift me up and cast me—using the root t-v-l again—into the sea" (Jon. 1:12). Yet, instead the sailors frantically try to row back to shore (v. 13), risking their own lives in order to spare his. Only when all hope is lost do they finally throw him into the sea in order to save themselves.[36] And even then, the sailors continue to hold out hope for the survival of the man who has imperiled them. They call out to God: "Do not hold us guilty of killing an innocent person" (v. 14). Although Jonah has explicitly admitted that he is *not* innocent (v. 12), they continue to consider him as such and to search for a way to spare his life. This exceptional ability to consider charitable alternatives to what their own eyes and ears perceive is the defining feature of the sailors.

A midrashic source offers an intriguing angle on the sailors' transformation into *anashim*, the Hebrew term for "men," or more inclusively, "people."

---

35. Ibid.
36. The extraordinary efforts of the sailors draw the attention of the authors of the midrash, leading them to the following embellishment of the story: "What did they (the sailors) do? They lifted Jonah and held him over the sides of the boat and said, 'God who is Lord of the world, do not hold us guilty of killing an innocent person, for we do not know the nature of this man—though he says he is the cause of this trouble.' They held him in the water up until his ankles, and the sea stopped raging. They brought him back to them, and the sea grew more and more stormy. They held him in the water up until his navel, and the sea stopped raging. They brought him back to them, and the sea grew more and more stormy. They held him in the water up until his neck, and the sea stopped raging. They brought him back to them, and the sea grew more and more stormy, until they threw him in completely" (*Pirkei de-Rabbi Eliezer* 9, Tanhuma 96). These sources are brought in Reiner, *Mo'adei Nehama*, 369.

In this view, the boat's occupants are *all* people; they are a symbolic micro-cosm of humanity at large.[37] Read this way, the moral excellence exhibited by the sailors hints at a universal potential for selfless, righteous behavior. More-over, the image of a floating universe with a prophet on board presents yet another contrast with the story of Noah. In the Flood narrative, the *prophet floated* safely in his boat as the world around him drowned. In the Book of Jonah, the *world floats* as the prophet faces death by drowning. Furthermore, in an ironic narrative twist, the world is now more moral and more compas-sionate than the prophet. Rather than leaving the doomed to die at sea—as Noah did with his contemporaries—the boat's inhabitants strive mightily to keep their fellow human being dry and safe.

The sailors ask nine questions, with the question "what," *mah*, recurring most often: "Because of *whom* is this evil; *what* is your business? *Where* have you come from? *What* is your country, and of *what* people are you? (Jon. 1:8) *What* must we do to make the sea calm around us?" (v. 11). These remarkable men are open and honest questioners. This is underscored not only by the interrogative inflection of their speech, but by the use of the word "*ulay*," perhaps, by the ship's captain. Though unfamiliar with Jonah's god, the captain is willing to consider the possibility of His unparalleled power and mercy: "perhaps [*ulay*] the god will be kind to us and we will not perish" (v. 6). The captain's use of the word *ulay*, with its sense of expansive potential, evokes Abraham's pleas on behalf of the people of Sodom. In both cases, there is no tangible sign to suggest that reality might be different than it appears. Yet Abraham is able to imagine the presence of righteousness lying hidden among the pervasive evil of the city. Likewise, the ship's polytheistic captain, who knows nothing of Jonah's God, is willing to con-sider the possibility that He will prove powerful, benevolent, and responsive enough to save their ship. The openness displayed by Abraham, the ship's cap-tain, and the sailors contrasts starkly with Jonah's stubborn certainty through-out the book. Unlike the sailors, who speak in questions, Jonah expresses himself with declarative certainty:[38] "for I *know* [*yode'a ani*] that this terrible storm came

---

37. When the text says, "Each man called out to his god," certain midrashim conclude that all 70 nations of the earth were represented on the boat. *Pirkei de-Rabbi Eliezer* 10, *Yalkut Shimoni* 550.

38. I first heard this contrast in the modalities of Jonah and the sailors presented in a lecture by Avivah Zornberg.

upon you on my account" (v. 12).[39] Later, he again speaks with absolute assured-
ness: "for I *know* that You are a compassionate and gracious God (Jon. 4:2)."[40]

The sailors' receptiveness to God reaches its peak at the chapter's end
when they bring sacrifices and make vows, *va-yideru nedarim*. Perhaps their actions provide a literary contrast to those of the close-minded prophet. In his
efforts to escape God and to cling to his certainties, Jonah began a moral and
religious descent, וירד, *va-yered*. With their extraordinary openness, the sailors
replace Jonah's downward motion with the phonetically inverse וידרו, *va-yidderu*,
they made vows. Their response to Jonah's descent is their emphatic display of
spiritual and moral ascent.

Jonah Son of Amittai

While the sailors are open and growing, evolving from simple "sailors" to
God-fearing "men," Jonah remains fixed and unyielding. The sailors, as representa-
tives of all of humanity, are ready to consider new truths, fearing a previously unknown God and ultimately worshipping Him. As suggested by his patronymic
"Amittai," derived from the Hebrew word for truth, *emet*, Jonah stays rooted to truth
as he defines it. He lives his life as the "son of Amittai," the offspring and purveyor
of his own inexorable truths.[41]

It is in this light that we might best understand Jonah's objection to delivering God's warning to the people of Nineveh. Jonah reasons that if human nature is fixed, if truths once learned are never questioned, then repentance is
impossible. To offer a second chance to the people of Nineveh would be to in-
dulge in an illusion.

Jonah's penchant for "truth" comes into conflict with his perception of God's
functioning in the world. In fact, when Jonah later articulates his reason for fleeing,
he hints at the absence of truth in God's actions:

---

39. The sailors break from their interrogative style only twice. The first time is when they state that they
    "know" that Jonah was fleeing God, because Jonah had told them. This statement reflects Jonah's
    certainty, not their own. The second time is when they plead to God for Jonah's life. They state, "For
    You, O LORD, by Your will, have brought this about" (Jon. 1:14). This declaration is really a submission
    of their own decision-making capabilities to God's greater wisdom and power.
40. Although it would seem that Jonah's certainty regarding God's mercy is laudable, we will see that
    Jonah pronounces these words as a complaint, not as praise.
41. I first heard this suggestion in a lecture given by Nehama Leibowitz.

That is why I fled beforehand to Tarshish. For I know [*yadati*] that You are a compassionate and gracious God, slow to anger, abounding in kindness, renouncing punishment. (Jon. 4:2)

With this statement, Jonah invokes the formula Moses used in addressing God after the sin of the Golden Calf in the Book of Exodus. There, Moses called God "a God compassionate and gracious, slow to anger, abounding in kindness and *truth*"[42] (Exod. 34:6).

But Jonah adopts this convention only to alter it for his own divergent intentions. Through his slight modification of Moses' words, Jonah sounds his objection to God's running of the world, in which God's attribute of "truth" is replaced by His "renouncing of punishment."[43] Jonah's rendition of God's attributes reads not as praise, but as an accusation. For Jonah, God has inexcusably strayed from His own exacting standards of truth.

Jonah's full name, "Jonah son of Amittai," a "dove the son of truth," suggests a deep conflict that lies at the heart of the book that bears his name. On the one hand, Jonah is to be God's faithful messenger, a quintessential *"Yonah,"* called upon to deliver God's message of mercy to the wayward people of Nineveh. But, on the other hand, Jonah is also a man of truth, the "son of Amittai" who yearns for a strict correlation between actions and consequences. Thus far, like Noah before the Flood, Jonah's sense of truth leads him toward detachment from his fellow human beings. He looks on from a safe distance, secure in his conviction that the guilty should receive what they deserve.

Jonah seems unaware of God's post-Flood forbearance and His pledge never again to destroy every living thing, despite the continued unworthiness of the human species (Gen. 9:21). The sailors act as God's messengers to Jonah, demonstrating humanity's capacity for self-transformation. These anonymous "men" respond to God's word, delivered by Jonah, with alacrity and sincerity. Yet Jonah himself remains firmly attached to his implacable "truth," the immutable nature of the human psyche.

Both Noah and Jonah are guided by their sense of certainty. They "know" that the human heart is unalterably as God describes it in Genesis: "only evil all the time" (Gen. 6: 5), and that death is the only corrective to such persistent depravity.

---

42. Author's translation.
43. Ibid. See also Reiner, *Mo'adei Nehama*, 374–75.

But this conviction faces serious challenge in the Book of Jonah, the sequel to the story of Noah. Instead of upholding the prophet's orderly world view, God sends messengers who provoke Jonah by posing question after question. In a very real sense, their mode of discourse is their message: life, conscious of its own possibility, is a question rather than an answer. Human motives are not simply self-reinforcing and static. They are hidden, unpredictable, and endlessly dynamic.

Nineveh: The Great City Overturned

For further insight into the development of Jonah's character, we examine his interaction with another population that is emblematic of humanity, the people of Nineveh. The third chapter of the Book of Jonah begins: "The word of the LORD came to Jonah a second time" (Jon. 3:1). Reading closely, we note the double entendre contained in these words. In one sense, God's word is intended for the people of Nineveh, as Jonah is again instructed to warn them of the coming destruction. Jonah, then, is God's agent, and the word of the LORD comes to him so that he might convey it to others. But on another level, Jonah *himself* is the intended recipient of God's word, and the people of Nineveh are God's messengers. Read in this way, the first time Jonah received God's "word" was in Jonah 1, through the remarkable behavior of the sailors. Now the text announces that the word of God is about to visit Jonah again, this time by means of the exceptional actions of another "messenger" population, the people of Nineveh.

We now turn to the full text of Jonah 3 in order to explore the effect that God's messengers, Jonah and the people of Nineveh, will have on one another. We will consider whether Jonah will manage to stir the people to repentance, and whether the people will cause Jonah to reconsider his unyielding position on the human capacity for change.

> The word of the Lord came to Jonah a second time: "Get up and go to Nineveh the great city, and call upon it the calling that I will tell you." Jonah got up and went to Nineveh in accordance with the Lord's command. And Nineveh was a great city to God—a three days' walk across. Jonah started out and made his way into the city the distance of one day's walk, and called: "In another forty days Nineveh shall be overturned!"
>
> The people of Nineveh believed in God. They proclaimed a fast, and great and small alike put on sackcloth. When the news reached the king of Nineveh, he rose from his throne, took off his robe, put on sackcloth, and sat

in ashes. And he had the word cried through Nineveh: "By decree of the king and his nobles: No man or beast—of flock or herd—shall taste anything! They shall not graze, and they shall not drink water! They shall be covered with sackcloth—man and beast—and shall cry mightily to God. Let everyone turn back from his evil ways and from the injustice of which he is guilty. Who knows [*mi yode'a*] but that God may turn and relent? He may turn back from His wrath, so that we do not perish."

God saw what they did, how they were turning back from their evil ways. And God regretted the evil He had planned to bring upon them, and did not carry it out (Jon. 3: 3–10).[44]

In Jonah 1, God had commanded Jonah to "get up, go, and call." But Jonah refused; he "got up" only to flee God's presence. When God now issues a nearly identical command, Jonah complies: "Jonah *got up* and *went* to Nineveh in accordance with the LORD's command ... and he *called*." We see the first stirrings of change in Jonah. But whether his outward obedience is accompanied by an internal shift remains to be seen.

To find out, we look closely at Jonah's speech to the people of Nineveh, remaining mindful from the outset of the symbolic value of that city. Twice within the space of two verses (Jon. 3:2,3) we are reminded that Nineveh is "the great city." In fact, this designation is given four times in the four chapters of this book, and once at the time of its inception as a city, immediately following the story of Noah in Genesis (10:12).[45] Nineveh is the quintessential metropolis, a place of teeming humanity, a symbol, like the ship in Jonah 1, of the entire world. In fact, the two words in Hebrew—אוניה and נינוה (ship and Nineveh respectively) are near anagrams. For the second time in his book, Jonah comes face to face with the world.

Jonah delivers a succinct prophecy: "In another forty days Nineveh will be overturned," which is astonishingly effective. Whole volumes of the prophets have been devoted to impassioned, verbose, and ultimately unsuccessful warnings intended to move the people to repent. Yet here, Jonah, the reluctant prophet, utters five Hebrew words and the city undergoes an immediate spiritual transformation. Why?

---

44. Author's translation.

45. It is unclear from the verse in Genesis to which city the term "great city" refers: Resen, Kelah, or Nineveh. Although in its context, Nineveh is the least likely referent, it is significant that from its very inception, Nineveh is tied to the adjectival phrase "great city."

Jonah uses language that draws on two known catastrophes. First, the forty day warning period recalls Noah's Flood, which continued for forty days and forty nights. Next, with the word "overturned," from the Hebrew root *h-f-kh*, Jonah's prophecy graphically evokes the devastation in Sodom:

> And God overturned [*h-f-kh*] those cities and the entire plain, and all the inhabitants of the cities and the vegetation of the ground ... God removed Lot from the upheaval [*h-f-kh*] where he overturned [*h-f-kh*] the cities in which Lot dwelled.[46] (Gen. 19:25,29)

It would appear that Jonah chooses these frightening images because they reflect his conviction that the people of Nineveh deserve to meet the same end as the victims of Noah's Flood and of God's destruction in Sodom. Jonah's terse, declarative tone supports the notion that he views the impending devastation as the city's inevitable and well-deserved fate: "In another forty days Nineveh *will* be overturned."

But Jonah's tenor reflects an attitude that is at odds with God's intentions. In the Flood narrative, God did not give His prophet any role in warning the people of the coming disaster. But here God twice orders the prophet to "call upon"[47] the people. As we have seen, it is likely that God's wish, which underlies His appointment of Jonah as messenger, is that Jonah's "calling" would lead to the people's repentance, which would, in turn, bring about their salvation.

Jonah finds himself in a difficult position, because he has been ordered to do something he does not believe in. And so he strikes a dubious compromise. In deference to God's power, he technically follows His orders, announcing the threatened devastation. But although Jonah may have no control over the basic content of God's message, he does control its mode of delivery. Instead of issuing a rousing address to inspire the people toward repentance, Jonah pares his words down to the barest minimum, revealing his own wishes by including graphic literary images of the Flood and of Sodom. And instead of offering the people a plan for escaping annihilation, Jonah announces their destruction as inevitable fact. In these ways, Jonah undermines the very repentance he has been summoned to initiate, as he continues to stubbornly resist the notion of sincere and enduring change.

---

46. Ibid. Author's translation.
47. In Jonah 1, God says *"u-kera aleha;"* in chapter 3, *"u-kera eleha."* Despite the shift from *ayin* to *aleph* in *aleha* and *eleha* respectively, the meaning is essentially the same.

If Jonah intends for his words to convey the certainty of God's punishment, how do the people of Nineveh receive them? Rashi points out that the root *h-f-kh* can denote not only destruction and devastation, but can also signal an overturning of actions and a reversal of consequences.[48] This bears itself out elsewhere in the Bible, such as in the verses "You turned [*h-f-kh*] my lament into dancing" (Ps. 30:12) and its converse, "Our dancing is turned [*h-f-kh*] into mourning" (Lam. 5:15). While Jonah may have intended a single, deterministic statement of fact, the people of Nineveh hear something else, an optimistic double entendre. On the one hand, they might persist in their evil ways. In that case they will be met with total Sodom-like destruction. But, on the other hand, they hold the power to avoid that destruction. If, within the space of forty days they *overturn* their actions and sincerely repent, their fate, too, will be *overturned*. Although he does not intend it, Jonah's words ring out with the sounds of untold possibility, of *ulay*. The people, open to life's mysterious potential, seize the possibility and immediately repent.

Like the sailors, the citizens of Nineveh show a remarkable capacity to explore and embrace the unknown, including a belief in God[49] (Jon. 1:16 and 3:5). Both populations, moreover, have leaders who play an integral role in their openness to the unforeseen. When the ship's captain said: "Get up! Call upon your god! Perhaps the god will be kind to us and we will not perish" (1:6), he modeled his sailors' open attitude toward the world. In a similar vein, the king of Nineveh says: "Who knows [*mi yode'a*] but that God may turn and relent? He may turn back from His wrath, so that we will not perish" (3:9). The captain and the king stand in contrast to Jonah and Noah, who, in their insistence on accepting only what is outwardly apparent, that which they "know," resist the challenge of effecting change. Instead, the two prophets stand apart from their charges, leaving them to meet a fate separate from their own.

Ultimately, though Jonah did not think it possible, the people of Nineveh achieve genuine repentance, their words backed up by unassailable deeds:

---

48. Rashi on 3:4, s.v. *"nehefakhet."* Rashi claims an intended double entendre on the part of Jonah. Both choices—destruction or turnabout through repentance—stand before you, and one will occur within forty days. When faced with such certainty, the people naturally opted for repentance and survival.

49. The sailors discover "the LORD," while the people of Nineveh speak of God (*Elohim*). The precise distinctions between these terms, while very significant, are beyond the scope of this work.

God saw what they did, how they were turning back from their evil ways. And God regretted the evil He had planned to bring upon them, and did not carry it out. (Jon. 3: 10)

In response to the people's renunciation of their evil ways, God annuls His evil decree. But it remains to be seen whether the people manage to affect Jonah as well, reversing his deeply-rooted assumptions about the immutability of the human psyche.

The Wings of the Dove

We have seen many inverse parallels between the Book of Jonah and the story of Noah. These literary inversions, along with the modeling of the outstanding heroes of the Book of Jonah, point to humanity's inexhaustible capacity to reverse its direction and its fate, a capacity insistently denied by the book's title character. What separates Jonah from the populations he encounters is the latter's ability to embrace a sense of *"ulay."* The sailors on the boat and the people of Nineveh, both of whom are worlds in miniature, hold the capacity for radical change, since they never cease to consider such change possible.

What, then, becomes of Jonah? Throughout his book, although God repeatedly exposes him to humanity in transition, Jonah clings to his absolutes, looking for consistency and truth instead of nuance and flexibility. As we have seen, the two worlds Jonah has encountered, the ship and Nineveh, beckon Jonah to recognize the world's transformative ability and then to view himself as a natural part of the equation. Jonah's name, *Yonah* in Hebrew, completes the book's play on names: יונה-אוניה-נינוה. In fact, the letters of the Hebrew name Yonah, יונה, are fully contained in both the words נינוה (Nineveh) and אוניה (ship).[50] This wordplay hints at

---

50. Moreover, on the basis of these similarities, one might suggest yet another possible reading of Jonah's decree: "In forty days נינוה will be overturned." The goal is for יונה (Jonah) to see himself in נינוה (Nineveh), an act symbolized by the transposing or "overturning" the letters of נינוה into the letters of Jonah's name, יונה. Read this way, Jonah's announcement is an unwitting proclamation of his own ability to be transformed along with the people. In another forty days, Nineveh will be "overturned," i.e., Jonah will come to see himself as a transposed form of the people of Nineveh; thus he will see himself as one who shares their fate. Not to be relegated to mere fanciful wordplay, this biblical technique of transposing letters in order to connect words and concepts is particularly evident in the Jacob stories of Genesis. See Shmuel Klitsner's analysis of the words Jacob and Jabbok, *minha* and *mahane*, *bekhora* and *berakha*, *gid* and *gedi*, etc., in *Wrestling Jacob*, 140.

a boundless opportunity for human growth shared by all its characters. If Nineveh and the ship are microcosms of an ever-evolving world, so too, is Jonah himself.

As we approach the end of Jonah's book, we wonder whether or not he will see things this way. If he is able to adjust his perspective, perhaps he could escape Noah's self-destructive descent into oblivion. Perhaps as a result, he might spread his wings and fly, like Noah's dove, to the promise of new beginnings.

Appropriately, the Book of Jonah ends with a question, this time posed by God.[51] God's rhetorical question comes after the appearance of additional "messengers" to Jonah. First, God caused a gourd[52] to grow spontaneously, offering Jonah shade and causing him great happiness. God then appointed a worm to attack the gourd and dry it up. Jonah is so distressed by the loss of the gourd that he expresses his wish to die. At this point, God responds with the question that closes the book:

> Then the Lord said, "You cared about the plant, which you did not work for and which you did not grow, which appeared overnight and perished overnight. And should I not care about Nineveh, that great city, in which there are more than a hundred and twenty thousand persons who do not yet know their right hand from their left, and many beasts as well?" (Jon. 4:10–11)

The interrogative form recalls the inflection of the sailors and the king of Nineveh in previous chapters. Moreover, it highlights God's role as the initiator and chief proponent of a new mode of operation in the world. Since the Flood, God has stretched His "heart" and made room for humanity to change its heart as well. As it turns out, what God declares need not come to pass; seeing the world in a godly way is often the very opposite of seeing it in absolute terms. Perhaps God hints at this by offering the rainbow as a symbol of non-aggression toward the world. After the devastation of the Flood, God signals that henceforth His will, like the rainbow, is pliant, and that colors can shade into one another with room for nuance.

In this sequel to the story of the Flood, doubt and possibility, gentler responses to the vagaries of human nature, replace declarative statements and inflexible judgments. This time, the world, following God's lead, conducts itself according to the principles of *mi yode'a*, who knows, and *ulay*, perhaps. God's use of the words

---

51. In fact, all of God's utterances to Jonah in chapter 4, though rhetorical, are in interrogative form.
52. NJPS offers "gourd" as a secondary definition of the difficult word *"kikayon,"* after "ricinus plant." The remainder of the above translation is in line with NJPS.

asher lo yada, "persons who do not yet know" (Jon. 4:11) points both to humanity's weakness and greatness as presented by the Book of Jonah. On the one hand, human beings are clueless. Like the animals, they are frequently given to expressions of their deepest, darkest nature and so will inevitably fail again and again. Yet, on the other hand, their lack of absolute "knowing" is their greatest strength. Like Abraham, the people in this book are endlessly imaginative about humanity's capacity to renounce its evil leanings and to reinvent itself.

Jonah hears God's final argument, but fails to respond. The messages have been delivered, first by God's agents and now by God Himself, but we do not know if Jonah receives them. It is not clear if Jonah can see himself as one with the world, with the same limitations, the same need for mercy, and the same inexhaustible capacity for improvement.

When we reach the end of his book, we are faced with Jonah's resounding silence, a silence that reverberates for us, and will reverberate throughout the stories we will analyze in this volume of subversive sequels. In this silence lies the hope and the opportunity of *ulay.* This word represents the potential of human beings to imagine themselves as other than they have always been and to undertake the courageous task of corrective repair that will reverse, *h-f-kh,* their standing before themselves and before God.

The open question with which the Book of Jonah concludes suggests that while there is no guarantee that humanity will embrace the opportunities for self-transformation, it is indeed possible for them to produce constructively subversive sequels within their own lives.

Chapter 2

The Rebirth of the Individual: The Tower of Babel and the Midwives of Israel

The only tyrant I accept in this world is the still voice within.
—Mohandas Gandhi

A t first glance, the Tower of Babel and the enslavement of the Israelites in Egypt seem to have very little in common.[1] In a search for stories and their sequels, other narratives strike us as more plausible and intuitive matches. The stories of Noah and Jonah, as we've just seen, share such basic elements as water, the destruction of humanity, prophets in crisis, and the evolving nature of the divine-human relationship. But in reading the Babel and Egypt narratives carefully, remarkable similarities in both language and theme become apparent. Both stories center on the building of cities, and both specify the same building materials. Both feature fear-inducing orations, and both display an unusual emphasis on the presence and disappearance of names.

This chapter will show how the biblical text employs elegant literary devices to pair these passages, setting them up to interpret and elucidate one another. As we will discover, both stories will address the centrality of individual identity in cultivating the divine-human relationship. Both will then demonstrate the adverse effects on that relationship when destructive forces attempt to suppress the individual.

---

1. I was first made aware of the intriguing connection between the two stories in a short article in a student periodical, Anisfeld, *Bikkurim Journal*, 7–17.

The Exodus narrative, as we will see, will also subvert the Babel story, harnessing its basic story line to arrive at unexpected new conclusions. In the subversive sequel to Babel, instead of succumbing to the seductive forces of conformity, humanity will seek the inner resources to resist, and to rediscover God in the process.

The Tower of Babel story is enigmatic. A group of seemingly well-meaning people seek to build a city and a tower "with its top in the heavens," so that they can "make a name" for themselves and avoid being scattered. For reasons not explicitly stated, their actions elicit God's anger, and as a result their greatest fears are realized. They never complete the tower, and the only "name" they acquire is one of confusion and obscurity. In the end, despite all their efforts—in fact, ironically *because* of their efforts—they are indeed "scattered over the face of all the land."

A crime has been committed and duly punished. But exactly *what* crime was it? The mere act of building a city and a tower? The grandiose goal of reaching the heavens? The desire to create a "name" and avoid scattering? Our search for the precise nature of the crime will provide the foundation for this chapter. In a thorough mining of this short passage, we will use the tools of literary analysis, with a special focus on the text's sophisticated word play, in order to identify the misdeed. Next we will consult the passage's parallel text, the enslavement in Egypt, which in many ways retells the same basic narrative, but with substitute names and locations. Through an array of literary and thematic comparisons, we will seek to confirm our thesis that the crime at Babel involves the quashing of the individual.

In our next stage of analysis, we will look to the Egypt narrative as a subversive sequel to Babel. We will note not only how it reinforces its central theme of a destructive conformity, but how it challenges and undermines that theme. Beyond asking *what* happened, the sequel will ask, what *might* have happened? Must the type of building exhibited in the Tower of Babel narrative have resulted in the undoing of an entire generation? Or could the human players have fought back? In the previous chapter, we examined God's role as catalyst in bridging the divine-human divide and in promoting the development of the individual. In this chapter, the individual takes center stage. This time humanity will take steps to heal itself and then will go on to forge, maintain, and repair the divine-human bond.

The Tower of Babel

We begin our inquiry with a close reading of the Babel narrative, paying keen attention to its structure and style. In order to appreciate the linguistic artistry of this passage, we present the full text in translation, highlighting outstanding recurring words and phrases and providing their transliteration from the original Hebrew:

> And all the earth [*kol ha-aretz*] was of one language [*safah ehat*] and of one set of words [*devarim ahadim*].[2] And as they journeyed from the east they found a valley in the land of Shinar and settled there [*sham*]. And they said to one another, "Come let us make bricks [*havah nilbena leveinim*] and burn them hard (lit. "burn burnings"), and the brick served them as stone, and bitumen served them as mortar [*ve-ha-hemar hayah lahem la-homer*]. And they said, "Come let us build a city [*havah nivneh*—from the root *b,n,h*—*lanu ir*] and a tower, with its top in the heavens, and we will make a name [*shem*] for ourselves, lest we scatter over the face of all the earth [*pen nafutz al penei khol ha-aretz*]. And the Lord descended to see the city [*ir*] and the tower that humanity had built [*banu benei ha-adam*]. And the Lord said, "If, as one nation [*am ehad*] and one language [*ve-safah ehat*] this is how they have begun to act, then nothing that they propose to do will be out of their reach. Come let us descend [*havah nereda*] and confuse their language there [*sham sefatam*] so that they will not understand each other's language [*ish sefat re'ehu*]. And the Lord scattered [*va-yafetz*] them from there over the face of all the earth [*mi-sham al penei khol ha-aretz*] and they ceased building [*b,n,h*] the city [*ir*]. Therefore, He called its name [*shemah*] Babel, because there [*sham*] the Lord confused the language of all the earth [*sefat kol ha-aretz*] and from there [*mi-sham*] the Lord scattered them [*hefitzam*] over the face of all the earth [*al penei kol ha-aretz*].[3] (Genesis 11:1–9)

Terse in its narration, this passage omits descriptive adjectives and even the names of its characters. As noted, its most basic premise shrouds itself in ambiguous brevity; God has been affronted, but the text withholds the details of the offense.

Yet along with this stylistic economy, the passage indulges in lavish redundancy, repeating specific words and phrases with remarkable frequency. The phrase *kol ha-aretz*, all the earth, appears five times; the word *safah*, language,

---

2. I am translating this ambiguous phrase in line with Alter's *Genesis, Translation and Commentary*, 46. For an elaboration on the possibilities inherent in this phrase, see note 9.

3. Author's translation.

appears five times; the root *b-n-h*, to build, appears three times; the word *ir*, city, appears three times; the root *p-v-tz*, to spread out, appears three times; the word *shem*, name, appears twice, with the identical consonantal construct *sham*, there, appearing five times, for a total of seven. The feminine and masculine forms for "one," *ehad, ahat*, appear four times.

These repetitions might be taken to reveal unimaginative writing that could be easily remedied with a sprinkling of synonyms. For instance, the Hebrew root *p-v-tz*, to scatter, recurs three times in these nine verses, even though a reasonable alternative appears in the verse immediately preceding the passage: *ume'ela **nifredu** hagoyim*, from these the nations branched out (Gen. 10:32).[4] The Bible frequently employs diversified language; why here does it fail to do so?

In this case, repetition is not an absence of style but a style in itself. The Bible frequently appoints and repeats a particular "guiding word," or *leitwort*, to use Martin Buber's term, by means of which it conveys its perspectives in subtle ways, "making a meaning available without articulating it explicitly."[5] The many guiding words in this passage combine to suggest a strong focus on the human drive for indivisibility. The people begin as one, and invest enormous efforts in safeguarding their unity, fearing that if they do not do so, they will be scattered throughout the earth. A closer look at the repeated words and phrases reveals the ways in which language encodes the people's goals:

Kol ha-aretz, safah, ehad (ahat), p-v-tz (all the earth, language, one, scatter): The people's oneness in speech and geography contributes to an unusual degree of unity. The people are referred to as the singular unit "all the earth," whose

---

4. Similarly, in the previous chapter the word *lashon* is used for "language" (Gen. 10:5,20,31) and could have been used interchangeably with *safah* in Genesis 11. Instead the same term, *safah*, is used five times in Genesis 11. Examples of word variation abound in the Bible. For example, after receiving God's sentence to roam the earth following his murder of his brother, Cain complains that all who find him will kill him, using the word *h-r-g*. Yet when the text goes on to paraphrase Cain's fear of being killed, it employs a different verb, *n-kh-h* (vv.14–15).

5. The *leitwort* is a key element of the Buber-Rosenzweig translation of the Bible into German. Everett Fox presents the *leitwort* as one of the three important techniques "with which biblical literature often conveys its message and which must influence the translation of the text … A leading word operates on the basis of sound: the repetition of a word or word root encourages the listener to make connections between diverse parts of a story (or even of a book), and to trace a particular theme throughout." Fox, *The Five Books of Moses*, xvi.

greatest fear is falling into the antithetical mode of being scattered "over the face of all the earth."

Ir, b-n-h (city, build): These words further highlight the people's belief that their geographic consolidation guarantees their unity. In their desperation to remain together, the people build a city—using the building materials *homer* and *leveinim*, mortar and bricks—hoping that doing so will shield them from dispersal.

Havah (come let us): *Havah* is a public call to action.[6] In this story, no one acts alone. These unnamed, undifferentiated people call out for a cooperative effort. The adjunct *pen* (lest) makes the threat emphatic: we had better unite, *lest* the dreaded dispersal occur.

Shem (name), *sham* (there): By their act of collective building, the people hope to prevent their scattering, and to create a "name," a sense of permanence, perhaps even immortality. Together, these identically constructed words are the passage's most oft-repeated, and, as such, have particular power to guide toward the heart of the passage. The people's enduring "name" depends on their staying "there," in the city that they intend to build.

As we continue to follow the trail of these guiding words, we find that curiously, the word "city," *ir*, recurs more often than the word "tower" (*migdal*), despite the title frequently bestowed on this passage, "the Tower of Babel." Later events support the primacy of the city in this tale. For one thing, God obstructs the building of the city, but makes no reference at all to the tower (Gen. 11:8). For another, the narrative affixes a pejorative name to the city, even as the tower escapes a negative label: "Therefore He called its name Babel, because there the LORD confused the language of all the earth ..." (v. 9). The passage's emphasis on the city suggests a preference by the builders, later repudiated by God, for horizontal rather than vertical construction. It is primarily the city, and not the tower, that acts as a central component in their effort to achieve geographic consolidation.

The passage's guiding words suggest a stylistic foundation for a basic plot line, in which a group of people seek unity and permanence through the building of a city. In addition, these words assure readers that a sin has, in fact, been committed. Traditional biblical commentators[7] detect an elaborate

---

6. Havah is a command form of the root *y-h-v*, and literally means "give!"
7. The theme of the passage's poetic justice appears in midrashim such as *Mekhilta Beshalah* chapter 2, Exod. 15:2, and is developed extensively and eloquently in Cassuto's *Commentary to the Book of Genesis*, 154–69.

quid pro quo,[8] in which each of the people's words and actions are met with divine retorts.

The people, referred to in the passage's opening as **all the earth,** *kol ha-aretz,* are of one **language,** *safah;* God later confuses the **language** of all the earth, *sefat kol ha-aretz.* The people call to **one another,** *ish el re'ehu,* to begin building; God confuses them so that they may not understand **one another's** speech, *ish sefat re'ehu.* The people summon each other to action with the words, **Come let us** make bricks, *havah nilbenah;* God's call for reaction is, **Come let us** go down, *havah nereda,* and confuse their language there. The people's greatest fear is lest we be **scattered** over the **face of the whole earth,** *p-v-tz al penei kol ha-aretz;* God responds as He **scatters** them over the **face of all the earth,** *p-v-tz al penei kol ha-aretz.* Finally, this literary action and reaction reaches its crescendo in the passage's stinging conclusion, which offers a literary response to the people's desire to make a **name** for themselves. In the words of contemporary Dutch Bible scholar J.P. Fokkelman:

> People want a name? Well, they can have it, but how different it will be from the name they had dreamt of: "therefore its name was called Babel, 'Muddle'!" This unexpected turn is like a judgment, so biting is its sarcasm.[9]

A structural analysis of this passage, then, makes a compelling case for reading it as a tale of cause and effect, misdeed and punishment. Yet, as we have seen, a reading that takes its cues from the guiding words suggests that the people of Babel enjoyed an unusual degree of unity. These two notions seem to be at odds. If the people lived in such great harmony, where is the sin? Should God not congratulate humanity on its rare state of oneness rather than condemn it? On the road to the subversive sequel, we must find a nexus between humanity's unity and God's anger. In search of this meeting point, we turn to the classical biblical exegetes.

---

8. The midrash was sensitive to this technique, applying the term *"middah keneged middah,"* measure for measure, to a punishment that suits the crime. For an example of the application of this technique to a literary quid pro quo, see *Midrash Tanhuma,* Buber, *parashat* Va-yese,' *siman* 11. When Jacob's reacts to his father-in-law, Laban's deceit in substituting Leah for Rachel, Jacob cries: *"Lammah rimmitani* [from the root *r-m-h*], why have you deceived me!" (Gen. 29:25). These words direct the reader back to Jacob's own deceit of his father. There Isaac lamented, *"Ba ahikha be-mirmah* [from the same *r-m-h* root], your brother came in deceit" (27:35). The poetic justice of Jacob's suffering is made clear by this method. Sean Herstein, a former student of mine, coined the term *"millah keneged millah"* ("word for word" as opposed to "measure for measure") to capture the literary nature of this type of quid pro quo.

9. Fokkelman, *Narrative Art in Genesis,* 14.

Rashi: A Rebellious Unity

Rashi looks to the opening words of the Babel story to understand the nature of the people's misdeed. The passage begins, "All the earth was of one language and *devarim ahadim*." The Hebrew term *"devarim ahadim"* is teeming with ambiguity. *Devarim* could mean *words, deeds,* or *things,* and *ahadim* could mean *few, several,* or *one.*[10] Rashi carefully defines both words, thereby providing a point of departure for the entire narrative. In his view, *devarim ahadim* means that the people were possessed by a single idea:

> They came with one counsel and said, "Not all depends on Him [i.e. God had no right] to choose for Himself the heavens. Let us ascend to the firmament and wage war with Him.'"[11] (Rashi on Gen. 11:1, s.v. *devarim ahadim*)

Although the people were indeed remarkably unified, they harnessed their unity in order to rebel against God. Rashi thus confirms the harmonious nature of the generation while at the same time finding the origin of its sin.

Rashi's view finds several reinforcements in the biblical text. First, the people describe the tower as having "its top in the heavens" (Gen. 1: 4). It is not difficult to read a mutinous intent into this detail, namely that the tower would invade God's perceived power base and challenge His authority. In this reading, humanity, in its hubris, sought to break the barriers between the human and divine spheres. The people's tower, *migdal,* phonetically plays on the Hebrew word *gadol,* great, pointing to their goal of aggrandizement through building.[12] The point is driven home by further wordplay, linking their stated goal of making a name, *shem,* for themselves, *sham,* there, in that place, by intruding on God's heavenly headquarters, the *shamayim.*[13] In a parallel passage in Isaiah, a king of Babylon boasts of his ability to "climb to the sky; higher than the stars of God I will set my throne" (Is. 14:13–14). This comparison suggests a history of competitiveness with God on

---

10. *Ahadim* in the Bible means "few," as in Gen. 29:20: "So Jacob served seven years for Rachel and they seemed to him *but a few days* [*ke-yamim ahadim*] because of his love for her." In addition, it could mean "quite a few" or "several," as in Gen. 27:44: "Stay with him *a while* [*yamim ahadim*] until your brother's fury subsides." Occasionally, *ahadim* means "one," as in Ezek. 37:17: "Bring them close to each other, so that they become one stick, *joined together* [*ahadim*] in your hand."
11. Rashi bases his comments on Genesis Rabbah 38:6.
12. Fokkelman, *Narrative Art,* 19.
13. Ibid., 25.

the part of Babylonians, resulting in occasional attempts to rise above Him physically with their lofty ziggeraut temple-towers. If this is indeed the people's goal, there is deep irony in the passage's report that "God *came down* to look at the city and tower that the children of Adam had built" (Gen. 11:5), a trope that is repeated two verses later (v. 7). Believing themselves to have challenged God's realm, the people exert themselves to build the highest tower possible; and yet God has to descend just to observe it.[14]

But why would this particular group of people seek to overtake God at this particular time? Reading further in Rashi, we find a connection between the tower builders and the great Flood that humanity has recently experienced:

> Another interpretation of *devarim ahadim* is: They said, "Once every one
> thousand six hundred and fifty-six years the firmament totters just as it did
> in the days of the Flood. Come let us make for [the firmament] a support.[15]
> (Rashi on Gen. 11:1, s.v. *devarim ahadim*)

In this view, in an act of preemptive self defense in the face of God's destructive power, the people built a tower, a steadfast beam meant to prevent any further eruption of the heavens. Perhaps their singular language and location, along with their fear of scattering, may be seen in this light. After the Flood, God had exhorted humanity to replenish the earth, using the terms *p-r-h*, be fruitful, *r-v-h*, increase, and *m-l,'* fill the earth (Gen. 9:1). God had seen to humanity's divergence into separate nations and languages: "From these the nations branched out over the earth after the Flood" (10:32).[16] But instead of diversifying, the people of Babel rebel by seeking to remain united. If they could combine their strength, they might protect themselves from God by thwarting His plan for humanity's natural dispersal.[17]

Rashi's notion of a mutiny against God finds further support in God's extreme response to the people's efforts. Unlike other crimes described in the Bible,

---

14. Berlin and Brettler, *The Jewish Study Bible*, 29. See also Sarna, *Understanding Genesis*, 77.

15. See note 10.

16. Sarna, *Genesis*, 72–73; Cassuto, *Genesis*, 167.

17. The notion that the people's actions in Babel were guided by their insecurity finds support in an aggadic passage in the Talmud, *Sanhedrin* 109a. In this passage, the people in Babel—perhaps as a result of post-Flood trauma—seek greater security by attempting to reach the heavens and wrest from God control of the rain. I am grateful to Ilana Kurshan for directing me to this source.

here God does not even wait for the completion of the act before striking. Instead, He decisively preempts the plan, saying, "If this is how they have *begun* to act, then nothing they do may be out of their reach. Come, let us go down and confound their speech there ..." (Gen. 11:6–7).

But Rashi's theory remains unproven, as there is no direct textual evidence of an attempted rebellion against God. The people's goals of achieving unity, permanence, and a name are stated quite clearly. But there are merely hints of a battle against God, who is not even mentioned in the first half of the passage where the crime is described. While it is clear from the plain sense of the text that the people's actions have invited God's wrath, it is not at all certain that the builders have deliberately rebelled against Him.

Naftali Zvi Yehuda Berlin: Excessive Unity

Lacking sufficient textual evidence to prove Rashi's theory of an attempted revolt against God, we turn to a second theory concerning the nature of the crime, offered by the 19th-century Lithuanian exegete, Naftali Tzvi Yehuda Berlin, known by his acronym Netziv, author of the commentary *Ha-amek Davar:*

> We must understand why they [the builders of Babel] feared some people leaving for another land. This was certainly related to the *devarim ahadim,* the "one speech" among them. They feared that since not all human thoughts are identical, if some would leave they might adopt different thoughts. And so they saw to it that no one left their enclave. Anyone who deviated from the *devarim ahadim,* the "one speech" that was among them would be sentenced to burning, as was done with our forefather, Abraham.[18] What emerges [from this text] is ... they decided to kill anyone who did not think as they did. (*Ha-amek Davar,* Gen. 11:4, s.v. *pen nafutz al penei kol ha-aretz*)

Like Rashi, and consistent with the passage's guiding words, Netziv understands the words *devarim ahadim* to refer to ideological consensus. And

---

18. Netziv refers to a famous midrashic story about Abraham's beginnings in which Abraham shatters his father's idols out of a newly discovered monotheistic world view. In his rage at his son's behavior, Abraham's father reports him to the king, who sentences Abraham to death by furnace. Abraham chooses to face the furnace rather than to recant his truth. God miraculously saves Abraham from the fire, making the truth of Abraham's claims apparent to all (Genesis Rabbah 38:13).

like Rashi, he finds this consensus to be the source of the people's crime. But here the similarity ends. Rashi condemns not their unity per se, but only its seditious focus. In finding fault with their unity *itself*, Netziv remains closer to the plain sense of the text, which does not cite God as a target of the people's efforts. In fact, he proposes that what they sought was not mere unity, but uniformity, in the form of an oppressively monolithic society.

To support this view, Netziv adduces various details supplied by the text:

> It is undoubtedly illogical to assume that there would be but one city in the entire world. Rather, they thought that all cities would be connected and subsidiary to that one city in which the tower was to be built. And the [purpose of] the tower was to look out upon the distance over all their dwellings [to ensure] that none would split off into another land. (*Ha-amek Davar*, 11:4, s.v. *ve-rosho ba-shamayim*)

This interpretation accounts for the passage's emphasis on the city, as opposed to the tower. The people's goal was to concentrate all of humanity into a single contiguous dwelling place, from which none would be permitted to leave. The great Tower of Babel was nothing more than a watchtower that was meant to keep foreign ideas from flowing in and people from fleeing out.

In line with Netziv's logic, we may glean more from the narrative's focus on the city. In much of the Book of Genesis, cities are places of alienation: from the earth's natural goodness,[19] from humanity,[20] from God,[21] and, as we will see in the Babel narrative, from one's sense of self-worth. In our story, there are hints of alienation in the unusual order of events described in the building effort. The

---

19. See Gen. 4:17. The first biblical city is built as an alternative to the idyllic agrarian life before the earth was cursed in Eden (3:17).

20. The cities of Sodom and Gomorrah are depicted as places of unmitigated evil, pitting human beings against each other (Gen. 19:4–5).

21. See Gen. 4:16–17. The first city is built by Cain, in defiance of God's command to wander the earth. For an elaboration on the evils of the city in the Bible, see the comments of Abravanel (15th century, Portugal), and his extensive negative treatment of the cities of Cain and Babel. In his view, the building of the city at Babel represented an effort to renounce the good life God offered in Eden and to substitute it with an artificial existence, filled with lust for possessions, often at the expense of living in harmony with others. Abravanel, *Commentary on the Bible*, Genesis, chapter 11, (in Hebrew).

people first call to one another to busy themselves with the details of construction: "Come let us bake bricks and burn them hard" (11:3). Only *afterwards* do
they announce the intended purpose of their activity: "Come let us build a city"
(11:4). Initially, the builders receive only a very partial description of the overall
plan. The minute details are not accompanied by an explanation of the larger
purpose of their exertions. In this way, individuals are kept at a distance from
their goals, from each other, and from any personal satisfaction they might derive
from their efforts.[22] Slaves to the whim of the city-building enterprise, human
beings lose their stamp of humanity.

A source in the midrash concurs with the view that the value of the individual was nullified in the collective building effort at Babel. By way of illustration, it
relates the following scenario. In building the tower, a laborer would climb steps
with bricks in hand. Losing his footing, he would slip and fall to his death, shatter-
ing the bricks. In response, onlookers would sink into deep mourning—for the
valuable broken bricks, not for the expendable human life. They would then cry,
"Woe is to us! When will we have another brick to replace it!"[23] In the city of Babel,
the collective was all. An individual was worth only as much as he or she contrib-
uted to the whole.

Netziv refers to Abraham, the next major biblical figure to follow the story
of Babel, in order to contrast his courageous individuality with the collective conformity of the builders of Babel.[24] With the words *lekh lekha*, which can literally be
translated as "go to yourself," God commands Abraham to leave behind everything that is familiar and to embark on a path that is uniquely his (Gen. 12:1).[25]
And in fact, throughout his trials, Abraham maintains his solitary stance, earn-
ing the title "Abraham the *Ivri*, Hebrew" (14:13), a term that throughout the Bible

---

22. For a classic exposition on alienated labor, see Marx, *Karl Marx: Early Writings*, 120–134.

23. *Pirkei De-Rabbi Eliezer* 24:7.

24. See note 18.

25. The idea that Abraham is to "go to himself" appears in the mystical commentary known as the
    Zohar (attributed to Rabbi Shimon B. Yohai and first published in the 13th century), "God said to
    Abraham, '*Lekh lekha*.' Rabbi Shimon said: 'The secret of wisdom is here. *Lekh lekha*: to correct (per-
    fect) yourself. From your land: from the place of dwelling within you, in which you consider the
    wisdom with which you were born. To the land that I will show you: there it will be revealed to you
    that which you seek, the power that is appointed over it (the land) which is deep and hidden.'"
    Zohar, *Parashat Lekh lekha*, 76b.

suggests singularity and otherness.[26] Abraham's status as lone seeker and trav-
eler thus contrasts with the stationary nature of the conformist multitude at Babel. Perhaps with this contrast in mind, the midrash cited above concludes with
Abraham's furious reaction to the building effort:

> Abraham son of Terah passed by and saw them building the city and cursed
> them in the name of his God saying, "Swallow them up, God! Divide their
> language!" (*Pirkei De-Rabbi Eliezer* 24:7)

By attributing this reprimand to Abraham, the original *Ivri,* the midrash pits
Abraham's distinctiveness in sharp relief against the monolithic nature of the people of
Babel and hints at a fundamental contrast between two philosophies. Abraham would
be the progenitor of an enduring nation of *Ivrim,* people who would be charged with
retaining their singularity in choosing God's path. On the opposite extreme were the
people of Babel, destined to be consumed by the forces of unanimity and anonymity.

There is much literary support for Netziv's hypothesis that the sin at Babel
was the creation of a coercively conformist society. We may find further evidence for
his view by *listening* to this passage as well as looking at it. Note the confounding
entanglement and hammering repetition of sounds, most specifically of the letters
B, V, N, and L employed by the people, God, and the narrative voice itself:

> *haVah NiLBeNah LeVeNim* [come let us make bricks]; *Lahem ha-LeVeNa Le-aVeN*
> [the brick served as stone] (Gen. 11:3); *haVah NiVNeh LaNu* [come, let us build

---

26. There are three hypotheses listed in *Genesis Rabbah* 42:8 as to the meaning of the epithet *Ivri.* It may
    identify Abraham's geographic origins: he is from beyond, *ever,* the River Euphrates. It may point to
    his lineage: he derives from Eber (*Ever* in Hebrew), grandson of Noah (see Gen. 10:24 and 11: 14). I
    have chosen to interpret it in line with the midrash's third suggestion: "R. Yehuda said, 'All the world
    was on one side, *ever ehad,* and he (Abraham) was on the other.'" This interpretation is supported by
    the use of the term *Ivri* throughout the Bible to denote Israelites as a group distinct from their sur-
    roundings. To take but one example, when the prophet Jonah boards a ship in an attempt to flee from
    God, God brings a great storm upon the ship. In their efforts to locate the source of danger, the ship's
    sailors ask Jonah who he is and where he came from. Jonah responds: "I am a Hebrew [*Ivri*] ... I wor-
    ship the LORD, the God of heaven, who made both sea and land. The men were greatly terrified ..."
    (Jon. 1:9–10). Jonah presents himself as an *Ivri,* distinct from all ethnicities and faiths the sailors had
    previously known. Nahum Sarna writes of three textual "clusters" in which the word "*Ivri*" bears this
    meaning: in the Joseph narratives in Gen. 39–43; In Exodus, chapters 1–3, 5, 7, 9; and 1 Samuel,
    chapters 4, 13, 14, 29. The term is sometimes pejorative, when Israelites are perceived as unwanted
    foreigners by those around them (see Gen. 43:34). Sarna, *JPS Torah Commentary, Genesis,* 377–78.

for ourselves] (11:4); *BaNu BeNe ha-Adam* [that humanity had built] (11:5); *Ve-NaVeLah* [(let us) confuse] (11:7).[27]

The sounds S and Sh are also used with tongue-twisting frequency and interchangeability:

> *Ve-roSHo ba-SHamayim ve-na'aSeh lanu Shem* [with its top in the heavens, and we will make a name for ourselves] (Gen. 11:4); *ve-navelah Sham Sefatam aSHer lo yiSHme'u iSH Sefat re'ehu* [and we will confuse there their language, so that they will not understand each other's language].[28] (11:7)

These sounds do not just play a formal role. They also reflect the content of the story:

> All of these repetitions create a throbbing, hypnotizing rhythm and a grating sense of sameness. All the people speak in the same manner, saying the same things with the same words because this is the communal refrain that has been inculcated into their consciousness through mesmerizing repetition.[29]

The insistently repetitive rhythms of the text point to a generation's intellectual and ideological homogeneity, in which every element of culture is mandated, from language and thought to meter and melody. Through structure and sound, this passage informs us that the sin at Babel is the achievement of consensus at the expense of individuality.

Between the Lines of Babel

In order to pave the way for seeing the Exodus narrative as subversive sequel to Babel, we have tried to distill the motives of the tower builders at Babel. We have closely looked at and listened to the story, overlaid with Netziv's conclusions. Yet his reading is not comprehensive. We recall Rashi's hypothesis that the people were engaged in a rebellion against God and the many textual nuances that support it. We note that

---

27. Cassuto, 233. Fokkelman adds the notion of a "sound-chiasmus," in which the sounds "l,b,n" are repeated six times in the passage, first in that order, then in reverse order. Fokkelman sees this form as helping to deliver God's message of reversing the people's intentions. *Narrative Art*, 15.
28. Author's translation.
29. Anisfeld, *Bikkurim Journal*, 9.

Netziv's views do not account for all these details. Why must the text inform us that that the tower's top was to be "in the heavens?" Why the repeated reminder that God had to descend (Gen. 11:5,7) in order to view humanity's grandest structure? And, most pressing, why is God so disturbed by the people's construction effort that He preemptively thwarts it? These details subtly suggest that God has been affronted, and as a result, the divine-human relationship has deteriorated. To fully understand this passage, we must revisit the conclusions of both commentators, considering a link between the uniformity described by Netziv and the rebelliousness suggested by Rashi. In order to do so, we turn to an earlier story in Genesis, the story of Creation, in which human autonomy is presented as a central component of God's ideal world.

The defining characteristic of human beings, biblically speaking, is that they are created "in God's image" (Gen. 1:28), endowed with the godlike ability to freely think, choose, create, and judge.[30] The human being is free to choose an independent path, even if that path leads to the defiance of God. After the first man and woman eat from the forbidden tree of good and evil, God proclaims: "Behold, the human being has become like one of us [ke'ahad mimmennu] knowing good and bad" (Gen. 3:22). The great 11th-century Spanish philosopher Maimonides finds in this statement evidence of God's pride in humanity's development, despite, and in part, *because of,* their act of defiance:

> The human being has become as one of us, that is ... singular in the world, and no other species resembles it in this way: that human beings, in their wisdom and understanding, know good and evil and do as they choose, with no one to restrain them.[31]

Similarly, the psychoanalyst Erich Fromm sees humanity's partaking of the forbidden fruit as a defining moment in the birth of the autonomous self:

> Acting against God's orders means freeing himself from coercion, emerging from the unconscious existence of prehuman life to the level of man. Acting against the command of authority, committing a sin, is in its positive human

---

30. See *Meshekh Hokhma* (R. Meir Simcha HaCohen of Dvinsk, 19th century, Russia) Gen. 1:27, s.v. *na'aseh adam:* "The divine image *is* free will, unencumbered by external pressures; it operates from independent intelligence and will."

31. Maimonides, *Mishneh Torah, Hilkhot Teshuva* 5:1. See also Rashi's comments on Gen. 3:22, s.v. *ke'ahad mimmennu.*

aspect the first act of freedom, that is, the first human act ... he has taken the first step toward becoming human by becoming an "individual."[32]

In order to fulfill God's intentions for humanity, each godlike person must develop as a unique individual, even if individuality will occasionally lead the human being away from God. An individual, even a rebellious one, is more godly than a mindless member of a human herd.

Since God wishes for human autonomy, any attempt to suppress the divine spark of individuality, such as the collective action of the tower builders, constitutes a rebellion against God. As the Mishnah states, "God has stamped each individual with the imprint of Adam, and there is no one person who is identical to another" (Sanhedrin 4:5). It is thus a religious imperative to maintain one's singularity.[33]

One aspect of the people's rebellion against God lies in their attempts at effacing the individual. Their attempts constitute a negation of God's plan for humanity to be unique as God is unique. But there is another facet to their mutiny. By quashing freedom of thought, the tower builders preclude any human-divine engagement. In the words of Buber, only an individual with a sense of an autonomous self can reach out to engage God:

> Not before a man ... can say I, can he ... to God—say Thou. And even if he does it in a community, he can only do it "alone."[34]

While religious behavior may be coerced or feigned, such acts by definition are meaningless.[35] Religious worship has meaning only when the individual freely and sincerely chooses to submit to God's authority. By eroding the individual, the builders in Babel render impossible any hope of a divine-human covenant.

The defining lines of the Babel narrative are purposefully blurred. The text's ambiguity on the question of whether the people sinned against God or against one another points to a complex truth: the people's suppression of their unique selves lay at the root of their disengagement from God. In tyrannizing one another by extinguishing the divine spark of individuality, the tower builders made standing before God impossible.

---

32. Fromm, *Escape from Freedom*, 50.
33. For an elaboration on the notion that coercion toward uniformity is a sin against God, see Korn, "Tradition Meets Modernity," 30–47.
34. Buber, "The Question to the Single One," 66.
35. The idea that only an autonomous individual can engage with God has been succinctly phrased by Rabbi Avi Weiss: "The term 'religious coercion' is an oxymoron."

The Planting of a Name

In the Bible, an essential ingredient in asserting a character's individuality is the assigning of a name. In fact, the Bible begins with God defining His inanimate creations by naming them. The heavens, the earth, the seas, the day, and the night are all given distinction through their names. Later, emulating God, Adam affirms the particular nature of individual species of animals and fowl by naming them. Significantly, man becomes ready to meet woman immediately after he names the animals. He can only fully appreciate her unique suitability for him after he has become intimately familiar[36] with each animal, as symbolized by his naming them. Only after he has rejected every other species could Adam recognize woman as the best possible antidote to his loneliness.[37]

But what's in a name? A name in the Bible is many things. It is a person's good reputation:

A good name is better than fragrant oil. (Eccles. 7:1)

Or bad reputation:

Both the near and the far shall scorn you, O besmirched of name, O laden with iniquity! (Ezek. 22:5)

A name also suggests ownership and control:

Joab sent messengers to David and said ... "now muster the rest of the troops and besiege the city and capture it; otherwise I will capture the city myself and my name will be connected with it." (2 Sam. 12:26,28)

Frequently a name represents a character's deepest essence. When Samson's father, Manoah, asks the angel who visits him for his name, the angel berates him:

---

36. For an exaggerated expression of the idea that Adam's naming was an act of intimate understanding, see Rashi's comments on Gen. 2:23, s.v. *zot hapa'am*. Rashi (basing his comments on *Yebamot* 63a) claims that Adam fully appreciated the appropriateness of his wife, because he first had sexual relations with all the animals.

37. See Rashi on Gen. 2:20, s.v. *u-le-adam lo matza ezer*: "When He brought them (the animals), He brought them before him species by species, male and female. He (Adam) said, 'Each one has a partner, but I have no partner.' Immediately, God caused him to sleep (and created woman)." This comment accounts for the strange order of events in the text: first God announces His intentions to create a "helper opposite" man, but then suddenly He presents the animals for man to name. Only after the naming of the animals does the story of the creation of woman resume. For a discussion of the more negative side of naming—its implications of hierarchy and control—see chapter 4.

Why do you ask my name? It is unknowable! (Judg. 13:18)

By refusing to reveal his name, the angel informs his questioner that human beings are not to grasp the essence of divine beings. In contrast, when the text divulges the names of its human characters, we are often given a window into the nature of the name bearer. For example, the mighty hunter Nimrod, whose name literally means "let us rebel," is tagged by Rashi as one who "caused the entire world to rebel against God" (Rashi, Gen. 10:8, s.v. *lihyot gibor*).

Sometimes a name's meaning is made explicit. Abigail, in speaking to her future husband, King David, apologizes for the rude behavior of her current husband, the "hard, evildoer" Nabal. She offers his name as explanation for his actions:

"Please, my lord, pay no attention to that wretched fellow Nabal. For he is just what his name says: His name means 'boor' and he is a boor." (1 Sam. 25:25)

For the most part, the Bible is insistent on naming its characters, particularly those who will approach God. Here again is Buber, this time on the significance of names in divine-human communication:

And indeed a man can have dealings with God only as a Single One ... This the Old Testament ... expresses by permitting only a person bearing a name, Enoch, Noah, to "have dealings with Elohim."[38]

The Bible uses names to preserve the memory and accomplishments of outstanding, and often godly, individuals. But names are not reserved for the extraordinary alone. The Bible provides extensive genealogical lists of characters whose stories are never fully told. These lists accentuate the Bible's partiality to names and to the individuals of all types that they represent.

The Babel narrative is surrounded on all sides by such lists. Yet the story itself strays from the formula of named characters, presenting instead a group of unnamed builders. This departure from the norm points to an effort on the part of biblical characters to seek distinction not through individual effort, but through collective identity. Thus the story of Babel describes a human tendency toward conformity. It concludes that, taken to extreme lengths, such behavior leads away from God and toward permanent anonymity. Without the unique defining characteristics of individuals, the only name the builders can achieve is associated with the confusion and obliteration of "Babel."

---

38. See note 35.

Yet strikingly, on the heels of the Babel narrative, the individual makes a decisive comeback: "This is the line of *Shem* [lit. name]. *Shem* was 100 years old ..." (Gen. 11:10). The text heralds the transition from the nameless to the named by offering a lead figure whose very name is "Name." With this verse, the anonymous tower builders are replaced by an emphatic return to named individuals.[39]

The genealogical list that Shem heads leads directly to Abraham the *Ivri*, the Hebrew, the quintessential "other," the man whose **name** is made great by God (Gen. 12:2) because of his willingness to break with conventional modes of behavior and thought.[40] Significantly, Abraham, the non-conformist, is the only patriarch to "walk before God" (17:1) and to earn the accolade "God's beloved" (Is. 41:8). Of his two distinctions, individuality and godliness, one builds upon the other. Only a unique individual, a person of "name," can enter the realm of the divine.[41] Perhaps it is not surprising, then, that the sequel to this story is to be found at the beginning of the book of the Bible that means "Names:" the Book of *Shemot*.

Exodus as Sequel

The Babel narrative, by its artful use of language, sound, style, and context, describes how God breaks apart an oppressively monolithic society because of its threat to the divine-human relationship. But if we are to ask not just what happened, but what *might* have happened, we must turn to the Bible's sequel to the story, the enslavement of the Israelites in Egypt. This latter narrative, too, focuses on a culture of tyrannical collectivization. But, as we will soon see, instead of merely paralleling the Babel story, it undermines it. As subversive sequel, the Exodus story will ask whether individuals might combat the tides of uniformity and suppression, and whether the divine-human relationship could survive in the face of society's attempts to silence the dissident voices within it.

We begin our investigation of these questions by examining a quote from the first chapter of the Book of Exodus, highlighting words that invite comparison with the Babel narrative:

---

39. Perhaps the doubling of the word *shem* presages God's intimate relationship with Shem's descendant Abraham. When God calls to Abraham at the Akeda, He does so by doubling his name. See Rashi on Gen. 22:11, s.v. *Avraham Avraham*.

40. The greatness of Abram—*va-agadelah shemekha*—plays on and contrasts with the failed attempt at greatness of the builders of the tower—*migdal*.

41. It is noteworthy that at three critical points in his life, Abraham, the man whose name is made great by God, in turn calls in *God's* name, *va-yikra be-shem Adonai* (Gen. 12:8, 13:4, 21:33).

These are the **names** [*shemot*] of the children of Israel who came to Egypt; with Jacob came each man and his household. Reuben, Simon, Levi and Judah; Issachar, Zebulun, and Benjamin; Dan and Naphtali, Gad and Asher. And all those who issued from Jacob were seventy, and Joseph was in Egypt. And Joseph died, and all his brothers, and all of that generation. And the children of Israel were fruitful [*p-r-h*] and they and they swarmed [*sh-r-tz*] and they increased [*r-v-h*] and became very mighty, and the earth was filled [*m-l-'*] with them. A new king arose over Egypt, who did not know Joseph. And he said to his nation, "Behold the nation of the children of Israel is greater and mightier than we are. **Come let us** [*havah*] deal cleverly with them [lit. him] **lest** [*pen*] they [lit. he] increase, and it will be when war occurs that they [lit. he] will join our enemies in fighting us, and rise up from the land." And they placed taskmasters over them [lit. him] to oppress them [lit. him] with their burdens; and they [lit. he] **built** [*b-n-h*] storage **cities** [*arei* (pl. of *ir*)] for Pharaoh, Pitom and Ramses. But the more they oppressed them [lit. him], the more they [lit. he] increased and spread out, so they came to dread the Israelites. The Egyptians enslaved the children of Israel with hard labor. And they embittered their lives with hard labor, with **mortar** [*homer*] and **bricks** [*leveinim*] and with all kinds of work in the field—they enforced all labor ruthlessly.[42] (Exod. 1:1–14)

The words emphasized above help bring to light several striking similarities between the two stories. First, Pharaoh's call to public action, "**come, let us** deal cleverly with them [*havah nithakema lo*]" echoes the tower-builders' charge, "**come, let us** build [*havah nilbenah*]" as well as God's rejoinder "come let us descend [*havah neredah*]." Second, Pharaoh's warning, "*lest* they increase [*pen yirbe*]," corresponds to the fear in Babel, "*lest* we scatter [*pen nafutz*]." The combination of *havah* and *pen* occurs only in these two chapters, and never again in the entire Bible.

Furthermore, the Israelites **build cities**, *b-n-h ir*, in Egypt, just as the people attempted to **build a city**, *b-n-h ir*, in Babel. The materials of the Egyptian enslavement are **mortar and bricks**, *homer u-leveinim*, evoking the **bricks and mortar**, *leveinim* **and** *homer*, used in Babel. This combination of building materials is another feature exclusive to these two narratives. The reversal of the order of the ingredients—from "mortar and bricks" to "bricks and mortar"—holds its own significance, hinting that these two stories will not merely parallel each other, but that in significant ways one will reverse the other as well.

---

42. Author's translation.

In addition to the linguistic similarities noted above, several outstanding thematic parallels connect the two passages. The first involves the appearance, disappearance, and reappearance of names. As we have seen, the absence of names in the Babel chronicle illustrates its undercurrent of a detrimental homogeneity. The people's sameness clashes with God's desire for an autonomous humanity. The Babel text is preceded by a detailed list of names: "These are the lines of Shem, Ham, and Japhet" (Gen. 10:1). The text then deftly moves to the tale of Babel, with its misguided emphasis on creating an anonymous society (11:1–9). This is followed by an emphatic, as well as highly ironic, return to named individuals, beginning with Shem, a man named "Name" (Gen. 11:10).

The second book of the Bible, called the Book of Names, *Shemot* in Hebrew, follows a similar pattern. It begins with a ceremonious tribute to names: "These are the names of the children of Israel who came into Egypt ..." (Exod. 1:1). But then the names are abruptly dropped. Instead of listing each of the seventy descendants of Jacob, as in a parallel text in Genesis (chap. 46), Exodus lists only the immediate sons of Jacob. After that, the book of names becomes a book of the nameless, with individual names replaced by the collective "children of Israel" (Exod. 1:6–14). As readers of the Babel narrative, we are braced for another attempt to suppress the individual. And in fact, all traces of leaders, heroes, or outstanding figures are entirely absent from the book's opening story of the enslavement in Egypt.

By omitting the names of its characters as in Babel, the text in Exodus hints at a loss of individual identity. To understand how this is so, we would do well to examine additional similarities between the two stories, beginning with the common theme of destruction and its aftermath.

They Were Fruitful and They Swarmed

As we have seen, the events in Babel occur on the heels of the great Flood and God's conciliatory blessing: "Be **fruitful,** *p-r-h,* and **increase,** *r-v-h,* and **fill,** *m-l-'* the earth" (Gen. 9:1). At first humanity complies, as "the nations branched out over the earth after the Flood" (10:32). But then, instead of continuing to disperse in order to replenish the empty regions of the earth, the people constrict themselves, and choose to live in one place, with one language and one set of ideas. Owing perhaps to the trauma of having survived wholesale destruction, an apprehensive society seeks security both in geographic contiguity and in the suppression of the individual.

In traditional sequel fashion, the Exodus narrative builds on this same pattern. First, a "world," in this case the foundational tribes of Israel (Exod. 1:6), disappears. Then the remaining people, the Israelites this time, multiply rampantly and disperse. Once again, God compensates the people for the loss of a generation by promoting renewal, using the same terms—fruitful, p-r-h, increase, r-v-h, and fill, m-l-' the earth—that He employed following the Flood (Gen. 1:28; 9:1,7). Again, the promise of regeneration fails to instill a sense of security within the vulnerable people. But this time, the source of insecurity is not to be found within the diminished people themselves. Instead it is projected upon them by a host country that will borrow a page from Babel, denying the Israelites their individual identities.

The first hint of trouble comes immediately after the death of the previous generation: "And the Israelites were fruitful and they swarmed, sh-r-tz, and they increased and became very mighty, and the earth was filled with them" (Exod. 1:7). At first glance, this verse optimistically reports that despite the death of their forebears, the people display great resilience.[43] As we have seen, the passage borrows its terms for proliferation from the blessed creation and re-creation of all living themes in the Book of Genesis. But darker currents lurk beneath the text's surface, as suggested by the additional verb sh-r-tz. This verb, which literally means "to swarm," made its first appearance in Genesis in the creation of the swamp creatures (Gen. 1:20-21) and bears a potentially negative connotation when associated with human beings.[44] Perhaps, by including this verb, the Exodus text has subtly shifted from the objective narrative voice to the subjective perceptions of the host society. Objectively, the Israelites multiplied greatly, but in the eyes of the wary Egyptians, they swarmed uncontrollably, like insects and rodents.[45]

---

43. An optimistic reading of these verses finds support in the NJPS translation, which defines the conjunction "vav" as "but" instead of "and." Thus, the two verses exist in negation to one another. Although the previous generation died, nevertheless the new generation was prolific.

44. See Lev. 11:43 in which the root sh-r-tz appears together with the root sh-k-tz, "abomination." If the Israelites eat of a creature that swarms, sh-r-tz, they will become an abomination, sh-k-tz. Aside from Exod. 1:7, there is only one verse in which the root sh-r-tz applies directly to human beings. In Gen. 9:7, God employs this term to command the people to proliferate; in this context the word is clearly positive. In support of a negative understanding of sh-r-tz in Exod. 1:7, see the comparison to Num. 23:5 in note 45.

45. Nazi propaganda films promoted this feeling by interposing pictures of a rapidly expanding Jewish population with shots of swarming rodents. Possible support for this reading may be found in Num. 22, in which Balak king of Moab borrows a page from Pharaoh's incitement speech against the Israelites. Balak tells Balaam that the nation is atzum mimmenni, greater than I (v. 6), adopting Pharaoh's phrase in Exod. 1: 9. In both stories (Num. 22:3, Exod. 1:12), the host nation "dreads, k-v-tz" the Israelites because they are "numerous, rav" (Num. 22:3, Exod. 1:9). Intriguingly, Balak uses the phrase khisa et ein ha-aretz, they have hidden the earth from view (Num. 23:5), the exact language used to describe the plague of locusts in Exodus (10:5). This parallel may indicate that, already in biblical times, invoking swarming insects was a common technique used in racist rhetoric.

The next verse presents further intimations of a souring Egyptian attitude toward the sojourners in their land. Following the death of Joseph and his generation, "a new king arose in Egypt who did not know Joseph" (Exod. 1:8). Rashi (v. 8) cites a Talmudic dispute that centers on this phrase.[46] Was this literally a new king, or the same king with new decrees?[47] In either case, says Rashi, Pharaoh "presented himself *as if* he did not know him."[48] Whether he was new or veteran, the king must have been dissembling. Rashi's position hinges on the logical assumption that any leader of a great country such as Egypt must have been aware of its most basic chronicles. These would most certainly have included the man who saved the country from economic ruin only a generation earlier. Pharaoh's attempts to reinvent the past mirror the purposeful amnesia often demonstrated by leaders of totalitarian states. By manipulating the people's collective memory, they seek to shape the parameters of all human thought.[49]

In the Exodus narrative, Pharaoh no longer admits to knowing Joseph, effectively eradicating from both Egyptian and Israelite consciousness any debt owed to the Israelite people. By his act of engineered forgetting, Pharaoh preserves respectability for his regime even as he lays the groundwork for dehumanizing and oppressing a once-valued minority. The Israelites' history has been expunged, and hence their legitimacy and their very identity have been called into question.

Dealing Cleverly

The new king proclaims: "Behold the Israelite nation is greater and mightier than we are" (Exod. 1:9).[50] Surprisingly, Pharaoh is the first character in the Bible

---

46. *Sotah* 11a.
47. The view that Pharaoh only pretended not to know Joseph is upheld by the absence of the formula: king *x* died and king *y* ruled in his place, as seen in Gen. 36:31–39.
48. See note 47.
49. The outer reaches of this phenomenon are chillingly explored in Orwell's *1984:* "By far the more important reason for the readjustment of the past is the need to safeguard the infallibility of the Party. It is not merely that speeches, statistics, and records of every kind must be constantly brought up to date in order to show that the predictions of the Party were in all cases right. It is also that no change of doctrine or in political alignment can ever be admitted. For to change one's mind, or even one's policy, is a confession of weakness ... If, for example, Eurasia or Eastasia (whichever it may be) is the enemy today, then that country must always have been the enemy. And if the facts say otherwise, then the facts must be altered. Thus history is continuously rewritten." Orwell, *1984*, 175–76. I am grateful to Nehama Leibowitz for drawing the connection between Orwell and Exodus.
50. Author's translation.

to recognize the independent nationhood of the Israelites, as he invents the term "Israelite nation." Yet Pharaoh addresses his comments about the "Israelite nation" to "*his* nation" (1:9), conferring nationhood upon the Israelites only to set them off as distinct from his own people. With his subtle rhetoric, Pharaoh portrays the foreigners as a fifth column living among the Egyptians.[51]

Pharaoh's claim that the Israelites are "*rav ve-atzum mimmennu*," greater and mightier than we are,[52] is absurd; they are but a small minority in a vast Egyptian empire.[53] But Pharaoh's words are not chosen to report verifiable statistics; they aim for an emotional, fear-inducing impact. Through his exaggerated claim, Pharaoh taps into and amplifies the anxieties of his people who *feel* as though they are being rapidly outnumbered by the prolific strangers.

But the words *rav ve-atzum mimmennu* can tolerate another interpretation as well, and as such may point to another insidious angle of Pharaoh's speech of incitement. Read literally, these words can mean "the Israelite nation is great and mighty *from us*." Thus Pharaoh intimates that the immigrants are parasites who deplete Egyptian resources for their own purposes. Resentment against the foreigners grows as their success is seen to have been attained at the expense of "real" Egyptians.[54]

Once he has presented the Israelites as alien and predatory, Pharaoh summons his people to address the problem: "Come let us deal cleverly with them, lest they increase, and it will be when war occurs that they will join our enemies in fighting us, and rise up from the land"[55] (Exod. 1:10). These worries seem contradictory. If the Israelite presence is indeed a threat, their leaving should be a welcome relief, *not* a cause for further concern.[56]

Although many exegetes have tried to resolve the contradiction, leaving it in place allows greater insight into the nature of inflammatory racist rhetoric. Since

---

51. I heard this insight in a class given by Nehama Leibowitz.

52. The letter *mem* as prepositional prefix usually denotes comparison: one is above and beyond the other. For example, see Gen. 25:23; 38:25; 48:19. Brown, Driver, and Briggs, *Lexicon*, 582.

53. The absurdity leads translators to seek alternative solutions. NJPS translates Exod. 1:9: "Look, the Israelite people are much too numerous *for us* [author's emphasis]."

54. I am indebted to my students at the Pardes Institute of Jewish Studies, who suggest this reading year after year. According to the plain sense of the text, this reading is unlikely, since the prepositional pronoun "מ" rarely connects adjectives and nouns in this causal way. Yet it is a possible reading, as it approximates such biblical statements as that made by Naomi in the book of Ruth (1:13): *ki mar li me'od mi-kem*, translated in Brown, Driver, and Briggs as "it is very bitter to me *because of you* [author's emphasis]." Brown, Driver, and Briggs, *Lexicon*, 580.

55. Author's translation.

56. The apparent illogic in the verse is addressed by Rashi (1:10 s.v. *ve-alah min ha-aretz*) and many others.

different segments of society hold diverse prejudices and fears, inciters toss out as many arguments as possible with no regard to consistency. It is often safe to assume that once one audience embraces an incendiary claim, it will ignore all others. Other groups, who are predisposed to different concerns and biases, will latch on to allegations that relate to their own fears. They too will overlook contradictory claims that do not speak to their prejudices. Pharaoh's illogical statement suggests that often the first casualty of rabble-rousing is consistency.[57]

As we have seen, the text in Exodus borrows its "come let us... lest" combination from the Babel narrative. The people of Babel molded themselves into singularity of thought, speech, and deed: "All the earth was of *one* language and *one* idea." Revisiting the model, the Bible depicts Pharaoh as seeking to collectivize the thoughts of his own people, gradually seducing them into genocidal behavior. At the same time, and indeed as part of that effort, Pharaoh portrays the Israelites as an illegitimate, amorphous mass, not worthy of the sympathy or pity that individual victims of oppression might deserve. Inexorably, the victims, too, gradually assume the characteristics ascribed to them. They become enslaved in mind, spirit, and body.

As part of his efforts to subdue the Israelites, Pharaoh calls to his countrymen to "deal cleverly with *him, lo*," using the grammatical form for the singular to refer to the entire Israelite nation (Exod. 1:10). When he speaks of his own nation, however, Pharaoh uses the standard plural form (vv. 10–14). Perhaps Pharaoh's uneven syntax is part of his rhetorical effort. Even as he is engaged in molding his people into adopting a uniformly xenophobic view of the Israelites, he speaks to them in the plural, conveying the sense that they, like all "normal" public groups, are diverse. In contrast, the foreigners, whom he portrays in the singular, are monochromatic and monolithic. Through the substance and style of his speech, Pharaoh seeks to present the Israelites as devoid of God's unique stamp, and thus as less human than the Egyptians. The more they are dehumanized, the easier it will be to begin oppressing them.

The first stage of the subjugation is the enforced building of cities,[58] which, in the view of biblical scholar Nahum Sarna, is an effective means of destroying any

---

57. The use of contradictory claims in inciting hatred is familiar from recent history. Jews in Nazi Germany were portrayed as Communists and as capitalist bankers, as ubiquitous power brokers and as pathetic parasites.
58. Building begins with making bricks. The verb form of the word "brick," *l-b-n*, appears in only two biblical stories: the Babel narrative (Gen. 11:3) and in two later verses in the story of the Egyptian enslavement (Exod. 5:7,14).

remaining sense of self among the indentured people. Sarna offers the following description of the life of the city-builder, based on ancient Egyptian sources:

> What we are dealing with is state slavery, the organized imposition of forced labor upon the male population for long and indefinite terms of service under degrading and brutal conditions. The men so conscripted received no reward for their labors; they enjoyed no civil rights, and their lot was generally much worse than that of a household slave. Organized in large work gangs, they became an anonymous mass, depersonalized, losing all individuality in the eyes of their oppressors.[59]

In Babel and in Egypt both, city building erases individuality and reduces free people to slaves. In Egypt, the people's enslavement is made even more acute by the despotic nature of the oppressor. The 20th-century Talmudic sage and philosopher Joseph B. Soloveitchik distinguishes slaves bound to individual masters, as in ancient Greece, from slaves of totalitarian states, as in Nazi Germany or Soviet Russia, or, we might add, as in the Egyptian society described in the Book of Exodus:

> In private slavery, some form of human relationship exists between the slave and his master. Two human beings interact, despite the difference in their station. It is possible for human empathy to enter their relationship, with occasional feelings of sympathy, confidence, identity, and trust. Such was the relationship of Joseph and Potiphar. It is a subordination, but not necessarily a subjugation. In corporate slavery, however, an impassive oppression precludes all human association; there is no friendship or human emotion. It is a depersonalized, faceless prison, with the inmates reduced to number identification.[60]

Building cities under the thumb of the all-controlling and tightly controlled Egyptian empire erodes the souls of the workers. It is the very essence of totalitarian slavery.

Where is God?

At this point in the narrative, all hope seems lost, as a broken Israel confronts a tyrannical Egyptian empire. Only divine intervention can bring redemption, but

---

59. Sarna, *Exploring Exodus*, 21.
60. Besdin, *Reflections of the Rav*, 203–4.

as in Babel, God is distanced from the human players in the narrative. If we are to borrow from the conclusions of Babel, we may deduce that here too the loss of human individuality has caused this chasm. Here, as in Babel, as the people drift farther from themselves they move farther from God as well. To invoke Buber's language, as their "I" is eroded, they are unable to reach out to a "Thou." The Book of Exodus makes this point dramatically by omitting all mention of God from its chronicle of the suppression of the individual. In this sequel to Babel, God is not merely alienated by humanity's lack of individual distinction. This story posits that if human beings are nameless, God must remain nameless as well.

Perhaps the Talmud had this divine-human breakdown in mind when it offered an alternative, homiletic interpretation of the verse, "Come, let us deal cleverly with *him, lo*" (Exod. 1:10).[61] The Talmud suggests that the singular *lo* does not refer to the Israelites, but rather to their God; the Egyptians plot to deal cleverly with the would-be savior of Israel. In Egypt, as in Babel, the forces of conformity "dealt cleverly" with God, keeping Him at bay by denying His presence within humanity. Without its stamp of uniqueness, humanity again proves unable to live in God's presence.

Yet suddenly, two flashes of light burst through the bleakness:

> The king of Egypt said to the Hebrew midwives, one whose name [*shem*] was Shifra and the other whose name [*shem*] was Puah. And he said, "When you birth the Hebrew women and you see them on the birthing stools, if it is a boy kill him, and if it is a girl let her live." And the midwives feared God, and did not do as the king of Egypt had said to them, and they let the children live. The king of Egypt called to the midwives and said to them, "Why have you done this thing, letting the children live?" And the midwives said to Pharaoh, "The Hebrew women are not like Egyptian women: they are vigorous. Before the midwife can come to them, they give birth."[62] (Exod. 1:15–19)

Initially, the first verse in this passage is puzzling, because it is entirely devoted to the introduction of a piece of dialogue—A said to B and C—without an accompanying quote. But the reader quickly understands that this verse

61. *Sotah* 11a.
62. Author's translation.

presents a groundbreaking novelty, the presence of two *named* characters. Finally, after a detailed account of the enslavement of the Israelites in which not a single individual name appears, the innominate mode of the Book of Names begins to break apart.

The Babel narrative, as we have seen, contains no names. No figure emerges to rescue the generation from the anonymity that it so craved. Instead, God grants and then exaggerates the people's wish for namelessness by sentencing them to permanent obscurity. Names are restored to the narrative only *after* the offending generation dissipates and when a new line, based on the very basis of named identity begins: "this is the line of Shem" (Gen. 11:10).

The subversive sequel provides a crucial departure from the original text. While beginning in much the same way, with a list of names and then their disappearance, the Exodus narrative questions the inevitability of its dire conclusions. By introducing courageous individuals, the story battles, and ultimately defeats, the magnetic force of conformity. Through their conscientious objection, the midwives salvage the identity and memory of the oppressed people.

So that we are sure not to miss the consequence of the moment, the midwives are introduced with a doubling of the word "name, *shem*," echoing the doubling used in Genesis at the moment of the reintroduction of names: "This is the line of *Shem*; *Shem* was 100 years old" (Gen. 11:10).[63] In both narratives, the emphatic re-entry of names signifies a significant shift in the story's direction and prepares the reader for a reversal of fortune. But in this, the subversive sequel to the Babel story, names return *before* the suppressed society is lost forever. This time, two lone figures appear in time to rescue the masses from the grasp of anonymity.

The adjective affixed to the women's occupation only heightens expectations. They are not simply midwives; they are the *Hebrew* midwives, *ha-meyalledot ha-Ivriyot*. These words are ambiguous, and have given rise to heated debate among commentators. Are they in fact Hebrew midwives, in which case the word *Ivriyot* (Hebrew) serves as an adjective modifying the noun "midwives"? Or are they Egyptian midwives *of* the Hebrews? Because the phrase could bear either reading, the debate turns on a logical point. If they are Hebrews, how could Pharaoh expect

---

63. The doubling of the word "name" in introducing two names is a common biblical convention (for example, see Gen. 4:19 and Exod. 18:8–9). Nevertheless, because there was no apparent need to name the midwives at all, the use and reuse of the word *shem* in relation to them is noteworthy.

them to comply with his infanticidal plans? And if they are Egyptians, how could they possibly defy their all-powerful king, as a result of "fearing God"?[64]

But such discussions miss the designed ambiguity of the text, which deliberately withholds any definitive ethnic marking of these women. Had the text chosen to be explicit, it could have used an adjectival form of the term *benei Yisrael* (children of Israel),[65] the designation used throughout the story.[66] By employing instead the words *ha-meyalleldot ha-Ivriyot,* a double entendre ensues. On one level, these words point to the women's vocation and their origins. They were midwives of either Hebrew or Egyptian lineage. More subtly, however, it might be said that no matter what their origins, they were in their essence *Ivriyot.* These courageous women were at odds with their surroundings much as Abraham and other *Ivrim* in the Bible were at odds with theirs.[67] As we have seen, the prevailing culture in Egypt imposes its conformity among oppressors and oppressed alike. The oppressed are cowed into a state of silent suffering, and the oppressors become gradually inured to the degradation and ultimately to the murder of unwanted foreigners. The midwives stand as *Ivriyot,* steadfastly resisting the corrupt conventions that have taken hold of their society.

But is not the statement that the midwives "feared God" proof that they were, in fact, of Israelite ancestry? Actually, the term "fearing God" is used repeatedly in the Bible to denote ethical behavior by non-Israelites.[68] When Joseph, dressed as viceroy of Egypt, tells his brothers that he will not harm them "because I fear God" (Gen. 42:18), he does not risk divulging his true identity, since God-fearing implied merely an adherence to basic moral standards. Hence the God-fearing nature of the

---

64. Rashi, drawing on the interpretation in *Sotah* 11a, upholds the first view; the Septuagint and Vulgate, Ibn Ezra, Malbim support the second.

65. See Lev. 24:10, Num. 25:14.

66. Exceptions are in Pharaoh's order to the midwives in Exod. 1:16, "when you birth the *Ivriyot,*" and in the midwives' response, "the *Ivriyot* are not like the Egyptian women." Pharaoh's order carries with it an implied justification: kill those children who are so different than our own (hence the term *"Ivri,"* which connotes Israelite as other to the surrounding culture). The midwives adopt Pharaoh's racist logic in their own defense, affirming Pharaoh's claim that the Hebrew women are indeed unlike the Egyptians—"*ki hayyot hennah,*" which could mean "they are vigorous," or more literally, "they are like animals" (1:19). Hence their birthing practices are uncontrollable.

67. See note 26.

68. See Yeshayahu Leibowitz, *Judaism, the Jewish Nation, and the State of Israel,* 392, and Sarna, *Exploring Exodus,* 25. See also Jon. 1:16, in which the non-Israelite sailors "feared the LORD greatly."

midwives is no indicator of their origin. On the contrary, the designation suggests that moral action, based on an instinctive recognition of God's expectations of humanity, can come from any quarter.[69]

In contrast with the Babel narrative, in which no individuals distinguished themselves, here the midwives restore both names and God's presence to the narrative by reaching through the silence and heeding God's moral calling. Significantly, on the heels of the distinguished actions of the midwives and in response to them, God joins the narrative in an active way for the very first time in the Book of Exodus:

> And God dealt well with the midwives; and the people multiplied and increased greatly. And because the midwives feared God, He made houses for them. (Exod. 1: 20–21)

Here, as in the Abraham story, individuality paves the way for godliness. Where there are *Ivrim*, individuals capable of choosing God, there God can reside.

Daughters of Redemption

With nothing more than the moral high ground for protection, the midwives face down the mighty king of Egypt. The text finds many ways to call our attention to the exceptional nature of this standoff, beginning with naming the midwives but not the king.[70] Nahum Sarna points out that the word "midwife" recurs seven times in this one passage, "an index of the importance that Scripture places upon the actions of the women in their defiance of tyranny and in their upholding of moral principles."[71]

Another measure of the midwives' importance may be derived from the fact that between them, the names Shifra and Puah contain all the letters of the name Pharaoh: (ש)פרה-פועה-פרעה. Through visual and phonetic wordplay, through word repetitions and the artful placement of names, these two women are pitted as equal to Pharaoh. In actually determining who would live and who would die, they ultimately emerge as superior to the mighty king of Egypt.

---

69. Nehama Leibowitz reaches a similar conclusion, while assuming the Egyptian nationality of the midwives. Leibowitz, *Shemot*, 36.

70. "Pharaoh" is not a proper name. It is a metonymic title meaning "great house." Sarna agrees that this asymmetry is intentional; it underscores the superiority of "these lowly women" over the great monarch. Sarna, *Exploring Exodus*, 25.

71. Ibid. , 25.

Further literary hints as to the remarkable strength of the midwives emerge from their defiant rejoinders to each of Pharaoh's orders. Pharaoh commands them to *kill* the baby boys, *va-hamitten;* they respond by giving *life, va-tehayyena.* As the text reports (Exod. 1:17), "they let the boys live" or perhaps even "actively sustained"[72] them.[73] More strikingly, Pharaoh commands them to "see" the children on the birthing stools, *u-re'iten;* they were to inspect them to determine their gender and then to kill the males. The midwives respond by scrambling Pharaoh's orders. Instead of "seeing," *u-re'iten*, the midwives "feared," *va-tir'ena*, creating an anagram: וראיתן becomes ותראין.[74] At every stage, the midwives' innate morality, their fear of God, bests Pharaoh.[75]

In a culture without names, these women are named. In a world bereft of God's presence, they find God, fear Him, and lay the foundation for His active engagement with His people. In a civilization in which silent—and at times, lethal—acquiescence to authority is the rule, the midwives protest Pharaoh's command with their act of defiance. When contrasted with the characterless society of Babel, these women appear all the more extraordinary. If Babel warns of the dangers of a society that fails to confront itself, the courageous midwives who challenge convention serve as the Bible's retort to that failed generation.

In Babel, the individual is blotted out, and as a result, so is the entire generation. In the story's subversive sequel, the enslavement in Egypt, the individual is seriously eroded, but two distinctive women arrive in time to reverse the process. Shifra and

---

72. See Ibn Ezra v. 17 s.v. *va-tehayyena.* Ibn Caspi (14th century, France) caustically objects to this perceived over-reading of the text's intent on the part of Ibn Ezra.

73. The irony in the midwives' response is emphasized by the otherwise lame excuse they offer for their disobedience: *ki hayot henna* (NJPS: "they are vigorous"). Perhaps the midwives imply a literal meaning to these words: we couldn't obey your orders to *kill* them because they are uncontrollably "live" people.

74. Cassuto, *Exodus*, 14.

75. Here, as in the Babel story, we have the elegant employment of the literary quid pro quo, or *millah ke-neged millah.* See note 8. In addition to playing off of the language and themes of the Babel story, the story of the midwives engages in dialogue with the larger Abraham narrative as well. Both the midwives and Abraham are held up as models of God-fearing behavior. After the binding of Isaac, an angel of God proclaims: "Now I know that you **fear God,** *y-r-' Elohim*" (Gen. 22:12). As a result: "I will bestow my blessing upon you and make your descendants as **numerous,** *r-v-h,* as the stars of the heaven and the sands on the seashore ..." (22: 17). The midwives, too "**fear God,** *y-r-' Elohim*" (Exod. 1:17). And like Abraham, they are blessed with the people's great proliferation: "And God dealt well with the midwives; and the people **multiplied,** *r-v-h,* and increased greatly" (1: 20).

Puah set off a chain of events that will ultimately lead to the defeat of the tyrannical Egyptian regime and to the salvation of the Israelite people. In Babel, an undifferentiated humanity forfeits its ability to live in God's presence. In its subversive sequel, although God was never evident to begin with, the heroic midwives discover Him and begin to construct an enduring divine-human relationship. Bested by the midwives, Pharaoh addresses his call for murder to the entire Egyptian populace:

> And Pharaoh commanded all his nation saying, "Every son that is born you shall throw into the Nile, but let all the daughters live."[76] (Exod. 1:22)

Although the narrative account of the midwives has concluded, the two women leave their imprint on a series of valiant female characters that feature prominently in the second chapter of Exodus:

> A man of the house of Levi went and married the daughter of Levi. The woman conceived and bore a son; and when she saw how good he was, she hid him for three months. When she could hide him no longer, she took a wicker basket for him and caulked it with bitumen and pitch. And she put the child into it and placed it among the reeds by the bank of the Nile. And his sister stationed herself at a distance, to learn what would be done to him. The daughter of Pharaoh went down to bathe in the Nile, while her maidens walked along the Nile. She saw the basket among the reeds and sent her slave girl to fetch it. When she opened it, she saw that it was a child, a boy crying. She took pity on it and said, "This must be a Hebrew child."[77] (Exod. 2:1–6)

In this passage, irony abounds. Pharaoh assumes the harmless nature of female Hebrew babies. After all, only the boys would grow into fighters who would threaten his regime. Consequently, he issues his murderous edict against baby boys alone, magnanimously proclaiming, "Let all the daughters live" (1:22). Yet almost immediately, his plans are thwarted by a series of "daughters."[78] These

---

76. Author's translation.

77. Ibid.

78. The text refers to two women as "daughters," the daughter of Levi and the daughter of Pharaoh. Although the third female character, Moses' sister, is not called a "daughter," she is, in fact, the daughter of a "daughter." All in all, immediately on the heels of Pharaoh's proclamation to "let the daughters live," the word *bat*, daughter, appears seven times. On the ironic use of this word, see Cassuto, *Exodus*, 17. Perhaps the recurrence of this *leitwort* helps explain the text's failure to name Moses' saviors: his mother,

women, like the heroic midwives who preceded them, defy Pharaoh by preserving the life of a baby boy, this time the young Moses. In an extraordinary development, one such daughter is *"bat Par'o,"* the daughter of the genocidal king himself. As we have seen, lone conscientious action is not bound by ethnic or religious affiliation; its mechanics are purely internal. This chapter presents Pharaoh's daughter as the latest in a list of *Ivriyot*.

Although Israel's savior is male, it is women who give him life and who see to his safety, sustenance, and upbringing. In addition, the selfless women in Moses' young life give birth to the independence of mind that will allow him to assume his role as leader. From them, Moses learns to examine the norms and values of his environment and to reject the corruption he sees among Egyptian and Israelite alike. As we will see in the next chapter of this volume, the daughters in this narrative lead Moses to an awareness of his otherness, and ultimately to a discovery of the heroism needed to conceive of and carry out the move to redemption. If we are to trace a line from the midwives to Moses, we find that time after time the solitary stature of courageous, conscience-driven individuals has paved the way to godliness.

Conclusion

The Egypt narrative helps interpret its more cryptic parallel, the story of the builders in Babel. Both emerge as chronicles of oppressively collective societies. But then, unexpectedly, two characters break the harmonious rhythms of the parallel. Instead of falling into their neatly laid-out positions, they appropriate the narrative and allow for a new story, one in which individual acts of defiance lead to a relationship with God and to the redemption of an entire people.

While the builders at Babel see their efforts end in ruin and rubble, the story of the midwives concludes with the reconstruction of the broken household of Israel. The outstanding women of Exodus undermine the Babel narrative to such an extent that in their story, the only structure to come crashing down is the textual account of uniformity, oppression, and godlessness.

---

his sister and Pharaoh's daughter. Surely such courageous women were deserving of names! In fact, two of the three will be named later (Exod. 6:20; 15:20). Perhaps the text refrains from naming them here, so that they must be repeatedly referred to as "daughters." Thus the narrative drives home the irony suggested above. This conjecture notwithstanding, the frequent omission of women's names from the biblical narrative remains most troubling and calls out for redress. See chapter 6, note 46.

Chapter 3

Mysterious Priests and Troubled Patriarchs: Melchizedek and Jethro and the Building of Leaders

קרא ... מארץ מרחק איש עצתי

I have summoned ... from a far off land the man of My counsel.

—Isaiah 46:11

O ur next narrative pair to be examined consists of two enigmatic non-Israelite[1] priests. Melchizedek, priest to God Most High, and Jethro, priest of Midian both appear at critical junctures in the lives of patriarchs. When the patriarch is weary, each priest offers bread, *lehem,* for physical sustenance and blessings, *b-r-kh,* for spiritual rejuvenation. Each priest encourages the patriarch to recognize God's hand, *yad,* in a miraculous delivery from harm. Both priests draw the patriarchs' attention to notions of justice, *tzedek,* which serve as the foundation of God's code of law. Significantly, too, each priest appears to the patriarch just prior to a terrifying, yet wondrous experience of divine revelation.

The similarities between these two priests will propel us toward a broader comparison of the patriarchs they encounter. Abraham and Moses are arguably the

---

1. For simplicity's sake, I am using the term "Israelite," though it is anachronistic in its context. Melchizedek makes his appearance in the Bible before the biblical character Israel, for whom the Israelites are named. My intent in using this term is to indicate that these priests come from outside the line of the forefathers. Even though Melchizedek is Abraham's contemporary, there is no evidence that he is included in the new religious identity that Abraham initiates. There are those who would disagree with this assumption and attempt to "Judaize" (again I use an anachronistic term) Melchizedek, most notably midrashic sources that label him as Shem, son of Noah, thus giving him status as a proto-Israelite. See Rashi 14:18, s.v. *u-malkizedek.* See also Targum Yonatan and *Nedarim* 32b.

most important figures in the chronicle of the emerging Israelite nation. Both will need outside counsel in order to successfully meet the challenges of their leadership roles, including the ability to take part in God's covenant. As the two stories unfold, we will find that the two non-Israelite visitors will help deepen the moral and religious sensibilities of God's chosen leaders, enabling them to assume effectively the many facets of their roles.

Once we have noted the similarities between the two narratives, we will observe their differences, looking for signs of the subversive sequel. As we sharpen our lens, we will note that the two stories present two separate leadership models, each of which is necessary at a different stage of nation building. The first, the story of Abraham, is a tale of an iconoclast, whose main challenge is to separate himself from others as he turns more fully inward toward his own ideals and goals. To become a symbolic leader of a nation not yet born, Abraham needs to retain an unobstructed focus on his internal truths and to resist external pressures that threaten to divert him from his path.

As we will discover, the story of Moses begins in a similar manner, with the leader standing apart from those around him. Raised in the gap between two cultures, Moses will have no natural community; hence from the earliest record of his life, his decisions will be entirely his own. Moreover, his main early influences will be two heroic women who will reinforce his sense of fierce moral independence. But once God calls upon Moses to serve as leader, he will have to learn to engage with others. Unlike Abraham, Moses will serve an actual nation, not a nation in potential. As a result, his challenge, which will be addressed by the priest Jethro, is to gradually shed his singularity to make room for a more inclusive, community-based leadership model.

At the end of this chapter, we will consider the significance of the non-Israelite status of the priestly advisors. Our inquiry will be aided by yet another story of priestly enablement. In connecting the third story to the previous two, we will discover a reciprocal relationship between Israelite and non-Israelite in which each holds the capacity to mentor the other in matters of justice and righteousness.

Abraham's Downward Spiral

In order to appreciate the impact of Abraham's priestly visitor, we must first understand who Abraham is as a leader, particularly at the moment in which he meets Melchizedek. From the beginning, Abraham's journey is a lonely one. In the words of the Talmudic sage Rabbi Yehuda, Abraham[2] receives the title of Hebrew, or *Ivri* (Gen. 14:13), because of his solitary stance in relation to others: "All the world was on one side, *ever ehad*, and he was on the other."[3] As we have seen, with the words *lekh lekha*, God commands him to go "to himself," on his own unique path as he draws closer to God.[4] The result of his journey will be a five-fold blessing, for himself and for those who are affected by him:

> The Lord said to Abram, "Go forth [lit., go to yourself] from your native land and from your father's house to the land that I will show you. I will make of you a great nation and I will bless you; I will make your name great and you shall be a blessing. I will bless those who bless you and curse him that curses you; and all the families of the earth shall be blessed through you.[5] (Gen. 12: 1–3)

God's insistent repetition of the verb "bless, *b-r-kh*," makes His promise emphatic and sweeping. Not only will Abraham be blessed; in his wake, so will the nations of the world. This causal connection will become apparent in two ways. First, the nations will reap God's blessings when they emulate Abraham's ethical behavior. And more concretely, at times they will benefit directly from Abraham's conscience-driven efforts on their behalf. While for the most part Abraham will function alone, nevertheless he will work tirelessly to tend to the needs of others (Gen. 18:1–8) and to protect them from harm (18:23–32). As we will soon see, God's principles of *tzedakah u-mishpat*, righteousness and justice, will frequently guide Abraham in deciding how and when to engage the world. Ironically, only by going "to himself," remaining clear of conflicting societal influences, will Abraham become better able to practice and model these godly values to the people around him.

In his continuing efforts to distill and adopt God's ways, Abraham distances himself from potentially negative influences. Along with this, in a more extreme and somewhat disturbing manifestation of his singularity, Abraham's life is marked by a

---

2. As in previous chapters, for the sake of simplicity we will not distinguish between the names Abram and Abraham, unless quoting directly from the text. At this point in the narrative—and until Genesis 17—the patriarch's name is still Abram.

3. See chapter 2 of this book, note 26. In Rabbi Yehuda's reading, the word *Ivri* plays on the similarly constructed *"ever,"* meaning "side."

4. See chapter 2, note 25.

5. Author's translation. Ramban agrees that the last five words of God's charge speak of others being blessed through Abraham. Ramban 12:3, s.v. *ve-nivrekhu vekha*.

series of departures from his loved ones. With God's approval and sometimes with His active prodding, Abraham splits from his nephew Lot (Gen. 13:9), from his first-born son, Ishmael, and from Ishmael's mother, Hagar (21:14). Twice he sets in motion chains of events that lead to his separation from Sarah, his wife. As we will see in the next chapter of this volume, when Abraham claims that Sarah is not his wife, but his sister, he contributes to her abduction by foreign kings (12:13–14; 20:2). Toward the end of Abraham's narrative, God orders the ultimate departure. He must sacrifice Isaac, the son who represents Abraham's future, whom God refers to as Abraham's favorite and remaining child (22:2).

God frames Abraham's life with the words *lekh lekha*, which appear at the beginning of his journey when he must take leave of his past, and at its end when he receives the order to forfeit his future. Thus, Abraham is commanded to end his career as he began, as one who stands as perpetual "other" to those around him. Arguably, Abraham was never destined to act as a model father, husband, or uncle. He was to be a solitary living symbol, prefiguring the history of his offspring:[6] a blessed nation with the potential to bring blessing to others, but dwelling alone.[7]

Abraham begins his leadership effort as God orders. He separates from others, while focusing more and more on his godly path. But soon after he responds to the first *lekh lekha*, Abraham enters a downward spiral, as his blessings and the vision that inspired them are called into question. External forces begin to insinuate themselves, threatening to derail Abraham's sense of a future-oriented divine calling. Instead, he is forced to focus on the immediate need to manage hostile surroundings. First, famine afflicts the recently-promised land and Abraham is forced into exile (Gen. 12:10). Then, out of mortal fear of the godless population of Egypt, Abraham lies, claiming that Sarah is not his wife, but his sister (12:13). Sarah is abducted nevertheless, and in a morally dubious conclusion to the episode, husband and wife are sent away with great riches (12:16). Abraham's material wealth leads to his next crisis: incompatibility with Lot, his next of kin and probable heir (13:6). Throughout these events, Abraham's clarity of purpose is blurred and diverted. He must deal with a series of intrusions that call for compromises and that demand primacy for political, rather than spiritual considerations.

---

6. For an elaboration of the notion of the actions of the forefathers foreshadowing future Israelite events—in rabbinic language *ma'aseh avot siman le-banim*—see Ramban on Gen. 12:6, s.v. *va-ya'avor Avram ba-aretz ad mekom Shekhem*. Similarly, see Rashi's comments on Gen. 12:6–9.

7. See Num. 23:9, in which Balaam declares about the Israelites: "There is a people that dwells apart, not reckoned among the nations."

Abraham's decline is briefly interrupted by a moment of upward focus. God tells Abraham to "lift your eyes and look" in all four directions, foreshadowing his descendants' acquisition of the land (Gen. 13:14). But almost immediately his eyes are again lowered to mundane reality. He is lured into a series of wars between two sets of allied armies, one comprised of five kings, the other of four. In an abstruse narrative, the text recounts a series of revolts, enslavements, and counter-revolts, all of which leave the reader wondering what possible relevance all of this might have to the ongoing narrative of the Bible's main protagonist, Abraham. Finally, the story's pertinence becomes clear. Abraham's nephew Lot, who had chosen to live among the wicked people of Sodom (13:13), is taken captive by the opposing forces. Abraham is then forced to choose between two unsavory options. He can either rescue his kinsman by aligning himself with Sodom, a nation notorious for its moral depravity, or retain the moral high ground by remaining militarily neutral, while forfeiting his "brother" (14:14).[8] Abraham chooses the former, winning the war for Sodom and her allies. It is at this point that the stage is set for the arrival of the mysterious priest Melchizedek.

A King Upstaged

In what is possibly the moral nadir of Abraham's experiences, he receives his priestly caller. But Melchizedek does not come right away. His visit is preceded by the arrival of Bera, the king of Sodom, leader and symbol of that wicked nation, a man whose very name means "in evil."[9] Presumably, the king is about to propose a victor's division of the spoils as part of a continuing association with his ally Abraham. Yet, instead, the text merely relates the following:

> When he returned from defeating Chedorlaomer and the kings with him,
> the king of Sodom came out to meet him in the Valley of Shaveh, which is
> the valley of the king. (Gen. 14:17)

Although we apprehensively await the king's offer, none is forthcoming. The king simply goes out "to meet" Abraham, and is then abruptly upstaged by

---

8. Despite their parting from one another with God's implicit approval (see Gen. 13:14, and Rashi s.v. *aharei hippared Lot*), Abraham continues to display fraternal feelings toward his nephew.

9. See Rashi, 14:2, s.v. *Bera*.

another visitor, of whom we have no prior knowledge. This new arrival is the priest Melchizedek, also known as the king of Salem:

> And King Melchizedek of Salem brought out bread and wine; he was a priest of God Most High. He blessed him, saying, "Blessed be Abram of God Most High, Creator of heaven and earth. And blessed be God Most High, Who has delivered [*miggen* (מגן)] your foes into your hand." And he gave him a tenth of everything.[10] (Gen. 14:18–20)

It is only after Melchizedek's cryptic appearance and mystifying utterance that the text's focus shifts back to the king of Sodom, finally confirming his motives for appearing in the first place. As expected, the king offers continued collaboration with Abraham, beginning with a division of booty between them:

> Then the king of Sodom said to Abram, "Give me the persons [*nefesh*] and take the possessions for yourself." (Gen. 14:21)

This textual sequence poses many problems, primarily the bifurcation of the narrative of the King of Sodom. Why does the text interrupt one narrative to interject another; why not finish with one king before presenting another? Even more troubling is the very presence of the second king, who has no apparent connection to the narrative flow of events. Melchizedek arrives with no explanation and no background. Following this passage he receives no further mention.[11] He is king of an unknown land, priest to an unfamiliar God. Why does the Bible include him here at all?

Melchizedek and the King of Sodom: A Study in Moral Contrasts

One theory as to Melchizedek's presence in this story posits that he serves as a foil for the evil king of Sodom.[12] The king of Sodom, who should have felt

---

10. The verse is ambiguous on the question of who gave the tithe to whom: Abraham to Melchizedek or vice versa. While the NJPS translation identifies the giver as Abraham, at this stage I have chosen to omit such identification, thereby leaving intact the ambiguous tone of the text. At a later stage, I will identify the giver as Melchizedek.

11. Melchizedek appears in only one other context in the Bible, in Ps. 110:4. There the word may be a description of a "rightful king" rather than a proper noun. Alternatively, it may be a proper noun that refers back to the king/priest of Genesis (see NJPS translation and footnote *b-b*).

12. See the comments of the 18th century Moroccan exegete Haim Ibn Attar, known by the name of his work, *Or Ha-hayyim*, on Gen. 14:18 s.v. *u-malkizedek.*

himself greatly indebted to Abraham for helping him win the war, greets him empty-handed. Yet Melchizedek, who owes Abraham nothing, brings bread and wine. By introducing the king of Sodom, then holding him in temporary abeyance while introducing a contrasting king, the text enables us to fully appreciate the moral failings of the man Abraham is about to confront. In support of this theory, we look to the meanings of the two names. Melchizedek's name means "king of justice," while as we have seen, the name of the King of Sodom, Bera, suggests his evil character. In fact, Bera's name suits his nation, which will become a biblical symbol of a corrupt society. As Isaiah chastises:

> Hear the word of the Lord, You chieftains of Sodom; Give ear to our God's instruction, you folk of Gomorrah! What need have I of all your sacrifices? Says the LORD ... Learn to do good; devote yourselves to justice; aid the wronged. Uphold the rights of the orphan; defend the cause of the widow. (Isa. 1:10,11,17)

Sodom will be guilty of a particular type of injustice: a self-satisfied withholding of food from the underprivileged, as described in this passage in Ezekiel:

> Only this was the sin of your sister Sodom: arrogance! She and her daughters had plenty of bread and untroubled tranquility; yet she did not support the poor and the needy. (Ezek. 16:49)

Like his people, the king of Sodom withholds bread. In contrast, Melchizedek freely offers bread to the war-weary Abraham. In fact, Melchizedek models a general ethos of giving, "bringing out" bread and wine and "giving" a tithe.[13] Yet unlike Melchizedek, the first words to escape the mouth of the king of Sodom are the self-centered "give me." The king's arrogance mirrors that of his people. In contrast, Melchizedek's message is one of humility. He attributes all material and martial success to God Most High, the true master of human destiny.

This comparison between the two kings notwithstanding, it is Abraham who commands our attention. While we may have a passing interest in contrasting the qualities of two marginal figures, the narrative has thus far focused on one main

---

13. On the ambiguity in this phrase, see note 10. Since Melchizedek is a priest, a strong argument could be made in favor of Abraham giving the tithe to him. Nevertheless, I prefer a reading that sees Melchizedek as the giver, as this is consistent with his overall generosity toward Abraham.

protagonist. We must therefore ask how Melchizedek's appearance, actions, words, and essence affect Abraham.

Melchizedek's Message to Abraham

As we have seen, this story appears in a context of chronic challenges to Abraham's integrity and divine direction. The most recent threat, the prospect of forging an unholy collaboration with the king of Sodom, leaves Abraham in a morally vulnerable state. If he agrees to the union, his moral crisis will continue and deepen. He will become further estranged from the divine ideals that first drove him and from their ensuing blessings.

But suddenly, a new figure interrupts the narrative flow of events. As if in a cinematic "freeze frame," the king of Sodom stands suspended while another character upstages him: Melchizedek King of Salem, Priest to God Most High. Melchizedek seizes this moment of suspended action in order to address Abraham before the evil king has a chance to speak. We now return to the text's presentation of the king/priest's appearance, noting how he has chosen his words and actions for maximal effect:

> He blessed him saying, "Blessed be Abram of God Most High, Creator of heaven and earth. And blessed be God Most High, Who has delivered [*miggen* (מגן)] your foes into your hand. (Gen. 14:19–20)

The first word Melchizedek utters is "blessed," from the Hebrew root *b-r-kh*. This word, which appears three times in this interlude, calls to mind the five-fold promise of blessing that Abraham received from God when he first set out on his path. In addition to recalling Abraham's blessedness, Melchizedek introduces a new name for God, *El Elyon*, God Most High, an appellation that appears three times in this passage. Perhaps this name is intended to remind Abraham of his early relationship with God and of its accompanying sublime ideals. With his repeated invocation of this name, Melchizedek urges Abraham to avert his gaze from the mundane protocols of the world around him and to re-affix it upon the heavens, the figurative dwelling place of God Most High.

Melchizedek further inspires Abraham by reminding him that God, and not the likes of the evil king of Sodom, is his only protector. Only God "delivers enemies into his hands." Perhaps with this phrase Melchizedek alludes not only to Abraham's victory over his enemies in war, but over an arguably more dangerous nemesis: Abraham's potential *ally*, the king of Sodom.

In addition to his evocative words, Melchizedek makes his point with deeds. By generously feeding the beleaguered patriarch, Melchizedek provides a model of the righteousness that his name intimates. With his name and his actions, Melchizedek foreshadows the theme of *tzedek*, righteousness, that will become central in the life of Abraham. Four chapters later, God explicitly states that His purpose in choosing Abraham is his potential to purvey justice and righteousness, *tzedakah u-mishpat*, to future generations (Gen. 18:19):

> For I have singled him out, so that he may instruct his children and his posterity to keep the way of the Lord by doing what is just and right [*tzedakah u-mishpat*] ... (Gen. 18:19)

The "way of the LORD" is defined as justice. It lies at the very core of God's future legal and moral systems. Abraham's election rests on his ability to serve as a model justice for his future generations.

In sum, at this critical juncture in Abraham's life, Melchizedek's name and essence, as well as his words and actions, remind the patriarch of his purpose and his calling. If Abraham could reconnect with the ideals that first motivated him, he would again look upward to God, the source of all blessing. Melchizedek fortifies and inspires Abraham by epitomizing the justice and righteousness that will serve as the foundations of God's covenant.[14]

---

14. As we will see in the coming pages, Abraham internalizes Melchizedek's messages, most significantly the notion of *tzedek* that is evoked by Melchizedek's name and his actions. Melchizedek's ongoing influence in Abraham's life may be observed in the story of God's destruction of the evil cities of Sodom and Gomorrah (Gen. 18). It is just before the destruction that God explains that His choice of Abraham rests on his potential to teach justice to his posterity. Immediately, Abraham sets about proving that God's assessment of him is correct and that he is indeed deeply infused with these values—values that were so ably demonstrated by Melchizedek. Abraham boldly and vigorously demands that God Himself abide by the principles of *tzedakah u-mishpat* in handling the evil people of Sodom (v. 25). In his impassioned plea, Abraham invokes the root *tz-d-k* seven times and he refers to *mishpat* twice. We might argue that in addition to drawing on the Melchizedek interlude, Genesis 18 acts as subversive sequel to Abraham's first encounter with the wicked kingdom of Sodom. In their first meeting, Abraham sought to save Sodom's people, even though aligning with them threatened his moral standing. In Genesis 18's replay of the Sodom-Abraham encounter, Abraham again seeks to save Sodom's people from annihilation. But this time, bolstered by Melchizedek's uplifting messages, Abraham is no longer at risk. Now confident in his ideals, *he* sets the moral tone for their encounter. This time, if the people of Sodom are to be saved, it will only be because they have traces of Abraham's core values of *tzedakah u-mishpat*.

The Internalization of the Message

The messages have been broadcast, but has the patriarch received them? We return to the text to weigh Abraham's reactions to all that he has heard. Following his brief inspirational performance, Melchizedek vanishes as abruptly as he arrived. The king of Sodom is released from suspension and is finally given license to speak:

> Then the king of Sodom said to Abram, "Give me the [*nefesh*] persons [or "soul"], and take the possessions for yourself. (Gen. 14:21)

The plain sense of this statement is the proffering of an exchange in which the king of Sodom gets his hostages and Abraham becomes rich. But a secondary reading is possible as well, since the word *nefesh* can mean either people or a soul.[15] Read the second way, the king of Sodom baits Abraham with a Faustian offer: "give me *your* soul by keeping the booty." An alliance with the king would bring Abraham material dividends, but he would forever lose himself in the process. Perhaps we might detect the subtlest reference to Abraham's earlier dubious material gains in Egypt, when, as a result of deceiving Pharaoh by claiming Sarah was his sister, he emerged a wealthy man.[16] Here again Abraham is offered tainted wealth that could further erode his moral standing.

At this decisive moment, in which he is potentially in danger of suffering an irreversible loss of his moral bearings, Abraham draws inspiration from his recent mysterious visitor, Melchizedek. Now keenly re-attuned to God's calling and His promises, Abraham finds the strength and the vocabulary with which to rebuff the advances of the evil king.

> But Abram said to the king of Sodom, "I raise my hand [in oath] to the Lord, God Most High, Creator of heaven and earth: I will not take so much as a thread or a sandal strap of what is yours; you shall not say, 'It is I who made Abram rich.' For me, nothing but what my servants have used up; for the share of men who went with me—Aner, Eshkol and Mamre—let them take their share."[17] (Gen. 14:22–24)

---

15. Although the primary meaning of *nefesh* in the Bible is "people," throughout the first chapter of Genesis its meaning is closer to the modern usage, "soul." The suggestion that this secondary meaning of *nefesh* could be applied to Gen. 14:21—as indicated by the brackets in the biblical quote cited above—is the author's.

16. For an elaboration on this story, see chapter 5 of this volume.

17. Author's translation.

The first sign of Melchizedek's influence comes with Abraham's references to God as "God Most High," the "Creator of heaven and earth," terms he has never before used. These new appellations for God point to His sublime, powerful standing, which contrasts starkly with the uninspiring nature of Abraham's recent experiences.[18]

Abraham adopts Melchizedek's terms of speech a second time when he refers to his *hand*. Melchizedek spoke of God as delivering Abraham's enemies into his hand. Abraham now raises that hand in solemn oath that he will never accept the largesse of unscrupulous figures such as the king of Sodom. Armed with God's protection, Abraham finds the strength to resist threats to both body and soul.

In his response to the king of Sodom, Abraham makes what is possibly a third reference to his encounter with Melchizedek, when he says that he does not want to allow the king of Sodom to say, "I made Abraham rich." The verb *he'esharti* (הֶעֱשַׁרְתִּי) plays phonetically upon the word for Melchizedek's tithe, *ma'aser* (מַעֲשֵׂר), with both words sharing the three Hebrew root letters, עשר, *'-s-r*.[19] Bolstered by both the tithe and Melchizedek's accompanying messages of empowerment, Abraham feels no temptation to accept the riches offered by the King of Sodom.

By drawing on Melchizedek's language of moral and spiritual rejuvenation, the text presents an Abraham who revisits the much-compromised spirit of *lekh lekha*, and who begins to remove the barriers that have obstructed his godly vision.

Out of the World's Hollow Spaces

Abraham is not the only one who takes note of Melchizedek's message. Strikingly, God too will evoke the language and actions introduced by the king/priest. Immediately following Melchizedek's visit, we read about the "covenant between the pieces," a celestial encounter in which God forges a sublime, unshakable covenant with Abraham and his descendants. Were it not for the opening words of Genesis 15, we might have read the passage in which the covenant is introduced as signaling the arrival of a new Abraham, whose coming adventures owe very little to earlier, more banal events. But the text instructs us otherwise. Genesis 15

---

18. Abraham independently adds God's particular name—the Lord—perhaps demonstrating his renewed relationship with the exalted, yet personal God of his early encounters.

19. Although it is likely that the two words stem from different languages—the tithe from the Arabic for "ten" and riches from Aramaic—it is also likely that by appearing in such close proximity to one another, word play is intended.

begins, *"After these things,* the word of the LORD came to Abraham," strongly suggesting the literary equivalent of an arrow pointing back toward the preceding
chapter and its chronicle of war and compromise.[20] Such linkage helps to explain God's enigmatic charge to Abraham in verse 1:

> Fear not, Abram, I am a shield [מָגֵן *(magen)*] to you;
> Your reward shall be very great. (Gen. 15:1)

God's words address Abraham's fear, yet no fear has been expressed. Rashi,
in an adaptation of Rabbi Levi's opinion in the ancient midrash Genesis Rabbah
(44:5), comments:

> [I will be a shield to you] from punishment, that you shall not be punished
> for all those souls you killed, and as to your concern about receiving your
> reward—your reward is very great. (Rashi, 15:1, s.v. *al tira Avram anokhi*
> *magen lakh*)

In this view, Abraham is concerned about the corrupting effect the war
has had on him. Killing, even in self-defense, is a morally debilitating experience, and Abraham feels vulnerable in the face of these challenges to his ethical standing. God's response to his unspoken apprehension is as unwavering
as it is reassuring. You have nothing to fear, says God. I am your shield against
any claims that those actions, necessary though they were, will define your
future. With God's protective shield, Abraham's undiminished rewards still
await him.

To deliver His encouraging messages, God, like Abraham in his encounter
with the king of Sodom, echoes and alludes to Melchizedek's words. First, we
recall that Melchizedek had blessed God who protects Abraham by handing
over his enemies to him—*miggen,* from the root *m-g-n.* God now adopts the
same Hebrew verb root, rarely used in the Bible, *m-g-n,*[21] to assure Abraham of

---

20. See Rashi on 15:1, s.v. *ahar ha-devarim ha'ele.*

21. The appearance of the root *m-g-n* in these two chapters represents two of the three times this root appears
(in both noun and verb forms) in all five books of the Pentateuch. This makes its doubling here especially noteworthy. The root *m-g-n* in the *pi'el* form (intensive action conjugation) means "to deliver," while
the noun form means "to act as a shield." God extends Melchizedek's thought by suggesting that not
only does He protect Abraham by handing over his enemies and enabling him to win wars; He also provides complete protection by acting as a physical shield against all other forms of adversity.

the veracity of this sentiment. God's message is: I am your shield, *anokhi magen lakh*, from both your moral and mortal enemies.

A second echo of Mechizedek's visit may be found in the text's reference to *tzedakah*, righteousness. This word featured prominently in the narrative of the priest whose name in Hebrew, *Malkitzedek*, means "king of justice." Now, the text in Genesis 15 states that God considered Abraham's belief to be an expression of his quality of *tzedakah* (15:6).[22] Justice and righteousness were the outstanding characteristics of Melchizedek, and they will now qualify Abraham to be God's elected leader.

We find yet another allusion from one story to the next in the phrase, "God **brought** Abraham **out**," from the Hebrew root *y-tz-'* (Gen. 15:5). Just as Melchizedek had "**brought out**, *y-tz-'*" bread and wine, providing physical succor to the weary patriarch, God now "brings Abraham out" in order to show him the stars:

> He brought him outside and said, "Look toward the heaven and count the stars, if you are able to count them. And he said, "So shall your offspring be."[23] (Gen. 15:5)

Melchizedek's offerings revived Abraham physically, while his words rejuvenated Abraham's spirit. Perhaps now, as a result, Abraham is ready to be "brought out" by God, from one frame of mind to another. The following midrash, cited by Rashi, hints at this deeper meaning in God's actions:

> He brought him out from the hollow space of the world and elevated him above the stars ...[24]

Abraham had long inhabited the world's "hollow spaces," the morally murky areas of life's unruly pathways that threaten to crush the spirit. God now offers him a return to the grand, celestial bearing of his early promises, using Melchizedek's terminology in the process.

---

22. Because of the particularly ambiguous nature of this verse, the commentators struggle to make sense of the word *tzedakah*. In line with Rashi and others, NJPS defines *tzedakah* as "merit," while Everett Fox provides the compound "righteous-merit." I prefer to understand *tzedakah* in the larger context of Abraham's narrative, in which it refers to justice and righteousness.

23. Author's translation.

24. Rashi, Gen. 15:5, s.v. *va-yotze oto ha-hutzah*. Rashi's comments are based on Genesis Rabbah 44:10.

A Subversive Sequel: From War to Covenant

The story of Abraham's quotidian struggle for survival finds resonance in the chronicle of his covenant with God. The latter text draws not only on Melchizedek's uplifting words following Abraham's battles, but on the language of the wars themselves. As we compare these passages, we will note the presence of the subversive sequel. In a grand literary reversal, words and phrases from the episode of the wars return with opposite intent to describe God's covenant. For instance, the two chapters share the names of such nations as *Refaim, Eimim, Goyim,* and *Emori* (Gen. 14:1,5,13; 15:12,14,16,20). While in Genesis 14 these nations were participants in Abraham's gritty war for survival, in Genesis 15 the names resurface as part of God's assurances that Abraham's descendants will inherit the land of Canaan. A second point of contrast may be found in the word *dan.* In Genesis 14, **Dan** is one of many war locations; it signifies Abraham's exertions to survive (14:14). In Genesis 15 the Hebrew word *dan,* which means to judge, suggests that Abraham can begin to let his guard down, since God will now take over as guarantor of his survival. In fact, God would exact **judgment,** *dan anokhi,* from the nation that would threaten Abraham's descendants (15:14). Both chapters speak of *rekhush,* **possessions** (14:21; 15:14). In Genesis 14, the looted **possessions** are reminders of Abraham's hard-fought struggle on the battlefield. In contrast, the **"great possessions,** *rekhush"* in Genesis 15 are part of God's reassurance that Abraham's descendants will be amply compensated following their enslavement. An additional literary link may be found in the word *berit,* covenant. In Genesis 14, a human alliance, *berit,* with his neighbors was Abraham's best hope for survival (14:13). By the next chapter, he advances toward a sublime, enduring *berit* in his partnership with God (15:18).[25]

Taken together, these two chapters literarily illustrate a reversal of Abraham's direction. Now armed with Melchizedek's uplifting messages and with God's explicit promises, Abraham is ready to follow his future as God's covenantal partner.

---

25. In addition to the above comparisons, the word *Dammesek,* **Damascus,** which appears only twice in all of the Pentateuch, is found in each of these two chapters (Gen. 14:15; 15:2). In Genesis 14 this term refers to a location in Abraham's war for survival: Abraham chased the enemy kings to **Damascus.** In Genesis 15 the word appears in the context of God's promise that Abraham will have a son who will be his heir to God's blessings; thus he need not worry that his legacy will fall to his servant, Eliezer of **Damascus.** For a more expansive treatment of these similarities, see Judy Klitsner, *The Torah of the Mothers,* 270–276.

Abraham as Archetype of the Jewish Nation

Melchizedek helps pave the way for more than just Abraham's personal emergence. Empowered by their encounter, Abraham will step into his role as a symbolic microcosm of the embryonic Israelite people, receiving his personal version of God's revelation. With dramatic foreshadowing, Abraham's individual theophany shares many of the basic components of the later national revelation at Sinai. First, the physical conditions are remarkably similar. Both stories feature **smoke** (Gen. 15:17; Exod. 19:9), **fire** (Gen. 15:17; Exod. 19:18), and a darkness-inspired **fear and trembling** (Gen. 15:12; Exod. 19:16). In both there is a statement of **belief** on the part of God's human audience (Gen. 15:6; Exod. 19:9). Perhaps the most impressive comparison lies in God's introductory words. At the foot of Mt. Sinai, God proclaims:

> I am the Lord your God who brought you out of the land of Egypt from the house of bondage. (Exod. 20:2)

In His covenant with Abraham, God says:

> I am the Lord who brought you out of Ur of the Chaldeans to give you this land as a possession. (Gen. 15:7)

These similarities highlight Abraham's function as lone symbol of the Israelite nation. To assume this momentous role, Abraham needed moral and physical reinforcement, as well as a reminder of the personal ideals and values, such as righteousness and justice, that first prompted him on his path. Faced with many prosaic challenges along his way and the threat of being swallowed up by "the earth's hollow spaces," Abraham benefited from the presence of another solitary figure, the mysterious king/priest. Melchizedek instructs Abraham in matters of righteousness and justice and helps him to keep his eyes fixed on the stellar firmament that beckons from above.

Abraham's encounter with Melchizedek underscores the notion of lone, conscience-driven action on the part of individuals. As we saw in chapter 2, the Pentateuch places special emphasis on those characters who oppose convention and follow a solitary path in their dealings with the world around them. In a sense, these defiant figures—Abraham, the midwives of Egypt, and Pharaoh's daughter, to recall a few—are all *Ivrim:* individuals who separate from the masses, and sometimes from their loved ones, as they uphold God's ways of justice. When Abraham finds himself temporarily diverted from his divinely inspired sense of integrity, Melchizedek helps him recover his direction.

But this leadership model seems inadequate in addressing the events to come. In the Book of Genesis, the Jewish nation exists in potential only. Thus it is enough for a symbolic leader such as Abraham to concentrate on the internal process of distilling his goals and values and on strengthening his relationship with God. But a nation will soon be born that will require a new leadership model, one that will reflect the shift from the individual to the community.

To begin addressing this concern, we turn to a parallel account of a patriarch and his priestly mentor, the story of Moses and Jethro. After uncovering the many similarities between the stories, we will note how the second story acts as a sequel to the first, at times reinforcing, and at times revising its messages. We will then turn to a third priestly passage, which plays on the tropes of both of these tales of an outside figure who provides counsel in a time of moral crisis.

Moses, Solitary Seeker

In a significant way, the story of Moses will begin where the story of Abraham ended. God's final address to Abraham contains the words *lekh lekha*, which suggest that Abraham is to end his career as he began, as a lone seeker of godly truths. Moses begins his life in a solitary manner, neither fully Hebrew nor fully Egyptian. Yet the young prince will receive priestly assistance to propel him away from his solitude toward a more inclusive stance. With Jethro's help, Moses will gradually grow into his role as leader of a nation.

Before we examine the function of the priest in Moses' development, we must first revisit the actions of the extraordinarily principled, independent women who left their indelible imprint on the young man's character. We return to a passage introduced in chapter 2 of this volume, Exodus 2, this time noting the prominence of two recurring "guiding" words. These words provide a key to understanding much about Moses' future. They will hint at the moral excellence that will define him as a human being and at his need for guidance in addressing the evolving needs of a nascent nation:

> A man of the house of Levi went and married a daughter of Levi. The woman conceived and bore a son; and when she **saw** [*r-'-h*] how good he was, she hid him for three months. When she could hide him no longer, she got a wicker basket for him and caulked it with bitumen and pitch. She put the **child** [*yeled*] into it and placed it among the reeds by the bank of the Nile. And his sister stationed herself at a distance, to learn what would befall him.

The daughter of Pharaoh came down to bathe in the Nile, while her maidens walked along the Nile. She **saw** [*r-'-h*] the basket among the reeds and sent her slave girl to fetch it. When she opened it, she **saw** [*r-'-h*] that it was a **child** [*yeled*] a boy crying. She took pity on him and said, "This must be a Hebrew **child** [*mi-yaldei Ha-Ivrim*]." Then his sister said to Pharaoh's daughter, "Shall I go and get you a Hebrew nurse to suckle the **child** [*yeled*] for you?" Pharaoh's daughter answered, "Yes." So the girl went and called the **child's** mother [*em ha-yaled*]. And Pharaoh's daughter said to her, "Take this **child** [*ha-yeled*] and nurse it for me, and I will pay your wages." So the woman took the **child** [*ha-yeled*] and nursed it. When the **child** [*ha-yeled*] grew up, she brought him to Pharaoh's daughter, who made him her son. She named him Moses, saying, "I drew him out of the water."[26] (Exod. 2:1–10)

The persistently repeated words *yeled,* child, and the root *r-'-h,* to see, allow us a glimpse into the forces most likely to inform Moses' later functioning as a human being and as a leader. As a boy, Moses is "seen" three times, once by his birth mother (Exod. 2:2) and twice by his adoptive mother (2:5, 6). In each of these instances, "seeing" represents the ability to look beyond social norms and to act in an ethical manner in defiance of convention and even external threat. Despite the danger to herself and the rest of her family, Jokhebed, after "seeing" the need of her newborn child, decides she must do everything humanly possible to save him. In a desperate act of defiance, she places him in the very river that Pharaoh has designated as the instrument of death, thereby redefining it as a place of *life*. Pharaoh's daughter is the next person to rest her eyes on Moses, and despite the death warrant that her own father has issued, she goes to astonishing lengths in order to keep him alive, including adopting him as her own. The two guiding words, "seeing" and "child," join with a third recurring word in this passage, "daughter,"[27] to encapsulate Moses' formative years. As a child he is seen, and consequently saved, by a series of selfless women. Thus the mother's milk imbibed by the young Moses is enriched with individualistic, fearless integrity.

As we trace Moses' growth into a leader, we will encounter the text's literary response to the actions of these courageous "daughters." Upon reaching maturity,

---

26. Author's translation.

27. For more on the significance of the guiding word "*bat,* daughter," see chapter 2, pp. 61–62, and note 78.

Moses too "sees" three times (Exod. 2:11,12). Like his maternal forebearers, he looks penetratingly and unflinchingly at the world around him. Moses is appalled by the injustice he sees and breaks with all known convention in order to protest the oppression. But as we will soon see, this type of lone behavior will not only enhance Moses' leadership abilities; in certain ways, it will impede them as well. Like Abraham, Moses will require the assistance of an outsider in order to realize more fully his leadership potential. But this time, instead of moving further inward, the leader will need to reach outward to embrace his community.

From Yeled to Ish: Moses' Lone Existence

Moses, like Abraham, faces the world alone, keenly attuned to the dictates of conscience. But the two leaders are opposites in a number of ways. For one thing, Abraham is the symbolic leader of a nation that has not yet been formed, while Moses is destined to lead an actual nation. In addition, as we have seen, Abraham's life is marked by a series of separations. Although he begins his life as part of a family, he must leave it in order to follow God. In contrast, Moses' early life finds him alone, neither fully belonging to his birth family nor in his adopted home.[28] Unlike Abraham, he must find his place within a community *before* he can engage God and embark on a path to successful national leadership. To fulfill this requirement, Moses, like Abraham, will need assistance. But unlike Abraham, Moses' counselor will have to help him become more, rather than less, a part of the world around him.

To highlight the problem that Moses will need to overcome, we now trace his first attempts at connecting to community. The text sets up a transitional narrative, in which Moses grows from *yeled*, child, to *ish*, man. This passage is marked by his search for the human connections that will enable him to lead. As part of his process of "growing up," a term that appears twice in this passage (Exod. 2:10,11), Moses twice "goes out" (2:11,13) in search of his people. But for Moses, an outsider from birth, embracing a community will be no simple task. Again, the passage's guiding words help to demonstrate the point:

> In those days, Moses grew up and went out to his brothers, and he saw [*r-'-h*] their burdens. He saw [*r-'-h*] an Egyptian **man** [*ish*] beating a Hebrew **man**

---

28. For an elaboration on Moses' solitary life as a young man, see Ibn Ezra's comments to Exod. 2:3, s.v. *va-tahmerah.*

[*ish*] from among his brothers. He turned this way and that and **saw** [*r-'-h*] that there was no one about [literally "there was no **man** (*ish*)"], and he struck down the Egyptian and hid him in the sand. When he went out the next day, he found two Hebrew **men** [*anashim* (plural of *ish*)] fighting; so he said to the offender, "Why do you strike your fellow?" He said, "Who made you a **man** [*ish*] who is chief and judge over us? Do you mean to kill me as you killed the Egyptian? Moses was frightened and thought: then the matter is known! When Pharaoh learned of the matter, he sought to kill Moses; but Moses fled from Pharaoh. He arrived in the land of Midian, and sat down beside a well.[29] (Exod. 2:11–15)

At this point in his young life, the frequently recurring term *ish*, man, together with a reprise of the Hebrew root *r-'-h*, to see, hold the key to Moses' quest. On one level, Moses literally seeks a "man," a male role model in his life. Although much has been said about the heroic women who raised him, Moses' father is curiously absent from the account of his upbringing, and perhaps now Moses seeks to fill that void. But on another more figurative level, Moses seeks a community of "men," of decent human beings who share his core values. If we were to translate the Hebrew term *ish* into colloquial Yiddish, we would say that Moses is a *mensch*, a morally upright, principled human being, on a quest for a community of like-minded people. To assume his role as leader, Moses seeks emotional and ideological affiliation with those around him. But which people will fill this role?

Looking first to the Egyptians, Moses is dismayed to find a culture of violence and oppression. The Egyptian "man" is a tyrant who delivers murderous blows—from the Hebrew root *n-kh-h*—to innocent victims. In response to this disturbing display, Moses looks around and finds that "there was no man." The plain sense of these words is that he first made sure that the coast was clear before striking down the Egyptian. But another possible reading has been put forth by Netziv in his Bible commentary *Ha-amek Davar*:

> He looked this way and that: He searched for ideas as to how to complain about the Egyptian who had gratuitously stricken the Hebrew, but he saw that there was "no man" before whom to report this inequity, as all around him were traitors and haters of the Israelites. (*Ha-amek Davar* Exod. 2:12, s.v. *va-yifen ko vakho vayar ki ein ish.*)

---

29. Author's translation.

Read this way, violence is not Moses' first course of action. Still hoping to find redeeming value in Egyptian society, he looks to its institutions of justice. But after exhausting the criminal and legal systems, he finds that there is "no man" among them. The society is irreparably suffused with corruption and injustice. Only when this realization sets in does Moses take unilateral action, protesting the violence by killing one Egyptian offender.

Despairing of finding a "man" among the Egyptians, Moses goes out a second time, this time focusing on the Israelites, whom he intuitively believed to be his "brothers" (Exod. 2:11). But Moses finds the Hebrews acting in much the same way as their oppressors. Like the Egyptian taskmaster who struck, *n-k-h*, a Hebrew slave, one Hebrew now strikes, *n-kh-h*, another. Despite the similarity in their behavior, Moses speaks to the aggressor rather than striking him. Perhaps he expects more from the Hebrew because of the blood ties he shares with him, or perhaps he assumes that the Hebrews, as victims of oppression will more readily accept his reproach. In any case, Moses attempts to reason with the assailant by asking, "Why do you strike your fellow?" (2:13). But again his hopes are shattered as the Hebrew lashes out with ironic invective: "Who made you an *ish* who is chief and ruler over us?" (v.14). This taunt is the unfortunate response to Moses' sincere search for an *ish*. Not only is there no other *ish* to be found, but he is now ridiculed for his own efforts to act as one.

Although he seeks a community, Moses operates alone. Single-handedly, he undertakes the virtually impossible task of combating the racist norms of Egyptian society as well as the self-hating stance of the Israelites. In neither society does one human being truly "see" the dangers of conformity; nor do the people open their ears to dissenting moral voices. In contrast, Moses looks and listens closely. He takes in the evils of oppression as he resolves to unilaterally combat the injustice that surrounds him.

But Moses' lone action is not effective. True, there are literary hints that killing was called for. There is poetic justice in his smiting, *n-kh-h*, the Egyptian who was himself smiting, *n-kh-h*, another.[30] But the Hebrew onlookers see his deeds out

---

30. Cassuto elaborates on the literary quid pro quo: "The Egyptian smote, therefore justice demanded that he too, should be smitten. However, the word *smite* is repeated with a somewhat different nuance: when first used it means 'to beat,' the second time it signifies 'to kill.' Nevertheless, the repetition points to the principle of measure for measure. By this act Moses showed the qualities of his spirit, the spirit of a man who pursued justice and is quick to save the oppressed from the hand of the oppressor, the spirit of love of freedom and of courage to rise up against tyrants. A man possessed of these attributes was worthy to become God's messenger to deliver Israel from the bondage of Egypt and to smite their oppressors with ten *makkot* (literally 'smitings')." Cassuto, *Exodus*, 22.

of context. From their vantage point, Moses has not defended a person in need, but has enacted a simple act of killing, *h-r-g* (Exod. 2:14).[31] As an individual, Moses demonstrates laudable courage. As a leader of others, however, his lone act of heroism is questionable at best. As we will see, his tendency to unilateral action will consistently threaten his leadership abilities. It is precisely this predisposition that will require the help of an outside counselor.

The following midrash explores the problematic nature of Moses' solitary actions in Egypt. It imagines a dialogue between Moses and God as the Israelites stand at the threshold to the Land of Canaan.[32] Although God has informed Moses that he will not accompany the people into the land, and that instead he is about to die, Moses pleads for his life:

> God said to him, "Moses, whose son are you?" He answered, "Son of Amram." God said, "And Amram, whose son is he?" He said, "Son of Izhar ..." God said, "Is any of them still alive?" He said, "They are all dead." God said, "And you want to live?" [...] God then said to him, "Did I tell you to kill the Egyptian?" Moses said, "You killed all the first born sons of Egypt, and I must die for one Egyptian?" God said to him, "Are you like me, taking life and giving life? Can you create life, as I do?"

This discourse portrays Moses as a man who blurs the lines between his own moral instincts and prerogatives and the divine right to create or terminate life. As a result of a recurring tendency to assign too much weight to his solitary decision-making, Moses ultimately falls short of accomplishing the most important task of his life, delivering God's people into the Promised Land.

At the very beginning of his leadership path, the text, through literary means, telegraphs Moses' greatest strengths and weaknesses as a future leader. On the one hand, Moses, like Abraham, will be a consummate individual. He will consult none but his conscience in making moral decisions. On the other hand, Moses will at times take Abraham's individuality to extreme lengths. His failure to consult or to enlist the input of others will occasionally lead him to lash out too

---

31. The verb *h-r-g* appears three times in this passage. It replaces the verb *n-kh-h*, presenting a much harsher perspective on Moses' actions on the part of his onlookers.

32. Midrash *Petirat Moshe, Otzar Midrashim*, section 2, 363. This source was taken from N. Leibowitz, *Exodus*, 38. Author's translation.

readily or to reach dubious conclusions that will work to the detriment of his overall leadership effort.

To help mitigate his solitude and to widen his perspective, Moses will need the help of an outsider. He will meet a solitary figure, an *ish* like himself, who will help him realize the promise of his leadership.

A Second Priest: Jethro Priest of Midian

We return to the young Moses in Egypt. Following his failure to influence either the Egyptians or the Israelites, along with his failure to find a community of people who share his vision of justice, Moses is forced to flee. When he arrives safely in Midian, we might expect that the thankless response he received for behaving as an *ish* will have deterred him from further acting as a lone purveyor of justice. But instead, his first act in his new land is heroically and single-handedly to rescue seven strangers in need. The daughters of Jethro, Priest of Midian—here referred to by one of several alternate names, Re'uel[33]—are the victims of intruding shepherds who prevent them from watering their flocks.

In describing Moses to their father, the young women refer to the gallant stranger as an *ish Mitzri*, an Egyptian *man*. Although they mistakenly identify Moses as an Egyptian, they correctly recognize his qualities as an *ish*, a person of moral substance. Impressed by what he hears, Jethro demands to know why his daughters have not brought this man home, where he would be welcomed and appreciated:

> "Where is he then? Why did you leave the **man** [*ish*]? Ask him in to break bread." Moses consented to stay with the **man** [*ish*] and he gave Moses his daughter Zipporah as a wife. (Exod. 2:21)

An *ish* himself, Jethro recognizes Moses as an *ish*, deeming him worthy of his company, his bread, and his daughter's hand. With his actions, Jethro begins to draw Moses out of his solitude. First, by welcoming him into his home, he offers him the community of

---

33. Jethro is the most well-known name of Moses' father-in-law to be, though curiously he is known by several other names as well: Re'uel (Exod. 2:18), Jether (4:18), and Hobab son of Re'uel (Num. 10:29; Judg. 4:11). The midrashic resolution to this problem is to assume that the variations are a deliberate method of representing the many facets of the priest's character. See Rashi's comments to Exod. 18:1, s.v. *va-yishma Yitro*, which are based on *Mekhilta Yitro masekhta de-Amalek*, chapter 1. Alternatively, a modern critical approach suggests that the different names reflect different traditions. See Sarna, *The JPS Torah Commentary, Exodus*, 240, notes 30, 31.

men that he has sought for so long. Then, by betrothing Moses to his daughter, Jethro provides him with the companionship of a marriage partner. Moses feels relief and gratitude at ending his isolation, as suggested by his pronouncement upon naming his son:

> She bore a son whom he named Gershom, for he said, "I was a stranger in a foreign land." (Exod. 22)

From the safety of Jethro's home, with his wife and son in tow, Moses looks back on his life in Egypt, the land of his two mothers and two nationalities, and of his vast, but failed potential for kinship. Only now, in this new land of Midian, does Moses realize that until his meeting with the priest Jethro, he has been estranged from everyone.

Men, Officers, and Judges

As we have seen, Melchizedek provided crucial assistance that helped Abraham assume his role as leader of a future nation. He appeared at a critical juncture, nurturing Abraham's body with bread and his soul with lofty messages that reminded him of his divine calling. In a parallel story of priestly enablement, Jethro has begun to fill a similar function for Moses. He too has offered bread, and he too will give the patriarch what he most needs to meet the challenges of leadership. We will find literary reinforcement of these themes later in the text, in another meeting between Moses and his father-in-law.[34] Following the ten plagues, the miraculous exodus from Egypt, and the parting of the sea, Jethro greets Moses with language that strongly resonates with the Melchizedek narrative:

> Blessed [*b-r-kh*] be the LORD ... who delivered you from the **hand** [*yad*] of the Egyptians and from the **hand** [*yad*] of Pharaoh, and who delivered the people from under the **hand** [*yad*] of the Egyptians. Now I know that the Lord is greater than all gods ... and Aaron came with all the elders of Israel to eat **bread** [*lehem*] before God with Moses' father-in-law.[35] (Exod. 18:10,12)

As in Melchizedek's meeting with Abraham, the foreign priest Jethro *blesses* God, who fortifies the *hand* of His subjects, delivering[36] them from harm. Again,

---

34. There is one brief exchange recorded between Moses and Jethro in the interim, in Exod. 4:18.
35. Author's translation.
36. Although both priests speak of God's deliverance of His people, they do not use the same Hebrew term. Melchizedek uses the word *m-g-n*, while Jethro chooses a form of the verb *n-tz-l*.

the priest breaks *bread* with the patriarch. And again the mysterious priest empowers the patriarch to persist in the difficult course on which he has embarked.

But the Jethro-Moses narrative will do more than mirror that of Melchizedek-Abraham. It will act as its subversive sequel as well. After strengthening the patriarch personally and helping him to become truer to his own ideals and goals, this priest will encourage the patriarch to forge a new path, one that requires looking not inward, but outward, toward the community that surrounds him.

In Midian, by offering Moses a family and a place of refuge, Jethro began to chip away at Moses' solitary existence. Now, in their next meeting, Jethro expands on his efforts, urging Moses to function in tandem with others. Jethro is appalled to find his son-in-law, now the leader of the nation, repeating the errors of his youth, again acting as a loner:

> Next day, Moses sat as magistrate among the people while the people stood about Moses from morning until evening. But when Moses' father-in-law saw how much he had to do for the people, he said, "What is this thing that you are doing to the people? Why do you act alone, while all the people stand about you from morning until evening?" Moses replied to his father-in-law, "It is because the people come to me to inquire of God. When they have a dispute, it comes before me, and I decide between one person and another, and I make known the laws and teachings of God." (Exod. 18:13–16)

Still the solitary activist, Moses leads by micromanaging the people. Every complaint, large and small, is judged by him alone. Here, as before, Jethro offers Moses a supportive buffer against his erosive solitude, this time by encouraging him to share the burden of leadership:

> But Moses' father-in-law said to him, "The thing you are doing is **not good** [*lo tov*]; you will surely wear yourself out, and these people as well. For the task is too heavy for you; you cannot do it **alone** [*levadekha*]. Now listen to me, I will give you counsel, and God be with you! You represent the people before God: you bring the disputes before God, and enjoin upon them the laws and the teachings, and make known to them the way they are to go and the practices they are to follow. You shall also seek out from among all the people capable **men** [*anashim* (pl. of *ish*)] who fear God, trustworthy men who spurn ill-gotten gain. Set these over them as **chiefs** [*sarei*] of thousands, hundreds, fifties and tens, and let them **judge** [*ve-shafetu*] the people at all times... Make it easier for yourself by letting them share the burden with

you. If you do this—and God so commands you—you will be able to bear up; and all these people too will go home unwearied." (Exod. 18:17–23)

Jethro advises Moses that taking too much upon himself is dangerous, not only for his own psychological well-being, but for the good of the people being judged. "The thing you are doing is **not good, lo tov**," says Jethro. "You cannot do it **alone, levadekha**." This statement resonates strongly with God's declaration in the Garden of Eden (Gen. 2:18): "It is **not good, lo tov,** for man to be **alone, levado.**" In fact, the word combination of lo tov and levad appears in only these two places in all of the Pentateuch. In harnessing God's words delivered at the dawn of creation, Jethro lets Moses know that he is no exception to the eternal human truth that a life of solitude is not good. To be a successful leader, he must first expand himself as a human being, by learning to include others.

Jethro's choice of language is significant in another way. He tells Moses to appoint *men* who are capable, honest, and God-fearing. He was to set over them *chiefs* of thousands, hundreds, fifties, and tens. The result of this careful delegation of responsibility would be an effective system of justice: "And they *judged* the people at all times" (Exod. 18:26). This word combination of **men, chiefs, and judges,** *anashim*—pl. of *ish, sarim, shofetim,* recalls the taunt of the Hebrew man in Egypt who was striking his fellow: "Who made you a **man** [*ish*] who is **chief** [*sar*] and **judge** [*shofet*] over us" (2:14)? With his understanding of Moses' problem and his suggestion for its solution, Jethro offers him the ammunition he needs to reverse the jeers of those who earlier had rejected him. By helping Moses to further shed his lonesome burden—a process begun in Midian and now expanded—Jethro helps him draw closer to his goal of worthy leadership. In a very real sense, Moses, under Jethro's tutelage, is now ready to operate as an effective **man, judge, and chief.**

Recidivism

Significantly, Moses' greatest success as a leader of his community follows on the heels of this encounter with Jethro. In the same Torah portion in which the above encounter occurs—aptly titled the portion of Jethro, *parashat Yitro*—Moses delivers the nation to Mt. Sinai. There, in a rare moment of unity, the people "answer as one" in pledging to uphold God's word (Exod. 19:8). Moses too, is one with his people at this momentous juncture. He prepares them spiritually for their meeting with the divine (vv. 10–15), and he serves as the people's faithful interlocutor with God (vv. 7,8,17,22–25). In his role as leader, Moses goes so far as to physically guide the people to their encounter: "Moses brought the people out toward God, and they took their places at the foot of the mountain"[37] (v. 17).

Yet in spite of his great success in fostering and becoming part of a covenantal community, Moses will continue to struggle against an internal pull toward lone decision-making and unilateral action. These tendencies take center stage in another encounter between Moses and Jethro, which is reported much later in the text, in the Book of Numbers. When Jethro informs Moses of his intention to leave the Israelites to return to his own land, Moses entreats his trusted mentor to remain with him:

> Come with us and we will do good [ve-heitavnu] for you; for the Lord has spoken the good [tov] about Israel.[38] (Num. 10:29)

When Jethro refuses, Moses continues to plead:

> Please do not leave us, inasmuch as you know where we should camp in the wilderness and can be our guide. So if you come with us, the good [ha-tov] that God makes good [yeittiv] with us, we will bestow [that good] [ve-heitavnu] upon you.[39] (Num. 10:31–32)

In his appeal to Jethro, Moses invokes different forms of the word "tov" five times. The recurrence of this word recalls and reverses Jethro's earlier pronouncement, "The thing you are doing [judging all the people all the time] is lo tov, not good" (Exod. 18:17). With Jethro's skilled arbitration, Moses was able to function in a "good" way, sharing the leadership burden with others. Moses now worries that this state of "good" will continue only as long as Jethro remains with him. If Jethro leaves, Moses might lose his resolve to include others, and might backslide into his solitary style of leadership, so aptly labeled by Jethro as "not good."

Moses' worst fears are almost immediately realized. Despite his supplications, Jethro leaves. Things begin to deteriorate, as suggested by the intrusion of a new guiding word. In place of the word tov comes its opposite, ra, bad.

> Moses heard the people weeping, every clan apart, each person at the entrance of his tent. The Lord was very angry, and to Moses it was bad [ra].

---

37. Author's translation. Note the similarity between this verse and Genesis 15:5 in which God "brought out" the patriarch Abraham—using the same root y-tz-'—in order to receive his symbolic revelation.

38. Author's translation.

39. Ibid.

Moses said to the Lord, "Why have you done **bad** [*ra*] to your servant, and why have I not enjoyed Your favor, that You have laid the burden of all this people upon me? Did I conceive all this people, did I bear them, that You should say to me, 'Carry them in your bosom as a nurse carries an infant,' to the land that You have promised on oath to their fathers? Where am I to get meat to give to all this people, when they whine before me and say, 'Give us meat to eat!' I cannot carry all this people **alone** [*lo ukhal anokhi levadi*], for it is too much for me. If You would deal thus with me, kill me rather, I beg You, and let me see no more of my **bad** state [*ra'ati*]!"[40] (Num. 11:10–15)

Jethro's absence has caused Moses to swing from "good" to "bad." Without his mentor, Moses acts like a harried parent. He feels he must address every need and every error of those in his charge, yet he feels incapable of managing alone. Confirming Jethro's prediction, "You cannot do it alone [*lo tukhal ... levadekha*]" (Exod. 18:18), Moses now cries, "I cannot carry this people alone [*lo ukhal ... levadi*] for it is too much for me" (Num. 11:14). In this state, when confronted by an angry, demanding people, Moses erupts into an emotional outburst. He accuses God of causing his wretched state and then begs for his own death. With no one to guide him and to critique his actions, Moses' lone tendencies get the better of him. As he continues in this vein, Moses will gradually, as foreseen by Jethro (Exod. 18:18), lose his ability to lead.

The tragic conclusion to the story of Moses' leadership comes in the twentieth chapter of the book of Numbers, when he faces yet another trial from a cantankerous nation. Moses receives God's instruction to quench the people's thirst by taking his rod in hand and speaking to a rock. But instead the overwrought leader does not comply:

Moses took the rod from before the Lord, as He had commanded him. Moses and Aaron assembled the congregation in front of the rock; and he said to them, "Listen you rebels, shall we get water for you out of this rock?" And Moses raised his hand and struck [*n-kh-h*] the rock twice with his rod. Out came copious water, and the community and their beasts drank. But the Lord said to Moses and Aaron, "Because you did not trust me enough to affirm My sanctity in the sight of the Israelite people, therefore you shall not lead this congregation into the land that I have given them." (Num. 20:9–12)

---

40. Author's translation.

Ending his career the way he began, Moses acts alone, heeding no voice but his own. But with this act, Moses' solitary stance brings him to new extremes. This time, as a result of his actions, he will be unable to complete his leadership mission. For the first time, Moses screens out not only human influences but God's orders, a situation that undermines the very essence of his calling. Moreover, his actions create an unfortunate symmetry to his life as a leader, with the word *n-hk-h*, strike, appearing at both ends. As with the Egyptian taskmaster, Moses strikes, *n-kh-h*, his target instead of speaking to it. We recall that in Egypt, even in his passion for justice, Moses had refrained from striking his own brother. Instead he had attempted to reason with the offending Hebrew: "Why do you strike your fellow?" But now, perhaps because of the cumulative effect of the people's complaining, Moses comes perilously close to fraternal violence. Instead of defending the errant people before God, as he has done consistently in the past, this time Moses lashes out, calling them "rebels." Then he raises his rod, perhaps to strike in a way he has dared not until now, against his own sacred flock. Although he never actually strikes the people, his furious action and accompanying angry words signal a new and unbridgeable chasm between Moses and the people. By striking instead of speaking, Moses hints that he has run out of words with which to communicate with them. In addition, his actions indicate his sense that like the Egyptian taskmaster, the Israelites are now irredeemable.

Despite Jethro's best efforts to encourage Moses' positive interaction with his people, in the end he reverts to his isolation. Instead of acting as a *man, officer, and judge* from within their ranks, Moses stands apart from them and judges them unworthy. Finally, because Moses cannot feel himself as one with his people, he can no longer serve as their leader. Instead, he must entrust his flock to another shepherd in order for them to reach their ultimate destination.

For better and for worse, Moses' legacy is one of intense, unflinching vision. On the one hand, Moses receives an unparalleled view of the divine, as God accedes to his audacious request, "Oh, let me behold Your Presence!" (Exod. 33:18). Moreover, the Pentateuch closes with a testament to Moses, the greatest Israelite prophet, who enables the people to see things no one else has ever beheld: "[God's] great might and awesome power ... displayed before the eyes of all Israel" (Deut. 34:12).

Yet on the other hand, Moses' acute vision reinforces his inclination to act alone, a tendency that will keep him from realizing the final stage of his calling. As a result of Moses' actions, God will let him "see" the promised land, but tragically, as God informs him, "you shall not cross there" (Deut. 34:4).

Beyond the Subversive Sequel

In many ways, the story of Jethro echoes the narrative of Melchizedek in order to subvert it. Abraham was in great need of inward focus, detachment from external influence, and uncompromising individualism. Yet these same factors threaten to undermine the character, mission, and effectiveness of Moses. Taken together, these stories suggest that solitude can be a virtue or a danger. While it may help the iconoclast to forge his individual trail, solitude may obstruct the path of the leader who seeks to build a community-based covenant.

Significantly, both types of leaders require outside counsel in order to meet their challenges. In both cases, the priest is a gadfly, an agent of discomfort who forces the patriarch into difficult psychological territory on the road to actualizing his leadership potential.

The subversive sequel model does not do full justice to the story of the encounter between the foreign priest and the Israelite leader. In previous chapters of this volume, we have noted how a second biblical narrative often undermines and revises its predecessor. But this need not always be the case. At times two stories will engage in a dialectical relationship in which each remains a relevant model for the future, depending on time and circumstance. We may infer from the stories we have studied that sometimes leaders will, like Abraham, need help becoming truer to what they already are. Others, like Moses, will require help evolving into what they must become in order meet the needs of a people. At times, people need a contemplative leader, one who remains free of sullying influences and who will inspire others to better themselves. At other times, and perhaps more frequently, people seek pragmatic leadership, in which the leader successfully engages the outside world, making necessary compromises in order to succeed. The chronicles of Abraham and Moses, with their shifting emphases, suggest the need for leaders to remain alert to ever-changing realities, and to be open to receiving help in meeting the particular needs of time and place.

Kings, Priests, and a Kingdom of Priests

The role of the priest as outsider who provokes, inspires, and guides finds surprising resonance in one additional biblical context. Although Melchizedek is the only individual in the Bible described as both a **king** and a **priest**, these two terms appear together again in the description of an entire people, a "holy nation" that is also termed a **king**dom of **priests**.[41] At the scene of God's revelation to the entire Israelite nation at Sinai, we read:

> Now, then, if you will obey Me faithfully and keep My covenant, you shall be my treasured possession among all the peoples. Indeed, all the earth is Mine, but you shall be to Me a kingdom of priests and a holy nation ... (Exod. 19:5)

At Sinai, God instructs the nation of Israel to take on the role of kingly priests. But does one not need to be born, or at least elected, into the priesthood? How can every Israelite be elevated to this status? Ibn Ezra explains that a *cohen* may stem from any one of the tribes of Israel and is to be distinguished purely by an ability to serve God.[42] The 15th-century Italian exegete Seforno expands on this idea:

> Even though the entire human race is dear to me ... you will be treasured above them all ... and the difference between you, more or less, is that although all the world is indeed Mine and the righteous Gentiles of the world are undoubtedly dear to me, you will be to me a kingdom of priests. In this you will be treasured over them all ... in that you will understand and teach the entire human race to call in God's name and to serve Him as one ... (Seforno, Exod. 19:5–6, s.v. *vi-heyitem li segullah*, s.v. *ki li kol ha-aretz*, s.v. *ve-attem tiheyu li mamlekhet cohanim.*)

Both Ibn Ezra and Seforno agree that the title *cohen* is not a privilege bestowed on, or inherited by, a select few. Rather, it is a sacred task offered to an entire nation. If the Israelites will recognize God and accept God's legal system—which is based on such notions as *tzedakah u-mishpat*, justice and righteousness—they will become God's "treasure" and His priests. The conditional nature of the biblical verse supports this reading: "*If* you will obey Me faithfully and keep My covenant, you shall be my treasured possession among all the peoples ... you shall be to Me a *kingdom of priests* and a holy nation ..." The chosen status of the Israelites is entirely dependent on their ability to adhere to God's word. Moreover, as

---

41. In the entire Bible, the dual title of king and priest is affixed to only Melchizedek and to the nation of Israel.

42. See Ibn Ezra *Ha-katzar* on Exod. 19:5, s.v. *mamlekhet cohanim*. It is significant that Ibn Ezra cites Melchizedek and Jethro as his examples of non-Aronide priests. Perhaps he too noted the similarities between them and their unusual function in the lives of patriarchs.

Seforno suggests, their elevation to priesthood is conditioned on their commitment to purvey God's word to the entire human race.

The revelation narrative offers an intriguing twist to the earlier models of the story of the patriarch and his mentor. In the first two stories, the troubled hero in need of help was the Israelite patriarch and the moral guide was the foreigner. In the new scenario at the foot of Mt. Sinai, these positions are reversed. This time it is the foreigners, the nations of the world, who need instruction, as God calls upon the Israelite nation as a whole to guide them toward *tzedakah u-mishpat*. This reversal hints at a dynamic and mutual relationship between the guided and the guide, between insider and outsider, and—to employ an anachronistic term—between Jew and non-Jew. Depending on the situation, Jew and Gentile may trade positions; each will need the other in moments of historic or personal crisis in order to maintain moral and pragmatic clarity.

If we venture past the pages of the Bible and into the pages of Jewish history, this model of a "kingdom of priests" as perpetual outsider, mentor, and agent of change has great resonance. Jewish annals are filled with examples of Jews as revolutionary guides in the halls of power, in the laboratory, and in the library. This model presents the Jew as one whose outside status allows for greater perspective, creativity, and moral clarity.

But there is a troubling element to accolades such as "kingdom of priests" and "treasured nation." At times these terms have evoked negative emotional responses— ranging from embarrassment on the part of Jews to resentment on the part of others—as they seem to suggest some sort of inherent racial superiority granted by God. We have attempted to reframe these expressions by viewing them as parts in a series; seen this way, they no longer present a relationship of supremacy and hierarchy, but of interdependence and reciprocity. When we view the third priestly narrative in the context of the other two, the Israelites are, in a sense, returning the favor bestowed on them by the non-Israelite priestly mentors to Abraham and Moses.

Moreover, these stories, when seen as sequels to one another, intimate that it is not the messenger, but the message that is of utmost importance. Only those who prove capable of providing moral and pragmatic guidance—whether Israelite or non-Israelite—will rise to the position of priesthood. In fact, the shifting identity of the priests implies that no one group has sole claim to this distinction. At different times different people will be able to discern God's will and to instruct others.

This idea finds poignant expression in an ancient midrash attributed to Elijah the prophet. Reacting to the surprising choice of Deborah as God's judge, prophet, and military leader, the midrash has this to say:

I call upon heaven and earth to bear witness that whether Jew or Gentile, whether man or woman, whether manservant or maidservant, the divine spirit rests upon one in accordance with the deeds that one performs. (Eliyyahu Rabbah, 9)

In the end, the combined stories of biblical priests challenge both Israelites and non-Israelites to learn from the many possible sources of wisdom and morality in the world. In addition, they challenge readers to seek guidance where it is most needed. At times, assistance is needed in focusing inward and upward, from the mundane realities of the earth's hollow spaces back toward the lofty ideals that dwell among the stars. Although this reorientation may come at the cost of isolation and loneliness, it is often necessary for inspiration and for clarity of purpose. At other times, help is needed in venturing out of solitude and engaging with the world. While such outward engagement may involve compromise, it also brings ideals down to earth, where they may form the basis of just and righteous communities.

Chapter 4

The Three Faces of Woman:
The Garden of Eden in Search of Sequels

He for God only; she for God in him.

—John Milton, *Paradise Lost*

The subversive sequel model is particularly useful in a study of biblical woman. Because there are so many disturbing aspects to woman's earliest portrayal, there is a compelling call for redress in the form of later narrative revisions of her story. In the Garden of Eden, it is the woman who succumbs to the serpent's seductions and who then leads man to disobey God. As a result of her actions, her status goes into steady decline as God chastises man for "listening to the voice of his wife," and declares that woman will now yearn for her husband who will "rule over" her. Throughout the generations, many have been satisfied with this depiction of woman. It was consistent with sociological realities, and at times it served as a convenient and authoritative rebuttal to any attempts to change woman's standing.

Instead of viewing the Garden of Eden story as isolated and definitive, we will identify it as the foundation for numerous sequels. Later stories that center on the struggles and triumphs of the Bible's women will refer back to it, sometimes reinforcing and sometimes overturning its assumptions and conclusions. Because of the unusually complex and basic nature of the Bible's first woman, we devote an entire chapter to her story; its subversive sequels will follow in subsequent chapters.

In our close examination of the Garden of Eden narrative, we will find that although we are accustomed to referring to primordial man and woman simply as "Adam and Eve," their actual portraits are far more sophisticated. Adam is split into two distinct characters,[1] while Eve is only one third of a tripartite creature we call woman. The various components of both man and woman represent different facets of their complex, and at times contradictory natures.

The First Face of Woman: Ha-adam—Majesty and Equality

The first incarnation of woman is as part of an androgynous human creature, referred to in Genesis 1 as *Ha-adam:*

> And God said, "Let us make a human in our image, after our likeness. They shall rule the fish of the sea, the cattle, the whole earth, and all the creeping things that creep on earth. And God created the human in His image, in the image of God He created him; male and female he created them. God blessed them and God said to them, "Be fruitful and increase, fill the earth and master it; and rule the fish of the sea, the birds of the sky, and all the living things that creep on earth.[2] (Gen. 1: 26–28)

Created in God's image, human beings, both male and female, resemble Him in numerous ways. Just as God is the creator of worlds, so are human beings called upon to create, to "be fruitful and increase and fill the earth."[3] And just as God is immortal, so do the human beings in this chapter achieve a measure of immortality. In addition to their ability to perpetuate themselves through the act of procreation, there is no mention of the specter of death. Moreover, just as God is the master of the physical world, so are human beings called upon to conquer and control—and to consume at will. Comprised equally of male and

---

1. For a full typological approach to the man of Genesis 1 as opposed to the man of Genesis 2, see Rabbi Joseph Soloveitchik's masterful essay, "The Lonely Man of Faith." Soloveitchik argues for a non-linear reading of the chapters, claiming that each presents an essential facet of the complex human being. For a similar approach, see Breuer, *Pirkei Beresheit,* 82–104.

   The character of primordial woman, which we will break down into three distinct parts, has not been systematically addressed in a similar way. Shira Wolosky has argued that Soloveitchik's typology applies equally to man and woman, with woman possessing the traditionally "masculine" human characteristics of Genesis 1 as well as the more "feminine" attributes of chapter 2. See Wolosky, "The Lonely Woman of Faith," 3–18.

2. Author's translation.

3. Like human beings, fish and fowl are blessed with fecundity (Gen. 1:22); but only humanity receives these blessings in the context of being godlike.

female components[4]—male and female He created *them*" (Gen. 1:27)—the human creature of Genesis 1 not only emulates God; it holds the sublime status as God's conversational partner as well. God directly commands and blesses both male and female of the species, addressing them equally in the plural: "God blessed *them* and God said to *them*, 'Be fruitful and increase …'" (1:28), indicating that they are indistinct in both their capabilities and opportunities. Indeed, from the fact that God delivers His word to woman and man alike, we can infer that neither sex has an advantage in the ability to communicate with the divine. In her original manifestation as *Ha-adam*, woman is fully half of the human creature who is master of the physical world, formed in God's image, and privy to His word.

The Second Face of Woman: Ishah—Hierarchy and Devotion

The next chapter of Genesis, however, provides another version of humanity's creation.[5] The same characters, God, man, and woman are present, but the story is told in a dramatically different way.[5] For one thing, the makeup of the character named *"Ha-adam"* has changed. Unlike the androgynous creature of Genesis 1, *Ha-adam is* exclusively male for most of the next chapter. The pronouns make the point. In Genesis 1, God spoke of humanity in the plural. "Male and female he created *them*, He blessed *them*, and said to *them*, behold I have given *you* [pl.] …" In this new account of creation, however, the male alone, still called *Ha-adam*, is formed from dust (2:7), as God "blew into *his* nostrils the breath of life" (2:7). And man alone is responsible for the garden: "The LORD God took

---

4. This is the plain sense of the verse, which says, "God created *Ha-adam* in His image, in the image of God He created him [*oto*]; male and female He created them [*otam*]" (Gen. 1:27). The use of the masculine singular (*oto*) followed by multiple references to humanity in the plural (*otam*) is most plainly understood if the word *Ha-adam* refers to humanity as a whole, with the pronoun *oto* being gender neutral, not masculine. Read this way, the verse states that God created humanity—which is comprised of both male and female parts—simultaneously.

5. Medieval commentators have attempted to resolve the contradictions by pointing to the Bible's technique of *klal u-frat*, a general outline followed by its specific details. Rashi (Gen. 2:8, s.v. *mi-kedem*) cites these two chapters as an example of one of the hermeneutical principles of Rabbi Eliezer, son of R. Yossi Ha-gelili, in which a general statement (i.e. Genesis 1) is followed by a detailing of that statement (Genesis 2). Similarly, Mieke Bal views Genesis 2 as a detailing and completion of the outline provided in Genesis 1. See Bal's *Lethal Love*, 118–19. In this view, the initial equality of Genesis 1 remains as a basis for understanding the developments of Genesis 2. However, because of its persistent male-specific language and focus, I view Genesis 2 as a separate, and at times, contradictory account of the creation story in which woman is no longer presented as equal to man but as his subordinate.

Ha-adam and placed *him* in the garden to till it and tend it" (2:15). God entrusts the male alone with direct receipt of His instruction, commanding him to refrain from eating of the tree of knowledge of good and evil (2:16–17).[6] Although the same word, *"Ha-adam"* is used in Genesis 1 to connote both male and female, the plain sense of Genesis 2 and most of Genesis 3[7] is that it refers to the male only. This becomes especially clear when God puts *Ha-adam* to sleep in order to construct woman (2:21–22). It is further reinforced when God rebukes *Ha-adam*, clearly the man only, for listening to *his wife* and for eating from the tree which God had commanded him: "*You* [masc., sing.] shall not eat of it" (3:17). For a large portion of this second creation story, woman, who was formerly an essential, equal part of humanity, is entirely absent. She has no part in tending to the garden, and she is excluded from God's conversation.[8]

When woman finally makes her way into the narrative, she bears little resemblance to the woman of Genesis 1.

> The Lord God said, "It is not good for man to be alone; I will make a helper corresponding to him."[9] And the Lord God formed out of the earth all the wild beasts and all the birds of the sky, and brought them to the man to see what he would call them; and whatever the man called each living creature, that would be its name. And the man gave names to all the cattle and all the birds of the sky and to all the wild beasts; but for Adam there could be found no helper corresponding to him.
>
> So the Lord God cast a deep sleep upon the man and while he slept, He took one of his ribs and closed up the flesh at the spot. And the Lord God fashioned the rib that He had taken from the man into a woman, and He brought her to the man. Then the man said, "This one at last is bone of my bones and flesh of my flesh. This one shall be called Woman

---

6. Phyllis Trible disagrees with the notion that in Genesis 2 *"Ha-adam"* refers to the male only. She claims that the text assumes humanity's androgyny throughout Genesis 2, up until the creation of woman from man. Trible, "Depatriarchlizing," 224.

7. Upon their expulsion from the Garden, man and woman are reunited as *Ha-adam* (Gen. 3:22–24). This is the plain reading of the text in its context, despite the fact that previously, with only one exception (1:28), man and woman as *Ha-adam* are referred to in the plural, while in these verses *Ha-adam* is singular.

8. Only later, in Gen. 3:16, will God directly address woman, and then only in context of delivering judgment and punishment for her disobedience.

9. Fox translates *ezer kenegdo* this way, which I find preferable to NJPS's "fitting helper." The most literal meaning of the term would be closer to the unwieldy "helper opposite him."

for from man she was taken." Hence a man leaves his father and mother
and clings to his wife, so that they become one flesh. (Gen. 2: 18–24)

Man is lonely; the animals are no solution. There exists no "helper corresponding to him," no creature who is similar enough to be his complement. And so woman
is created. But unlike the fully enabled *Ha-adam*, woman depicted in this chapter is
derivative.[10] She exists in relation to man: *his* loneliness leads to her creation; she is
bone of *his* bones and flesh of *his* flesh (Gen. 2:24), a "helper corresponding to *him*" (v.
18). Even the seemingly idyllic description of the future union of males and females as
becoming "one flesh" is phrased from the point of view of the male, who will "leave *his*
father and *his* mother and cling to *his* wife" (v. 24). Woman's perspective on this meeting is entirely absent. Is she as elated as man? Does she consider him to be *her* perfect
complement, her *ezer kenegdah*? Woman's silence in this passage only intensifies these
questions and affirms the male-centered lens of Genesis 2.

In addition to being the focal point of the narrative, man in this account is in
some ways, like the *Ha-adam* figure of Genesis 1, godlike.[11] In Genesis 2, man's godlike
status is evident in his naming the animals (2:19), an act that in Genesis 1 represented
a type of creative power that was reserved for God alone. As we have seen, naming can
be an act of intimacy; when one names another, one recognizes and asserts the other's
individual identity. But naming can also signify dominion and possession, as demonstrated by God's calling the names of things as part of His act of creating them. (1:5,8,10).
In Genesis 2, man assumes the divine role of designating the names of the animals,
thereby completing their creation (2:19). But in this second version of the creation story,
man does not rule his surroundings together with woman. This time his control extends to her, as he names not only the animals, but his wife as well (v. 23).[12]

---

10. Despite the many efforts on the parts of the ancients and moderns to find greater mutuality between
    man and woman in Genesis 2, this is the plain sense of the text. See note 5.
11. In fact, man continues to bear the name *Ha-adam* throughout most of this chapter, while woman
    does not.
12. We might find further evidence of man's godlike status in relation to woman by comparing the two
    descriptions of humanity's creation. In Genesis 1, God bestows His likeness, *tzelem,* upon *Ha-adam.* In
    Genesis 2, although God is still the chief artisan of humanity, it is Adam who lends his likeness to his
    fellow human being, the woman, with the phonetically similar *tzela,* rib. In a further expression of his
    sovereign status in relation to his surroundings, man stands at the center of creation, while all other
    creatures, both animal and human, are brought to him for his pleasure. First, God **"brought, b-v-'"**
    the animals to man (2:19). Then strikingly, God **"brought, b-v-'"** woman to him as well (2:22).

Although hierarchy and control have crept into the second account of humanity's creation, there is another component to the perspective of Genesis 2. Whereas in Genesis 1, human beings, both male and female, were to "fill, master, and rule" the earth, in this rendering of events, man is placed in the Garden of Eden "to till it and to tend to it" (2:15).[13] Man's humbler, more relational stance toward his physical surroundings extends to woman as well as the earth. Although to some degree he will control her, his need for her mitigates his position of power. As we have seen, this man, unlike the uniformly masterful creature of Genesis 1, is lonely without his mate (2:18).[14] The full import of man's naming his wife must be seen in this context. In naming her, he does not only exercise control over her. This act suggests that he also recognizes her deep essence, as the only one of God's creatures appropriate to be his life-partner.

Upon meeting the woman who is so much like him, Adam bursts into spontaneous, rapturous song, calling her "bone of my bones and flesh of my flesh" (Gen. 2:23). The text, adopting a rare editorial voice, then lends its own approval to man's optimistic grasp of the male-female relationship with the words: "Hence a man leaves his father and mother and clings to his wife, so that they become one flesh" (v. 24).

Ramban elaborates on the unique emotional bond that informs the union of man and woman:

> In my opinion, beasts do not cling to their females; any male will come upon any female and then move on ... The text relates that because the female of the human species is bone of his bone and flesh of his flesh, he clings to her as if she were his own flesh, as he desires to be with her constantly. Just as the first man was like this, so was it embedded in the nature of his descendants for males to cling to their females, leaving their fathers and mothers and viewing their wives as if they were of the same flesh. (Ramban, 2:24, s.v. *ve-hayu le-vasar ehad*)

In other words, in addition to introducing hierarchy into the male-female equation, this version of the creation story conveys the hope for profound emotional intimacy between the sexes as well, employing the metaphor of total physical synthesis. Genesis 1 dwelled on the pragmatic rendering of their sexual union, with

---

13. See Soloveitchik, "Lonely Man," 24.

14. Ibid., 22, 26, 27. Soloveitchik understands God's statement, "It is not good for man to be alone" (Gen. 2:18), to refer to man's state of existential loneliness.

its command to "be fruitful and increase." Genesis 2 now introduces the emotional state that informs their partnership with its expectation that they would "be as one flesh." The relational element between man and woman is further highlighted by woman's new name, *"Ishah,"* an integral, highly valued portion of man, *Ish.*

The creation account in Genesis 2 has two components, hierarchy and emotional closeness. It seems from man's song of exultation at woman's birth that despite the inequality between them, he is content with both aspects of their relationship. It remains to be seen whether woman, who has not yet spoken, is as satisfied as man with this uneven status quo.

Ishah—*Woman in Search of Self*

Thus far we have seen that in Genesis 1, human beings are full and equal partners in their godlike capacity to create and subdue. They are equal too in their godliness, as both are capable of receiving God's direct word. In Genesis 2, the equality between man and woman is lost, but an emotional component is gained. Although man now eclipses woman in significant ways, he also views her as a unique and irreplaceable gift, and as one who gives him a sense of completion as a human being.

By presenting its story in non-linear installments, the biblical text has so far offered two perspectives on woman, each punctuated with a different name.[15] First there is woman as one half of the sublime *Ha-adam.* Together with man, she is humanity itself—indeed the name *Ha-adam* means "humanity"—in all its unbounded potential. In her second manifestation she is *Ishah,* man's unequal, yet greatly appreciated emotional complement.

As we will soon see, there is yet another dimension to the Bible's first woman. All three of her components will provide a frame of reference in which

---

15. Alter sees the paradoxical nature of Genesis 1 and 2 in a similar way. He compares the two accounts to "a post-Cubist painting which gives us ... a profile and a perspective of the same face ... The Hebrew writer takes advantage of the composite nature of his art to give us a tension of views that will govern most of the biblical stories—first, woman as man's equal sharer in dominion, standing exactly in the same relation to God as he; then, woman as man's subservient helpmate, whose weakness and blandishments will bring such woe into the world. Alter, *The Art of Biblical Narrative,* 146. Methodologically, Alter's reading resembles that of Soloveitchik and Breuer. In addition, he closely approximates our understanding of the first two presentations of woman. We differ mainly in our analysis of the woman of Genesis 2. Alter sees her only as weak, while we have noted another component, her emotional value to her husband.

to understand the female characters of the Bible's later stories. Thus it is well worth studying her facets more closely. We return to the second manifestation of woman, the *Ishah* of Genesis 2,[16] who has just been created from man's rib. Man has expressed his delight at her arrival, and as we have noted, she has remained silent. When this woman finally speaks, it is to the wily serpent. By paying close attention to the nuances of their dialogue, we will find indications that her earlier silence was fraught with dissatisfaction and restlessness.

> The two of them were **naked** [*'-r-m*] the man and his wife, yet they felt no shame. Now the serpent was the **shrewdest** [*'-r-m*] of all the wild beasts the Lord God had made. He said to the woman, "Did God really say: You shall not eat of any tree of the garden?" The woman replied to the serpent, "We may eat of the fruit of the other trees of the garden. It is only about the fruit of the tree in the middle of the garden that God said: 'You shall not eat of it or touch it, lest you die.'" And the serpent said to the woman, "You are not going to die, but God knows that as soon as you eat of it your eyes will be opened and you will be like God, who knows good and bad."
>
> When the woman saw that the tree was good for eating and a delight to the eyes, and that the tree was desirable as a source of wisdom, she took of its fruit and ate. She also gave some to her husband, and he ate. Then the eyes of both of them were opened and they perceived that they were naked; and they sewed together fig leaves and made themselves loincloths. (Gen. 2:25–3:7)

We can adduce several things about woman's frame of mind even before she opens her mouth. For one thing, in the introduction to her dialogue with the serpent, the text twice employs the flexible adjective *'-r-m*, which can mean either naked or shrewd.[17] Man and woman are *arummim*, naked; the serpent is *arum*, shrewd. Woman is faced with a choice between them. She could continue to live in a state of "nakedness" with her husband, that is in a naïve and pure,

---

16. The *Ishah* is also present throughout most of Genesis 3. For the sake of simplicity, I will refer to *Ha-adam* as the woman of Genesis 1 and the *Ishah* as the woman of Genesis 2.

17. Or, in the translation of Everett Fox, the human beings are "nude" and the serpent is "shrewd." Through this rhyme, Fox preserves the text's phonetic play. Fox, *The Five Books of Moses*, 21.

though unequal partnership. Alternatively, she could opt for the shrewdness of the serpent, with its promise to elevate her to godlike knowledge. Apparently in search of change, woman chooses the serpent.

We may detect a second clue as to woman's unrest in the very fact that the serpent aims his wiles at her, and not at the man.[18] The Talmud offers an intriguing direction for understanding the woman-serpent dialogue, viewing the serpent as a symbol of inner human urges.[19] Thus it is not the serpent who seeks out woman, but the reverse. The passage can be read as a kind of interior monologue in which the woman summons, and then wrestles with the "serpent" within. Through this interior monologue disguised as dialogue we are given access to the psychology of the *Ishah.* This woman, fashioned by God's own hand and jubilantly received by her male counterpart, is burdened by an inner void that clamors to be filled by the forbidden.

But what is the nature of the longing that leaves her susceptible to temptation? So far we have seen two parts of woman. She is the godlike, immortal creator of Genesis 1, full partner to man and fully equal before God. She is also the subordinate, derivative, and cherished helper of Genesis 2, who receives no direct communication from God. Perhaps dissatisfied with her circumscribed role, woman yearns for the kind of equality and immortal godliness described in Genesis 1.

Literary clues as to the source of her of her longing are discernable between the lines of dialogue. First, there is the name of the tree in question. Although God calls it "the tree of knowledge of good and evil" (Gen. 2:17), woman never does. Instead, in replying to the serpent's overtures, she calls it "the tree *in the middle of the garden*" (3:3). There is, in fact, only one tree that has been described as standing "in the middle of the garden," and it is not the tree of knowledge, but rather the tree of *life:*

> And from the ground the Lord God caused to grow every tree that was pleasing to the sight and good for food, with the *tree of life in the middle of the garden,* and the tree of knowledge of good and bad. (Gen. 2:9)

---

18. In viewing woman's actions as proof of her moral inferiority, Bible critics and traditionalists are remarkably in step. For example, Trible cites Paul Ricoeur, who claims that woman "represents the point of moral weakness." Trible, Depatriarchalizing, 226. Similarly, the 13th century Yemenite Midrash Ha-Gadol writes: "The serpent made the following calculation: 'If I go and speak to the man I know he will not listen to me ...' What did he do? He said, 'I will go and talk to the woman, who I know will listen to me, since women are more flexible and are easier to entice.'"

19. *Baba Batra* 16a. The Talmud states that the serpent is the evil inclination.

Although she physically reaches for one tree, woman's subconscious grasps for another. The true object of her desires is apparently the tree that will grant her eternal life, an approximation of the godlike and godly status she seeks.

Support for this notion may be found in another slip of her tongue, one that suggests her psychological displacement of one object onto another. Although God has forbidden eating from the "*tree* of the garden" (Gen. 2:16,17), she tells the serpent they are forbidden to eat of the "*fruit* of the tree, *mi-peri ha-etz*" (3:3). Her addition of the word "*peri*" evokes the image of childbearing, as in God's instruction in Genesis 1 to "be **fruitful** and increase, *peru u-revu*." Perhaps with her subtle allusion to life-giving potential—the human version of godlike immortality—woman conveys her deepest expectations of the forbidden tree that lies so enticingly "in the middle of the garden."

A further clue lies in the serpent's surprisingly categorical declaration: "You will not die" (Gen. 3:4). With his words, the serpent bluntly negates God's earlier explicit statement, "On the day that you eat from the tree, *you will surely die*" (2:17). If the serpent is really an externalization of the woman's inner thoughts and desires, eternal life emerges again as her most keenly felt wish.

In fact, says the serpent, not only will the tree protect the woman from death, it will also make her as she wishes to be, "like God" (Gen. 3:5). But what was she to do with the prohibition against eating from the tree? The serpent provides the answer by revealing, and thereby discrediting, God's rationale. God, he explains, forbade the fruit out of fear for His exclusive hold on power: "But God knows that as soon as you eat of it your eyes will be opened and you will be like God who knows good and bad" (3:5). The serpent, as inner voice of woman, projects onto God a competitive motivation. Reading back into the mind of woman that manufactured such a projection, we again find signs of her frustration with her secondary status, and perhaps a hint of competitive feelings toward God, the source of all power. It is in fact woman, and not God, who yearns for mastery and control, but her projection masks her vulnerability. Her interior "serpent" successfully disparages God, while at the same time building her feelings of rivalry and resentment against Him. Psychologically, the *Ishah* is now ready to conclude that God has neither the right nor the authority to keep her from the forbidden tree.

Although she yearns for godlike mastery and immortality, the woman grasps not for the tree of life, but for the tree of knowledge of good and bad. Perhaps she sets her sights on this tree because of its very forbiddenness. Perhaps its dimensions grow as she ascribes to it the power to cure all her ills. Or perhaps she assumes that before she can reach the ultimate goal of the tree of life, she must first be privy to the godlike knowledge that this other tree would provide.[20] In any case, the forbidden tree was "good," a "delight," and "desirable" in her eyes. Succumbing to its lure, "she took of its fruit and ate" (Gen. 3:6).

Woman is the clear catalyst for transgression; man follows her lead. Here the distinction between them is crucial and reflects the yearning described above. While both man and woman harbored a piece of the divine, and while both communicated with God in Genesis 1, in Genesis 2, only man is godly. The male is still a creator, "calling" creatures into being (2:20,23) and receiving God's word. Woman, to the contrary, has no creative role in this version of the story, nor does she receive God's instruction. This difference might explain man's initial ability to avoid temptation. From his privileged position, he does not share woman's desperation to be more "like God." In her exclusion, woman covets, and then partakes of the forbidden fruit. Ironically by doing so, instead of becoming closer to God, she only increases her distance from Him. Because her husband follows her lead, both are banished from God's garden and are blocked from approaching the true object of woman's desire, the tree of life (3:24).

The Third Face of Woman: Havvah—Mother of All the Living

The mutinous act of eating from the forbidden tree brings immediate and harsh consequences to the serpent, man, and woman. In our continued attempts to deepen our understanding of woman, we will dwell primarily on the repercussions that affect her. To do so, we temporarily skip over God's reproaches to the serpent and to man and begin with His words to woman. For a fuller picture of woman's position in the aftermath of her disobedience, we note the verse in which Adam renames his wife:[21]

> And to the woman he said, "I will make most severe your pangs in childbearing; in pain shall you bear children. Yet your urge shall be for your husband, and he shall rule over you." (Gen. 3:16)
> The man called his wife's name *Havvah*, because she was the mother of all the living.[22] (Gen. 3:20)

---

20. See Gen. 3:22
21. In the next section we will return to God's comments to the serpent and man.
22. Author's translation.

The most overt and devastating results of woman's actions are that she now faces pain in childbirth and subservience to her husband. Because man heeded her in disobedience, he will heed her no longer (Gen. 3:17). Man's act of renaming woman belongs in this context. To begin with, the very act of naming, as we have seen, can signify dominion, and Adam now confirms his authority over his wife. But in addition, the name man chooses for her, *Havvah,* also reflects a deterioration in woman's status.

Havvah, like the *Ha-adam* figure of Genesis 1, will be capable of virtually limitless procreation. But there are crucial differences between the two portrayals. In Genesis 1, woman as life-giver functioned in a context of equality with man and with mastery over her environment. Her name, *Ha-adam,* reflected the gamut of her possibilities as a person, of which her role as procreator was one, albeit essential, part. In contrast, *Havvah's* life-giving abilities are now devoid of other contexts. As a result of her actions, she is now distanced from God and inferior to man. Her new name reflects her potential for motherhood only. As we will see in the sequels to this story, giving birth is a most sublime calling. But we will also see that when the other components of woman are absent or eroded, this role cannot compensate for her losses.

Havvah: *Grandeur and Immortality*

After noting the negative turn woman has taken, we must recognize that in some ways, she has actually drawn closer to her goal of godlike immortality. In order to do so, we return to God's pronouncements following humanity's rebellion. This time we quote the text in full, including God's comments to the serpent, man, and woman. We include again, this time in full context, Adam's renaming of his wife.

> Then the Lord God said to the serpent,
> "Because you did this,
> Out of all the cattle
> And all the wild beasts
> You are *cursed:*
> On your belly shall you crawl
> And dirt shall you *eat*
> *All the days of your life.*
> I will put enmity
> Between you and the woman,
> And between your offspring and hers;
> They shall strike at your head,

And you shall strike at their heel."
And to the woman he said,

> "I will make most severe
> Your pangs in childbearing;
> In pain shall you bear children.
> And your urge shall be for your husband,
> And he shall rule over you."

To Adam he said, "Because you heeded the voice of your wife and *ate* of the
tree about which I commanded you, 'You shall not *eat* of it,'

> *Cursed* be the ground because of you;
> By toil shall you *eat* of it
> *All the days of your life:*
> Thorns and thistles shall it sprout for you.
> But your food shall be the grasses of the field;
> By the sweat of your brow
> Shall you *eat* bread,
> Until you return to the ground—
> For from it you were taken.
> For dust you are,
> And to dust you shall return."

The man called his wife's name *Havvah,* because she was the mother of all
the living.[23] (Gen. 3:14–20)

In very nuanced ways, the text hints that although woman instigated the
crime of eating, God exhibits greater sympathy for her than for her husband or
for the serpent.[24] To begin with, God condemns both man and serpent for their
act of **eating**, *'-kh-l* (Gen. 3:14,17,18). As a fitting consequence, both will now **eat**,
'-kh-l, with pain and difficulty (3:14,19). In addition, God **curses**, *'-r-r,* both. The
serpent itself is **cursed** while the earth is **cursed** for man (3:14,17). But, in pun-
ishing woman, God omits all mention of the crime of eating and of the ultimate

---

23. Author's translation.

24. Although we have chosen to view the serpent as an externalization of woman's thoughts (above,
Talmud), literally they remain separate; its curse is not the woman's curse. Alternatively, the
16th-century Italian exegete Seforno, who views the serpent metaphorically (see his comments
on Gen. 3:14–15), reads the curses to the serpent as metaphoric curses to humanity.

negative consequence of "accursedness."[25] Moreover, while both serpent and man will carry their curses "all the days of your life, *kol yemei hayyekha*" (3:14,17), there is no such open-ended time frame applied to woman. In addition, while man will now become more aware of his imminent *mortality*—"for dust you are and to dust you shall return," (3:19)—given her childbearing abilities, woman will achieve a measure of the *immortality* she has so desperately sought.

God's sympathy for woman is later echoed by Adam. As we have seen, his act of naming suggests his dominion over her, and the name he gives her limits and defines her. Yet the name *"Havvah,* mother of all the living," also bestows incomparable grandeur upon woman. With this name, Adam recognizes and affirms the eternal life she has been seeking and has now achieved.

Why has woman, arguably the primary culprit in humanity's disobedience, merited this deferential treatment by both God and man? Perhaps their responses point to an attempted corrective repair of her marginalization. For reasons that are never explained, an initial portrait of man and woman as equals with each other and before God gave way to a story of hierarchy and exclusion. We have argued that woman's diminished status led her to disobedience. Because she was no longer creative, equal, or godlike, she sought another way to become "like God." She reached for an enchanted, forbidden tree, with thoughts of partaking of another tree, the tree of life. In a sense, both God and man now affirm the godlike capacity woman has so ardently pursued. God's address to woman focuses on her ability to bear children, albeit in pain. And Adam confers upon her the life-giving name *Havvah.* Despite her descent, woman achieves the exalted, godlike capacity to create human beings.

Hints of Subversive Sequels

In addition to the corrective repair implied by the words of God and man, the text hints at more reversals to come. One such hint may be detected within God's severe pronouncement to woman, "To your husband is your desire and he shall rule over you." It seems that these words are a *prescription* for future male-female relations. But there are those who argue that these words are instead a *description* of sociological realities that are to play out through much of human history.[26] Together

---

25. Trible, *Rhetoric,* 126.
26. Trible, "Departiarchlizing," 227.

with this prediction of inequality comes an implied call for change. In the words of Phyllis Trible:

> We misread if we assume that these judgments are mandates. They describe; they do not prescribe. They protest; they do not condone. Of special concern are the words telling the woman that her husband shall rule over her. This statement is not a license for male supremacy, but rather it is a condemnation of that very pattern. Subjugation and supremacy are perversions of creation ... Through disobedience the woman has become slave. Her initiative and her freedom vanish. The man is corrupted also, for he has become master, ruling over the one who is his God-given equal.[27]

Trible argues that hierarchy is not a result, but a breakdown, of God's plan for humanity. After all, God initially created human beings—the dual *Ha-adam*—in a state of harmonious equality. Thus the oppressive hierarchy of Genesis 3 must be viewed as a deviation from God's wishes. In this light, God's words may be seen as an implicit call for reversal. To be sure, God's harsh words to woman, "He shall rule over you," represent a further distancing from the majestic and autonomous portrait of woman recorded in Genesis 1. Yet this nadir, when read as description rather than prescription, functions as a call to man, woman, and even to God Himself to begin the long historical struggle for social and spiritual restoration.

We might find support for Trible's distinction between the descriptive and the prescriptive in a comparison of God's words to woman with His decree to man, "By the sweat of your brow shall you eat bread" (Gen. 3:19). It would be unreasonable to suppose that God is condemning man exclusively to manual labor for all time. In fact, the Bible itself almost immediately records subversive sequels to this pronouncement by presenting its male heroes, beginning with Abel and continuing with most of the patriarchs, as shepherds, not farmers.[28] These developments leave us with the strong impression that if man can overcome God's curses, finding other ways to eat than by the sweat of his brow, surely

---

27. Ibid.

28. See Shapiro, *Studies in the Jewish Thought*, 367. Shapiro asserts that the Bible's trend away from manual labor foreshadows the Messianic era. In private conversations with Shmuel Klitsner in the early 1970s, Shapiro extended this logic to the advancement of women's equality. He saw the women's movement as a herald of messianic times—an overturning of the divine pronouncements in the Garden and a return to the ideal human relationships of God's initial creation.

woman must have alternatives to giving birth in pain and to serving her husband. Logic dictates that a reversal is possible and is desirable for both man and woman. In both cases, God's pronouncements at Eden describe human experiences at their worst, while at the same time implying a call for improvement and repair.[29]

At the story's end, the text offers another hint of humanity's potential to correct the damage done in the Garden:

> So the Lord God banished *Ha-adam*[30] from the Garden of Eden, to till the soil from which he was taken. He drove *Ha-adam* out, and stationed east of the Garden of Eden the cherubim[31] and the fiery ever-turning sword, to guard the way to the tree of life. (Gen. 3: 23–24)

On the one hand, humanity no longer has access to the godlike immortality that the tree of life would provide. Yet, on the other hand, the path that has been paved, though obstructed, still exists. Moreover, God's sword, with its constantly alternating motions, both bars the way to the tree and points in its direction. Perhaps, like the sword, man and woman can be ever-turning, or more literally "self-overturning,"[32] as they strive to rewrite woman's story of exclusion and hierarchy back into one of equality, mutuality, and godliness.

---

29. For a similar sentiment, see Rashi on 3:16 s.v. *"ve-kotz ve-dardar tatzmiah lakh."* While a plain reading might have suggested that, no matter what his efforts, man would always produce inedible plants, Rashi insists that the text offers a challenge to man and a call to overcome this situation. Left to its own natural devices, the earth will produce thorns and thistles, but they may be eaten through the human act of *tikkun*.

  Even without this type of logic, if we are to assume that at least some of God's declaration is eternally binding, there is a distinction to be made between man and woman. As we have seen, God appends the words, "all the days of your life" to man's consequences, but not to the woman's. Thus it appears that even if some of the results of the disobedience are permanent mandates, those meted out to woman are not.

30. While NJPS translates *Ha-adam* as "man," I prefer to leave the original Hebrew in place, which sends us back to Genesis 1, where the term *Ha-adam* encompasses both man and woman.

31. In fact, ancient Jews have viewed the cherubim as symbols of male-female equality. The Talmud (Yomah 54a) describes the cherubim as two angelic figures—one male and the other female—lovingly intertwined with one another. Like the first cherubim that guard the entrance to Eden, the later cherubim guard the entrance to the holy Tabernacle. Seen this way, the cherubim symbolize male-female equality as a prerequisite to entering, or reentering, God's holy places. I am grateful to Daniel Schwartz for directing me to this source.

32. For the larger meaning and implications of the root *h-f-kh*, see chapter 1 of this volume, pp. 25–26. This root is used in the book of Jonah to refer to humanity's overturning of itself in favor of a better path.

Chapter 5

Forbidden Fruit and the Quest for Motherhood: Havvah *and* Sarah

A locked garden is my sister bride, a hidden well, a sealed spring.
—Song of Songs

Biblical woman is initially a creative, godlike creature addressed by God and equal to man. But her story is presented a second time, in which she is derivative of man and is marginalized from both man and God. Her desire for greater equality and godlike immortality leads her to a longed-for elixir, the tree of life, which ironically distances her even more from her hopes. Her third manifestation, as "mother of all the living" grants her a measure of the divine creative power she has craved. But it comes devoid of the exalted, godly context of the *"peru u-revu"* blessing given the equal human partners of Genesis 1. In eating from the forbidden tree, woman had sought to bridge gaps between herself and God and between herself and man. But now, despite her miraculous life-giving abilities, she is further removed from God and further subordinated to man.

Havvah's Subversive Sequel: **She Will Rule Over Him**

In the aftermath of God's harsh pronouncements and humanity's banishment from the Garden, *Havvah* attempts to combat her new reality. But her chosen method of battle will lead to counter-productive results:

> Now the man knew his wife *Havvah,* and she conceived and bore Cain, saying, "I have gained [*kaniti*] a man [*ish*] with the Lord."[1] (Gen. 4:1)

---

1. Author's translation.

Havvah's short statement brims with ambiguity, as the words *kaniti* and *ish* both have dual meanings.[2] The verb *kaniti* can mean either "I have created" or "I have acquired." *"Ish"* might refer to the male child *Havvah* has just borne;[3] it could also refer back to her husband, the *Ish* of the Garden of Eden. Thus one possible reading of her statement is: I have *created a son* with the LORD. Another is: "I have *acquired a man*—that is Adam—with the LORD.[4]

We have much to gain by embracing both readings, rather than choosing between them. Taken together, they offer insight into *Havvah's* complex frame of mind at the moment in which she bears her first child. On the surface, she is triumphant and grateful. With God's help she has finally fulfilled her dream to be godlike, like the sublime *Ha-adam* figure of Genesis 1. With her statement, *Havvah* celebrates this milestone of creative majesty in her life.

Yet on another plane, *Havvah's* words undermine the hoped-for relationship between *Ish* and *Ishah* that was expressed in Genesis 2: "Hence a man, *ish*, leaves his father and mother and clings to his wife, *ishto*, so that they become one flesh" (2:24). We recall that as a result of their rebellion, man and woman were distanced from this dream, as *ishah* became subservient to *ish*: "*El ishekh teshukatekh*, to your *man* is your desire and he will rule over you" (3:16). Now, at the moment of her greatest power, *Havvah* attempts a subversive sequel to God's pronouncement. She flaunts her ability to reverse man's dominion over her—that is to possess *him*—through her godlike ability to create human beings.

Havvah's intimation of acquisition and ownership does nothing to repair the wounded male-female relationship left by God's declarations in Eden. Instead, with her statement about possessing man, *Havvah* attempts to perpetuate hierarchy, but in the opposite direction. Her attempt at reversal is headed for failure. As long as

---

2. NJPS translates *kaniti* as "I have gained," which artfully straddles the two meanings of the word. The Hebrew root *k-n-h* generally means "to create" when applied to God. See Gen. 14:19, 22; Deut. 32:6.

3. If *ish* refers to the child, this would be anomalous. In the Bible, women give birth to "sons" or "daughters," not to "men." The unusual use of this word provides motive to seek a second interpretation of the word *ish*.

4. See Pardes, *Countertraditions*, 47–48. Pardes sees woman's proclamation as a rejoinder to man's song in Gen. 2:23. In Adam's naming speech, he claims to have had a part in creating woman; she now responds with a counterclaim, that she has helped to create him. A similar connection is drawn in a comment to Gen. 2:23, attributed (perhaps mistakenly) to the 12th-century French exegete Rashbam. When woman is formed, Adam proclaims: "*This* time bones of my bones ..." Rashbam comments: "This time *only* (is woman taken from man). Henceforth, the opposite will be true: man will come from woman."

Havvah seeks ownership of others, she compromises God's image, the *tzelem Elohim* within herself, actually eroding and *weakening* her sense of self. Ultimately, this erosion will make her less, and not more, godly. Eric Fromm addresses the destructive acquisition-based mode of being:

> My property constitutes myself and my identity ... In the having mode, there
> is no alive relationship between me and what I have. It and I have become
> things, and I have it, because I have force to make it mine. But there is also a
> reverse relationship: it has me, because my sense of identity, i.e. of sanity,
> rests upon my having it.[5]

In Fromm's view, *having* is a poor substitute for *being*. Placing one's energies into possessing others objectifies both the acquisition and the acquirer. Gradually but inexorably, one who lives in the acquiring mode is diminished and limited, until one's very sense of self is at risk.

In contrast, a person in the *being* mode cannot lose his or her identity. In that case, Fromm argues, "my center is within myself; my capacity for being and for expressing my essential powers is part of my character structure and depends on me."[6]

Havvah views her child as a means to acquiring her husband. With this attitude, she devalues her son, her husband, and herself. Woman had fervently wished for immortality and godliness, yet now the opposite occurs. Instead of expanding her self-definition with the miraculous act of childbirth, *Havvah* constricts it.

Sarah: Infertility and Exclusion

The next female character to receive the Bible's close attention is Sarah. Since her story will center on her infertility and her efforts to overcome it, we approach it with a sense of foreboding. We wonder if in her quest for her slice of immortality, she will repeat the mistakes of her predecessor. Or perhaps alternatively, with the help of God and man, she will begin to rewrite woman's story of subordination and attempted acquisition.

Sarah's story stands out immediately from the eleven chapters that precede it, wherein the Bible assumes unimpeded fertility. The reassuring repetitions of *"va-tahar, va-teled, va-yoled,* she conceived, she bore, he begat," lead us to expect a continual yield

---

5. Fromm, *To Have or to Be?* 65.
6. Ibid., 97.

from ever-fertile wombs. But with Sarah the norm is suddenly called into question: "Now Sarai was barren, she had no child" (Gen. 11:30).

Commentators have long been struck by the redundancy in this verse. If Sarah was barren, is it not obvious she had no child? Some say the repetition serves to emphasize the all-encompassing nature of her condition: Sarah was absolutely barren, having no child whatsoever. Others draw the opposite conclusion, viewing the redundancy as limiting the scope of Sarah's infertility. Read this way, Sarah was barren *in that* at this stage she lacked children. The implication is that although she is barren now, she will not be so forever.[7] Alternatively, we might see the repetition as a dramatic technique intended to call our attention to a remarkable and previously unknown state: behold, this woman is barren; she has no children! This surprising development expressed in double language challenges us to revise our assumptions about procreation. From now on, in some cases it will be God, and not nature alone, that will open and close a woman's womb.[8]

With the Bible's first woman as background, this new reality portends trouble for Sarah. Like the *Ishah* figure in Eden, Sarah yearns to partake of the elusive "tree of life," which in her case means overcoming her infertility and conceiving. Yet like the *Ishah*, Sarah is excluded from all divine-human dialogue. As a result, Sarah's chances for writing a subversive sequel to the story seem remote. The characters, God, man, and woman, are the same. Many of their actions seem the same as well. Here, as in Eden, God speaks to man alone as He promises Abraham: "I will make of *you* (masc. sing.) a great nation, and I will bless *you*; I will make *your* name great and *you* shall be a blessing. I will bless those who bless *you* and curse those that curse *you*; and all the families of the earth shall bless themselves by *you*" (Gen. 12: 1–3). And later, "to *your* seed will I give this land" (12:7). But what of Sarah?[9] At this stage, God does not speak to her, or of her. As with the woman in the Garden, God does not even instruct His male prophet to convey His word to her. Abraham, in turn, seems to accept Sarah's exclusion, adopting God's singular language in his plea for offspring: "What can you give *me*, seeing that *I* shall die childless" (Gen. 15:2). At the beginning of her narrative, it seems that the infertile Sarah stands alone.

---

7. For example, see Radak on 11:30, s.v. *ein lah valad.*

8. For explicit statements to this effect, see: Gen. 29:31; 30:22; I Sam 1:5.

9. At this point her name is still Sarai, and so it remains until Genesis 17, when God changes her name to Sarah. At that same point, Abram's name is changed to Abraham. For the sake of simplicity, unless quoting a verse directly, we will refer to the couple as Abraham and Sarah throughout.

Abduction

Sarah's exclusion will be further highlighted in a story of her objectification and abduction. When a famine hits the recently promised land of Canaan, Abraham moves his family to Egypt, a land then filled with licentiousness[10] and danger. Yet surprisingly, this narrative will provide hints of a subversive sequel to the Eden narrative and will begin a reversal of Sarah's disadvantaged role. We present the story in full:

> There was a famine in the land, and Abram went down to Egypt to sojourn there, for the famine was severe in the land. As he was about to enter Egypt, he said to his wife Sarai, "I know [*hinneh na yadati*] what a beautiful woman you are. If the Egyptians see you and think, 'She is his wife,' they will kill me and let you live. Please say [*imri na*] you are my sister, that it will be good for me because of you, and that I may remain alive thanks to you."
>
> When Abram entered Egypt, the Egyptians saw how very beautiful the woman was. Pharaoh's courtiers saw her and praised her to Pharaoh, and the woman was taken into Pharaoh's palace. And because of her, it was good for Abram; he acquired sheep, oxen, asses, male and female slaves, she-asses and camels.
>
> But the Lord afflicted Pharaoh and his household with mighty plagues on account of Sarai, the wife of Abram. Pharaoh sent for Abram and said, "What is this you have done to me! Why did you not tell me that she was your wife? Why did you say, 'She is my sister,' so that I took her as my wife? Now, here is your wife; take her and be gone!" And Pharaoh put men in charge of him, and they sent him off with his wife and all that he possessed.[11] (Gen. 12:10–20)

This story has troubled readers of the Bible throughout the centuries. Some critical scholars have accused Abraham of cruel unilateral action, endangering his wife for his own personal gain.[12] Other, more traditional commentators have exonerated Abraham completely, claiming he had no choice other than to go to Egypt, and that his

---

10. See Lev. 18:3–30. The Israelites are warned not to emulate the behavior of the Egyptians; the following verses then elaborate on the types of behaviors, mostly incestuous, that are to be avoided.

11. Author's translation.

12. Cassuto cites Holzinger, attributing anti-Semitic motives to his fierce indictment of Abraham's actions. Cassuto translates: "Abraham, out of shameful baseness abandons his wife to the lust of a foreign potentate, and derives material advantage from this dirty business." Cassuto, *Genesis*, 348.

deception was a morally defensible and reasonable course in which to save Sarah and himself.[13] But perhaps a more moderate response is in order. We might sympathize with Abraham's difficult situation while finding implicit condemnation of his behavior from the text's presentation of this story as a sequel to the Eden narrative.

In several ways, Abraham is indeed quite deserving of our sympathy. After all, he does not deliberately seek to harm Sarah. He takes her to Egypt in what he perceives to be their best chance of surviving the famine.[14] Then he produces a plan that he thinks will protect them both as much as is possible given their dire situation. If he reveals their true relationship, Abraham will almost certainly be killed, in light of ancient near-Eastern practices and mores, as a 20th century Bible scholar explains:

> The speech of Abram to his wife is an instructive revelation of social and moral sentiment in early Israel. The Hebrew women are fairer than all others, and are sure to be coveted by foreigners; but the marriage bond is so sacred that even a foreigner, in order to possess the wife, will kill the husband first. Hence the dilemma with which Abram is confronted: if Sarai is known as his wife, her life will be safe, but he will probably be slain; if she passes as his sister, her honor will be endangered, but his advantage will be served.[15]

According to this account, in the ancient world adultery was taboo, while murder was not. Forced to choose the lesser of two evils—Sarah's dishonor or his own death—Abraham decides to risk his wife's virtue in order to defend his life. But how could Abraham protect himself at his wife's expense? Some argue that Abraham's survival is, in fact, the only way for him to help Sarah. If he is killed, she will become public property, left to service the sexual demands of the Egyptians. But if he can just remain alive, as her "brother" he might have some chance of protecting her. This reading finds support in Abraham's expression of his fear in dual language, "They will kill me and let you live." The doubling points to Abraham's twofold fear: he might be killed, while Sarah is kept alive to lead an unspeakably terrible existence.[16]

We may sympathize with Abraham, but we cannot exonerate him so easily. His actions, no matter how honorable their intent, ultimately compromise Sarah's safety

---

13. Malbim 12:13 s.v. *imri na ahoti at lema'an yitav li.*
14. For another example of Egypt as a refuge from famine, see Gen. 42: 1–5.
15. Skinner, *International Critical Commentary,* 248–9.
16. Cassuto, 12: 12 s.v. *ve-haregu oti ve-otakh yehayyu.*

and well-being, as she is left to fend for herself in the palace of Pharaoh, after he takes her "as a wife" (Gen. 12:19). To begin with, Abraham endangers her merely by bringing her to Egypt's borders.[17] Had he sufficiently considered the threat posed by her beauty *before* their approach to the land, perhaps he might have gone elsewhere, to a land without such predatory intentions toward foreigners. Moreover, once they reached Egypt and he fully understood the danger, perhaps he could have devised another plan, one that would not risk having Sarah taken from him. Sarah's silence only heightens our discomfort with Abraham's actions.[18] Is she left with no choice but to support a plan that will result in her abduction? Although Abraham's behavior may have seemed warranted given the nature of his situation, the text, as we will see, does not endorse it.

Sarah as Forbidden Fruit

Throughout the story of Sarah's abduction, Abraham's failures are highlighted by the passage's unexpected use of Eden-like language. Such similarities invite us to draw parallels between the two stories, and consequently to view Abraham's behavior as deserving of the Bible's subtle literary reproach. The first example, which will only indirectly implicate Abraham, is the verb combination of *seeing* and *taking*. In the Garden, the forbidden fruit was a beautiful object of desire, to be inappropriately *seen and taken:*[19]

> When the woman *saw* that the tree was good for eating and a delight to the eyes, and that the tree was desirable as a source for wisdom, she *took* of its fruit and ate (3:6).

---

17. See Ramban, 12:10 s.v. *hinneh na yadati.* Ramban claims that Abraham sinned by not having sufficient faith that God would provide for him in the promised land of Canaan. He should have stayed where he was and prayed to God for salvation.

18. Abraham uses the biblical convention of *"hinneh na"* followed by a request (in the command form, combined with an additional *"na"*). This convention, which calls for someone to act in a certain way within a particular context, is evident in Gen. 16:2 and 27:2–3. In both of these instances, the person being petitioned responds positively to the request: "Abram heeded Sarah's voice" (16:2), and "Esau went to the field to hunt game to bring home" (27:5). Yet despite the fact that Abraham invokes the convention in Genesis 12, Sarah does not respond. On the basis of the above comparisons, it is reasonable to make an argument from Sarah's silence. Although Abraham asks her to cooperate in his deception, the expected statement of affirmation does not follow. I am grateful to Martin Lockshin for directing me to this possible reading. See note 20.

19. The combination of the verbs "to see, r-'-h" and "to take, l-k-h" in the Book of Genesis consistently points to improper, impulsive taking of that which is not to be taken. See Gen. 3:6; 6:2; 34:2; 38:2.

In Egypt, Sarah is the beautiful object to be *seen* and *taken:*

When Abram entered Egypt, the Egyptians *saw* how very beautiful the woman was. Pharaoh's courtiers saw her and praised her to Pharaoh, and the woman was *taken* into Pharaoh's palace. (12:14–15)

The text's choice of language suggests that the Egyptians view Sarah not as a human being, but, like Eden's fruit, as a commodity to be desired and seized. But the text hints at something more. In assessing their situation at the portal to dangerous territory, Abraham, like the unscrupulous Egyptians, sees only one thing: Sarah's physical beauty:[20] "I know what a beautiful woman you are" (12:11).

It would appear that in devising his plan for their survival, Abraham considers Sarah's beauty, but not her indispensability to him. In his assessment of the potential dangers facing them, he mentions only the risks of having Sarah by his side, but not those inherent in claiming she is his sister. As a result of his incomplete analysis of the situation, he adopts a strategy that will likely separate them, possibly forever. Instead of doing everything possible to keep Sarah at his side, Abraham's actions lead to Sarah's being "seen" and "taken" like Eden's fruit.

In what is perhaps another nod to Eden, the narrative makes ironic use of the word *tov,* good. At the start of the biblical record, all of God's creations were pronounced *"tov"* (Gen. 1:12,18,21,25,31). Yet as we have seen, Genesis 2 introduces a state of *lo tov* by stating, "It is not good for man to be alone" (2:18). God rectifies that situation by creating woman, in essence declaring that only man and woman together could bring a sense of *tov* into the world. In Egypt, Abraham turns God's sentiment on its head with his words *"imri na ahoti at lema'an yitav li,* please say you are my sister so that it will be *good* for me." Although Abraham's

---

20. Is this the first time Abraham notices? Rashi (12:11 s.v. *hinneh na yadati*) suggests that it is. In his view, *hinneh na yadati* means "now I know." As a result of this "new" reality, please say you are my sister. Ramban (12:11–13, s.v. *hinneh na yadati imri na ahoti at*) disagrees, as does Rashbam. Lockshin interprets Rashbam's comments to Gen. 27:2–3 in line with Rashbam's interpretation to Gen. 12:11. According to Lockshin, the first *na* in both passages is "the formulaic introduction to a request, unconnected to the verb immediately following." The second *na* then introduces the request itself. Read this way, Abraham states reality as it has always been: "I am well aware that you are a beautiful woman." As a result, "please say you are my sister." Lockshin, *Rabbi Samuel ben Meir's Commentary on Genesis,* 150–51.

plan would result in the separation of husband and wife and would return him to a lone existence, he mistakenly thinks that his actions will lead him to *"tov."*[21]

Pharaoh as God

In a very strange and surprising turn, God's role in the story of the Garden of Eden is performed here by Pharaoh, the morally tainted King of Egypt. In rebuking the woman after her disobedience in Eden, God asks rhetorically, "what is this you have done, *mah zot asit!*" (Gen. 3:13). Pharaoh now echoes these words in chastising Abraham, *"mah zot asita li,* what is this you have done to me! (12:18).[22] Moreover, when God drives humanity from His Garden, the text says:

> So the Lord God **sent him off** [*va-yeshallehehu*] from the Garden of Eden,
> to till the soil from which he was taken.[23] (Gen. 3:23)

Similarly, Pharaoh "sends off" the recalcitrant man and his wife, away from his land of plenty:

> And Pharaoh put men in charge of him, and they **sent him off** [*va-yeshallehehu oto*][24] with his wife and all that he possessed. (Gen. 12:20)

Why does the text cast Pharaoh in the role of God? This unscrupulous character, who forcibly takes another man's wife into his home (Gen. 12:15), now assumes the position of Abraham's accuser, judge, and moral superior. It seems that through this act of subtle literary association, the text equates Abraham with Adam, a fellow errant who is banished from a naturally fertile land (13:10). But Abraham

---

21. Seen this way, the ironic use of the word *"tov"* in this chapter follows several other ironic uses since God's initial creation. In the Garden of Eden, the woman deems the forbidden fruit to be *"tov,"* (Gen. 3:6) even though it represents the very opposite of "good" as previously defined by the text, i.e., the manifestation of God's will. Similarly, in a linguistic sequence that bears great similarity to that in the Abraham-Sarah narrative, divine beings "see" the daughters of men as "good," and as a result of their misjudgment, they inappropriately "take" them (6:2).

22. The word combination of *"mah zot,* what is this" and the root *"'-s-h,* do," is relatively rare in the Pentateuch, appearing seven times in all. Once is in God's rebuke to woman in the Garden of Eden, and twice more in the wife-sister stories of Genesis.

23. Author's translation.

24. Both verses use this verb in the emphatic *pi'el* form. In the first verse, the object is appended to the verb, *va-yeshallehehu,* while in the second the object pronoun, *oto,* is separate.

receives an extra sting. Perhaps because he upset God's desired balance of *"tov"* by giving up Sarah, Abraham faces eviction not by God, but by the evil Pharaoh.

Pharaoh's words then carry the insult even farther. While expelling Abraham, Pharaoh makes sure to correct Abraham's misrepresentation of Sarah as his sister by proclaiming, "Now here is *your wife, ishtekha;* take her and be gone!" (Gen. 12:19). In fact, the word for wife, *ishah,* appears ten times in this one passage, lending a tone of sardonic criticism to Abraham's actions. We are reminded time and again of the couple's true relationship, one that Abraham has denied. In addition, the repetition of the word *ishah* serves as an ironic reminder of the hoped-for relations between the original *Ish* and *Ishah* of the Garden of Eden. Rather than clinging to Sarah "as one flesh" (2:24), Abraham's actions lead to their separation.

By the story's end, Abraham has traveled a long and troubling distance. He began by following God's order of "*lekh lekha,* go forth" (Gen. 12:1), "taking, *l-k-h*" Sarah his wife on the divine journey (12:5). Yet along the road, Abraham has denied Sarah's identity as his wife, contributing, albeit unintentionally, to her being taken by others. It is now Pharaoh, the Bible's quintessentially evil king[25] who orders Abraham to "take, *l-k-h*" Sarah and "go, *lekh,*" not for any godly purpose, but in the shame of banishment.

The story of Abraham and Sarah's sojourn in Egypt ends on a familiar and regrettable note. Old patterns continue as man exercises control over his wife, man and woman are alienated from each other, and both are banished from a land of plenty. Yet, rather than following the expected script, the story begins to veer in a surprising, and subversive new direction. Instead of objectively reporting its tale, assuming that, in light of Eden's conclusions, man must naturally rule over woman, the text *attacks* that assumption through well-crafted literary substitution. First, woman replaces Eden's fruit as object, as *she* is now the beautiful object that is inappropriately "seen" and "taken." Then Pharaoh replaces God as man's judge, as suggested by his echoing of God's language when he cries: "*mah zot asita li,* what have you done to me," and when he banishes, *sh-l-h,* Abraham from his land. Through the similarities in language, the two stories are drawn together. Then, by the substitutions, their differences come to light. These differences whisper to the reader that it is one thing for fruit to be objectified and inappropriately taken. But it is far worse for a woman to be treated in this way. When man allows for this to happen, he is rebuked and expelled not by God, but by a morally debased mortal being.

---

25. His title carries associations of the Bible's greatest villain, the Pharaoh of the Israelites' enslavement.

In these subtle literary ways, the narrative voice is the first to intimate a call for change. But as the story reaches its conclusion, man and woman, the characters *in* the story, have not yet recognized these new winds. We now return to Sarah's narrative, in search of the beginnings of corrective repair.

Attempted Reconstruction

At first, it is hard to find signs of repair, as God and Abraham continue their exclusive dialogue about Abraham's future progeny. But then, in her desperation to have a child, Sarah speaks and acts for the first time:

> Sarai, Abram's wife, had borne him no children. She had an Egyptian maid-servant whose name was Hagar. And Sarai said to Abram, "Look [*hinneh na*] the Lord has kept me from bearing. Consort [*bo na*] with my maid; perhaps I shall be built up [*ibbaneh*] through her."[26] (Gen. 16:1–2)

Sarah's plea to Abraham, "*Hinneh na ... bo na*, look-consort now," recalls the syntactic construction used by Abraham in his short speech to Sarah as they approached the Egyptian border: "*Hinneh na ... imri na*, I know that you are a beautiful woman ... please say you are my sister." In what is perhaps a belated reaction to her silent compliance until now, Sarah replicates Abraham's speaking style for her own very divergent purposes. Abraham had urgently requested her cooperation in his plan for survival in Egypt, and she had wordlessly given it. Now she responds with a pressing request of her own. She asks Abraham to allow her to recover her dignity by helping her to become a mother. Sarah identifies her sole source of strength as her fertility. She feels that only through childbirth will she be "built" (*b-n-h*), much like the woman in Eden who emerged from her amorphous state to be "built" (*b-n-h*) from the side of man (Gen. 2:22).[27] This verb hints at Sarah's feelings of incompleteness: without fertility she remains inchoate and purposeless. To her mind, childbirth, even vicariously through a surrogate, is her only hope of reconstruction.

But Sarah's plan takes an unexpected turn:

> Sarai, Abram's wife, took her maid, Hagar the Egyptian—after Abram had dwelt in the land of Canaan ten years—and gave her to her husband Abram

---

26. Author's translation.

27. In the book of Genesis, three women are, or seek to be, "built." God builds woman from man's rib, Sarah seeks to be built up through surrogacy, as does Rachel (30:1).

as a wife. He cohabited with Hagar and she conceived; and when she saw
that she had conceived, her mistress was lowered in her esteem. And Sarai
said to Abram, 'The wrong done me is your fault! I myself put my maid in
your bosom; now that she sees she is pregnant, I am lowered in her esteem.
The LORD judge between you and me!" Abram said to Sarai, "Your maid is in
your hands. Deal with her as you think right." Then Sarai treated her harshly, and she ran away from her.[28] (Gen. 16:1–6)

Hagar was supposed to facilitate the "building up" of Sarah. But instead, as a
result of Hagar's pregnancy, the vulnerable matriarch crumbles even further, as the
handmaid begins to look down on her mistress. In impotent despair, Sarah lashes
out at Abraham, crying, "The LORD judge between you and me!" Sarah's situation
and her contentious words draw us back to *Havvah* and her statement, "I have acquired a man with the LORD" (Gen. 4:1). Both women feel weak and both look to
childbirth to give them power. Both speak in adversarial tones about their husbands,
while invoking God as their allies. The similarities between Sarah's story and that
of *Havvah* signal an unhappy direction: a perpetuation, rather than amelioration, of
marital strife, with the question of fertility at the center of the fray.

Maltreated by Sarah, Hagar flees. Later, upon the instruction of God's angel she
returns, and gives birth to a son. In repeating Hagar's name three times in its announcement of Ishmael's birth, the text hints at her new-found centrality in Abraham's life:

Hagar bore a son to Abram, and Abram gave the son that Hagar bore him
the name Ishmael. Abram was eighty-six years old when Hagar bore Ishmael to Abram. (Gen. 16:15–16)

It appears that childbirth has redeemed Hagar, not Sarah. If anyone is "built
up" from Hagar's pregnancy, it is Hagar. What is left for Sarah, now that Abraham's
personal prayers have been answered through another woman?

At this point, just when she seems most doomed to irrelevance, God, who has
been silent in relation to Sarah, begins to speak of her. In the midst of God's male-
centered instruction to Abraham regarding the covenant of circumcision, He says:

As for your wife Sarai, you shall not call her name Sarai, but her name shall
be Sarah. I will bless her; indeed I will give you a son by her. I will bless her

---

28. Author's translation.

so that she shall give rise to nations; rulers of peoples shall issue from her.[29]
(Gen. 17:15–16)

Not only will the long-awaited covenantal child emerge from Sarah's womb, but the very nature of the *berit* itself will be affected by her presence. Although the covenant calls for the cutting of male flesh, it will be upgraded to a *berit olam*, an everlasting covenant, only with the appropriate woman as mother (Gen. 17:7,13). God emphasizes Sarah's critical position by choosing this pivotal moment to rename her. Both Abraham and Sarah, formerly Abram and Sarai, are symbolically reborn at this moment as the progenitors of God's royal nation (17:5, 16).

On the face of things, God simply informs Abraham of Sarah's name change: "You shall not call her name Sarai, but her name shall be Sarah." But perhaps there is a hint of something deeper. In the Garden of Eden, one expression of man's dominance over woman was his naming her: "And the man *called* his wife's *name Havvah, va-yikra Ha-adam shem ishto Havvah*" (Gen. 3:20). By now instructing the patriarch not to *call* Sarai's *name, "lo tikra et shemah ...,"* perhaps God symbolically revokes *all* male privilege in naming woman, leaving that act of dominion to God alone.

In a further signal to Abraham of Sarah's essential position within the covenant, God twice blesses her (Gen. 17:16). By blessing both Abraham and Sarah, God reenacts His blessing of the androgynous *Ha-adam* when the world was first created (1:28).[30] The moment in which God forges His covenant with humanity is also a creation of sorts. Abraham and Sarah are blessed as the prospective parents of a new kind of "world," the incipient Israelite nation.

Sarah's blessings, moreover, recall the five-fold blessing given to Abraham at the beginning of his journey toward God (Gen. 12:1–3). The message to Abraham is clear: you were blessed before, but now, with the addition of Sarah, your blessings are eternal. United through God's *berit,* Abraham and Sarah would give birth to a much blessed new entity.

---

29. Author's translation.

30. Seforno draws the connection between the blessings given to Sarah and the curses given to *Havvah*. He claims that with her childbirth-related blessings, Sarah would now reverse the curses given in Eden. Seforno 17:16, s.v. *u-verakhtikha*. See Seforno's source, *Sanhedrin* 19b, with Rashi and Tosafot.

Where is Sarah?

In this subversive sequel to the Eden story, God has begun the process of repair by signaling an end to woman's exclusion. Although God does not speak directly to Sarah, He speaks of her pivotal position in His *berit.* Yet, surprisingly, upon hearing the promise of Sarah's future pregnancy, Abraham shows signs of resistance to her inclusion in God's plan:

> Abraham fell on his face and laughed, as he said to himself, "Can a child be born to a man a hundred years old, or can Sarah bear a child at ninety?" And Abraham said to God, "O that Ishmael might live before you!" God said, "Nevertheless, Sarah your wife shall bear you a son, and you shall name him Isaac, and I will maintain my covenant with him as an everlasting covenant for his offspring to come. As for Ishmael, I have heeded you. I hereby bless him, I will make him fruitful and exceedingly numerous. He shall be the father of twelve chieftains, and I will make of him a great nation. But my covenant I will maintain with Isaac, whom Sarah shall bear to you at this season next year."[31] (Gen. 17: 17–21)

Despite the illustrious promises he has just received, Abraham laughs. It seems to him absurd that at their advanced ages he and Sarah will produce a child (Gen. 17). Abraham then intimates that God's promise is unnecessary, since he already has a son. As long as Ishmael "lives before God" (v. 18), Abraham sees no need for God to make unlikely promises about his bearing another child with the aged Sarah.

As Abraham continues to question Sarah's place in his covenantal destiny, God's educational efforts become more direct. When God sends three messengers to Abraham to announce Sarah's approaching pregnancy and childbirth, they ask Abraham, "Where is Sarah your wife?" (Gen. 18:9). The visitors use an unusual Hebrew word for "where." Instead of the more common *"eifo,"* which denotes a simple quest for information, they use the word *ayyey,* a term that is used to ask rhetorically why someone or something is not where it should be.[32] For instance, when God asks Adam, "where are you?" a form of *ayyey* is chosen[33] (3:9). The term signifies that God knows where Adam is, but wants to prompt him to look inside himself and repent. The true intent of God's question to Adam

---

31. Author's translation.
32. See Nehama Leibowitz, *The Study of Bible Commentators,* 6. Leibowitz claims that *ayyey* expresses "a complaint, a demand, a rebuke or wonder: where is the person or object? Why is it not where it ought to be?" As examples of the Bible's use of *eifo,* she cites Gen. 37:16, Job 38:4, and Ruth 2:19. As examples of the use of *ayyey* she cites Judg. 6, 13, 2 Kings 18:34, 2 Kings 2:14, and Jer. 2:28.
33. *Ayyeka,* Gen. 3:9.

following his rebellion in the Garden is: What has become of you? What have you done? Why are you not where you ought to be, obediently following God's path?[34] Similarly, the divine guests are not asking for Sarah's geographic whereabouts,[35] but rather are implying that Sarah should be at Abraham's side, hearing God's word. Their question is really a demand. Where is Sarah in your life? Why is she not here where she belongs, receiving the prophecy that is of such vital consequence to both of you? For emphasis, the three visitors add the word *ishtekha*, your wife, accentuating Sarah's role as the only woman whose destiny God has inextricably linked to Abraham's.

Abraham's response consists of two words: *hinneh ba-ohel*, she is in the tent. His simple, seemingly instinctive answer suggests that in Abraham's mind the tent is where Sarah has always resided and is where she naturally belongs, tending to interior concerns. All nuance is lost on Abraham. The subtle rebuke of "where is Sarah your wife?" remains unheard.[36] In this passage (Gen. 18:1–10), the guiding word *ohel*, tent, appears five times, punctuating the entrenched routine of their union. While Abraham stands at the outer border of the tent waiting to engage the world and God, Sarah remains deeply within it, receiving whatever portion of events Abraham imparts to her.

Abraham seems impervious to the signs of change coming from God and His messengers. But Sarah's actions indicate a change in her self-perception. Sensing that the men's words will have dramatic bearing on her life, she ventures from the inner recesses of the tent toward its opening (Gen. 18:10), Abraham's traditional sentry point (18:1). No longer content to wait inside until summoned, Sarah acts independently to hear God's word as directly as possible. As Sarah overhears the message brought by the men of God, she reacts with incredulity, much as Abraham did (17:17) when he first heard the news:

> And Sarah laughed to herself, "Now that I am withered, am I to have enjoyment [*ednah*][37]—with my husband so old?" (Gen. 18:12)

---

34. See Rashi on Gen. 4:9, s.v. *aye Hevel ahikha*.

35. For an equation of the men's question to Abraham with God's probing question to Adam in Eden, see Rashbam, Gen. 18:9, s.v. *ayyey Sarah ishtekha*.

36. Abraham's decision to overlook the rhetorical intent of God's question recalls Cain's literal response to God's rhetorical question (Gen. 4:9). When God asks, "Where [*aye*] is Abel your brother," He means for Cain to confess his crime. Instead, Cain responds as if God had asked him for Cain's whereabouts: "I do not know. Am I my brother's keeper?" (Gen. 4:9)

37. Alter suggests that Sarah's use of the word *ednah* evokes the Garden of *Eden*: "the term *ednah*, עדנה, is cognate with Eden, עדן, and probably suggests sexual pleasure, or perhaps even sexual moistness." Alter, *Genesis*, 79. Other than in the Garden itself, Sarah's statement constitutes the only place in the Pentateuch in which the root '-d-n appears.

With her words, Sarah doubts not only herself, but God as well. Angered by Sarah's questioning His abilities to alter the biological facts, God delivers a reproach:

> Then the Lord said to Abraham, "Why did Sarah laugh, saying, 'Shall I in truth bear a child, old as I am?' Is anything too wondrous for the Lord? I will return to you at the same season the next year, and Sarah shall have a son." (Gen. 18:13–14)

These verses raise two difficult questions. First, why is Sarah so surprised by this news? Is it possible that Abraham, who has already received word from God as to Sarah's impending pregnancy (Gen. 17:19,21), has neglected to share the information with her? And second, why does God reprimand Sarah through Abraham, instead of rebuking her directly? Addressing the first question, Ramban offers a possible rationale for Abraham's failure to inform Sarah of the miraculous events to come:

> It is noteworthy that Abraham did not reveal [to Sarah] what was said to him earlier [in Gen. 17:19]: "But Sarah your wife will bear you a son." Perhaps he was waiting for God to (directly) send her the message at a later date ... or perhaps, out of his great alacrity in performing God's commandment, he was busy circumcising himself and the members of his household. Then, in his weakness he sat at the doorway to the tent, with the messengers arriving before he could tell her anything.[38]

In Ramban's view, Abraham indeed neglected to inform Sarah of God's promise, and as a result, she now reacts to the news with incredulity. But *why* did Abraham not tell her? Perhaps he expected God to inform Sarah Himself, or perhaps Abraham's circumcision temporarily distracted him from relaying God's tidings. Ramban's suggested solutions are improbable, but they confirm our sense that Abraham *should* have communicated God's promise to Sarah.

Perhaps Abraham's failure to include Sarah provides a key to resolving the second difficulty posed by this text, God's channeling His rebuke of Sarah through Abraham. Perhaps God addresses Abraham because it is the patriarch who bears ultimate responsibility for Sarah's inappropriate response. Had Abraham included his wife when he first received the miraculous tidings, she would not laugh in disbelief now. Viewed this way, God's rhetorical question "Why did

---

38. Ramban, Gen. 18:15 s.v. *va-tekhahesh Sarah lemor.*

Sarah laugh?" joins with the earlier rhetorical question posed by God's emissaries to Abraham, "where is Sarah your wife?" Taken together, these questions pose an emphatic divine challenge to Abraham's continued exclusion of Sarah.

Once Again: She is My Sister

Before arriving at the resolution of Sarah's fertility problem, the text detours into familiar ground.[39] Again, Abraham and Sarah travel to a foreign land, and, feeling threatened by its inhabitants, Abraham claims that Sarah is not his wife, but his sister (Gen. 20:2). As in the first story, Sarah is "taken" by the king, this time Abimelech, King of Gerar, who replaces Pharaoh, King of Egypt.

Yet despite the similarities, there are numerous distinctions to be drawn between the two accounts. To begin with, in this story, Abraham has the benefit of experience. As readers who have seen this before, we expect him to have learned from the failure of his strategy in Egypt. Given his background, we might argue that Abraham should have either stayed away from any land that would endanger Sarah, or devised another plan for protecting her. In addition, in Gerar, Abraham is even less solicitous of his wife than he was in Egypt. There, although he did not wait for her response, he offered her an explanation of his plan and a request: "You are a beautiful woman ... please say you are my sister" (Gen. 12:11–13). This time Abraham utters a terse, declarative statement to others, about her: "*Va-yomer Avraham el Sarah ishto ahoti hi*, Abraham said of[40] Sarah his wife, 'She is my sister'" (20:2).

If Abraham is less sensitive to Sarah in this story than he was in the first, God is more so. In the first account, it is not clear whether or not Sarah escapes her imprisonment unscathed, and Pharaoh's cryptic statement is cause for concern: "I took her as a wife"(Gen. 12:19). Although God brought plagues upon Pharaoh's household "on account of Sarai, wife of Abram" (12:17), they may have come too

---

39. There is a much larger detour before this, the story of God's destruction of Sodom and its surroundings.

40. This is the plainest reading of Abraham's words. Although the preposition *el* usually means "to," there are cases in which it means "of." See Ibn Ezra on v. 2, s.v. *el Sarah ishto*. This reading is supported by Gen. 20:13, in which Abraham again uses a preposition that usually means "to" to mean "of": *imri li ahi hu*. An alternative would be to define *"el"* in the more usual manner: "Abraham said *to* Sarah his wife, 'She is my sister.'" With a nod to her, he informs her that they are again performing their "she is my sister" act.

late to fully protect her. In the second wife-sister story, the text makes it very clear that God intervenes *before* any harm can come to her:

> But God came to Abimelech in a dream by night and said to him, "You are
> to die because of the woman you have taken, for she is a married woman."
> Now Abimelech had not approached her. (Gen. 20:3–4)

God's expanded protection of Sarah is further evident in the second story, when for the first time He issues an explicit warning of certain death to the offending king:

> Therefore, restore the man's wife—since he is a prophet, he will intercede for
> you—to save your life. If you fail to restore her, know that you shall surely
> die [*mot tamut*] you and all that are yours. (Gen. 7–8)

God's words: "*mot tamut*, you shall surely die," recall His identical warning to Adam against eating from Eden's forbidden tree (Gen. 2:17).[41] With this literary allusion, the text hints that the treatment of Sarah as a mere object of desire is objectionable in the extreme and is likely to yield consequences as dire as those threatened in the Garden of Eden.

God's increased efforts on behalf of Sarah contrast with Abraham's continued inaction. The passage's theme of prayer helps to make the point. Early in the story, God tells Abimelech that Abraham is a prophet whose prayers could help save him (Gen. 20:7). Later, in a curious epilogue to the story, there is a reprise of this notion, this time with a focus on infertility:

> Abraham then prayed to God, and God healed Abimelech and his wife
> and his slave girls, so that they bore children; for the Lord had closed fast
> every womb of the household of Abimelech because of Sarah, the wife of
> Abraham. (Gen. 20:17–18)

Abraham uses his impressive spiritual abilities to benefit the infertile women of another land. These efforts prove ironic within the broad context of the Abraham-Sarah narrative. The reader cannot help but wonder why, if Abraham has the capacity to successfully petition God to unseal closed wombs, he has

---

41. While the construction of verb *m-v-t*, death, preceded by the infinitive absolute is common in the Bible, in Genesis the combination appears in only two contexts: the Garden of Eden and in wife-sister narratives. See 26:11 for the use of this phrase by Abimelech, after Isaac has misrepresented Rebekah as his sister.

never done so on behalf of his own wife. Although Sarah will nonetheless soon give birth, this interlude draws our attention to Abraham's persistent failure to help her.[42]

Sarah's Voice

No longer waiting for Abraham's intervention, God at long last responds to Sarah:

> The Lord took note of Sarah as He had said, and the Lord did for Sarah as He had spoken.[43] (Gen. 21:1)

This verse refers to two actions on God's part, both of which are directed at Sarah: God "took note" of her and He "did" for her. But the verse puzzles in its double reference—with no stated object—to God's speech. To whom had God "said" that Sarah would conceive? To whom had God "spoken" of Sarah's childbirth? Since Sarah is the only proper name in the verse, it seems reasonable to assume that the reference is to her. But if this is true, when did such dialogue take place? The textual record points to only three words spoken directly by God to Sarah, words of rebuke at that: "*Lo ki tzahakt,* no, but you laughed" (Gen. 18:15). In addressing this problem, Rashi suggests that God spoke not to her, but *of* her, to Abraham.[44] This line of thought is consistent with the Abraham-Sarah dynamic as we have observed it. Although God has barely spoken to Sarah, He has found numerous ways in which to speak *about* her to Abraham. For example, God spoke to Abraham about incorporating Sarah into His *berit.* Less directly, He spoke of her again—on His own and through His emissaries—with the subtle reprimands, "Where is Sarah your wife?" and "Why has Sarah laughed?" In a sense, God spoke of Sarah in the palaces of Pharaoh and Abimelech

---

42. Alternatively, Abraham's praying for the infertility of others might be an indication that, although Sarah will reap no benefits, Abraham has learned something from his past neglect. Note that nowhere had God actually commanded him to pray for Abimelech's household, and even in Gen. 20:7, when God predicts that Abraham "is a prophet and will pray for you [Abimelech]" (author's translation) the prayers were to be for the sake of sparing Abimelech's life, not to cure his household from barrenness. Thus, Abraham seems to show initiative in interceding with God with regard to the infertility of others. I am grateful to Daniel Schwartz for this insight.

43. Author's translation.

44. Rashi, Gen. 21:1, s.v. *Va-ya'as Adonai le-Sarah ka'asher dibber.* This reading is consistent with the passage's strong emphasis on Abraham. His name appears six times in the space of eight verses, while ten additional pronouns refer back to him.

when He intervened in order to protect her. God's efforts now culminate in His re-deeming Sarah through a miraculous act of childbirth. Despite the absence of audible dialogue between God and Sarah, the communication between them grows wider and deeper as the narrative unfolds. God's determined inclusion of the matriarch points to a dramatic, though incomplete, corrective to the hierarchy and exclusion that were the legacy of Eden.

With the grand gesture of granting this miraculous pregnancy and birth, God's actions on behalf of Sarah are now direct and apparent to all. But will God's gift provide an adequate response to Sarah's longing? It is not clear whether the wondrous birth will enable her to assume her position as God's chosen matriarch, and whether her status will be acknowledged and appreciated by Abraham. Now that she has been fulfilled as *Havvah*, "the mother of all the living," we wait to see if Sarah might actualize the other dormant facets of her womanhood: her potential as *Ha-adam*, man's equal partner, and the part of the *Ishah* that is his cherished and indispensable emotional complement.

It seems that for Abraham, rather than clarifying Sarah's covenantal status, Isaac's birth confuses it. Abraham now faces conflicting claims from two sets of mothers and sons:[45]

> Sarah saw the son whom Hagar the Egyptian had borne to Abraham making sport. She said to Abraham, "Cast out that slave-woman and her son, for the son of that slave shall not share in the inheritance of my son Isaac. The matter was exceedingly bad[46] in Abraham's eyes regarding his son. But God said to Abraham, "Do not let it be bad in your eyes concerning the boy or your maid-servant;[47] whatever Sarah tells you, heed her voice,[48] for it is through Isaac that offspring shall be continued for you. As for the son of the slave-woman I will make a nation of him, too, for he is your seed." (Gen. 21:9–13).

Abraham needs a divine reminder that his destiny will be fulfilled through Isaac, while to Sarah this remains perfectly clear. As a result, Sarah orders Abraham

---

45. See *Tosefta Sotah* 6:3, and R. Shimon's disagreement with R. Akiva. In R. Shimon's view Ishmael and Hagar challenged Isaac's right to Abraham's inheritance. By extension, this challenge applied to Sarah's position as matriarch as well.

46. Everett Fox translation.

47. Ibid.

48. Author's translation.

to banish Ishmael, whose presence is blurring her husband's vision. Abraham, re-acting not out of covenantal concerns, but with natural paternal emotion, views Sarah's demand as "exceedingly bad" (Gen. 21:11). Yet despite the cruelty involved in her pronouncement, God supports Sarah's grasp of the situation.[49] He affirms that Ishmael, who will have an illustrious, but completely separate future, must leave in order for Isaac to assume his rightful position. God instructs Abraham with the words, "Everything that Sarah tells you, heed her voice, *shema be-kolah*, for it is through Isaac that offspring shall be continued for you" (v. 12).

Strikingly, God's order to Abraham to heed Sarah's voice echoes and reverses God's rebuke to Adam in the Garden of Eden. "Because you heeded the voice of your wife, *ki shamata le-kol ishtekha*, cursed be the ground because of you" (Gen. 3:17).[50] If, at the beginning of Genesis, listening to his wife led to man's banishment from God's presence, now it is deemed essential that he heed her in order to maintain his place in God's presence. Heeding woman's voice, previously a misguided and disastrous choice, has now become God's mandate.

Although, at long last, Abraham and Sarah have a child together, the negative tension between them persists until the last lines of the narrative they share. In this, their final recorded interaction, Abraham heeds Sarah. But it appears that he does so not because he sees the merit of her claim or because he views her voice as the voice of authority. Instead he heeds her in deference to God's explicit command. Now, as in much of their story, God signals the need for change, which Abraham resists. Abraham and Sarah do not interact directly after this point, suggesting, per-haps, that Abraham is not able to relate to Sarah in the way that God has urged. God has wished for Abraham to begin overturning the consequences of Eden, but it seems that throughout Abraham's life with Sarah, he is not ready.

Conclusions, Beginnings

In two ways, we have viewed Sarah's story as a subversive sequel to the Garden of Eden narrative. In one sense, her narrative points to a negative reversal, away from the majestic, fully enabled *Ha-adam*, as well as from the cherished, albeit subordinate,

---

49. Addressing the full moral implications of Sarah's demand and of God's support for it is beyond the scope of this work.

50. Some have argued that due to the different prepositions, *le-kol* vs. *be-kol*, the two words are not identi-cal. For example, see *Ha-amek Davar* on 21:12, s.v. *shema be-kolah*.

Ishah. Although Abraham leaves his father's home (Gen. 12:1), he never achieves the ideal of Genesis 2: "Therefore shall a man leave his father and mother and cling to his wife and they shall be as one flesh." In fact, instead of leaving his original family in order to cling to a wife in creating a new family, Abraham does the opposite. Twice, he relinquishes Sarah, claiming that she is his sister, thereby symbolically *leaving* his wife in order to return to his birth family.

Throughout their lives together, Abraham and Sarah remain separate and un-equal, a situation that is occasionally and temporarily rectified by God's intervention. The gap between husband and wife is highlighted by the geographic distance between them at the time of Sarah's death. "Abraham stayed in Beer-Sheba" (Gen. 22:19), while Sarah dies in Hebron (23:2). Yet upon her death, Abraham suddenly seems more concerned with Sarah than ever before. He takes great pains in—and the biblical text devotes fully seventeen verses to recording—the negotiations for a suitable burial place for her. Abraham inters Sarah in the Cave of Makhpelah, the burial site destined to hold Abraham's remains as well as those of most of the other patriarchs and matriarchs of Genesis. With this act, Abraham at long last bestows full recognition upon Sarah as the first matriarch of God's nascent nation.

The text's syntax supports the notion of Abraham's increased connection with Sarah after her death. In the description of his efforts to procure her burial plot, Sarah is referred to seven times in the possessive, as *Abraham's* deceased (Gen. 23:4,6,8,11,13,15). If fuller appreciation of Sarah arrives only at her death, this provides a sad contrast to Adam's expression of regard for his wife that comes at the moment of her "birth:" "This one at last is bone of my bones and flesh of my flesh ..." (2:23).

Yet Sarah's story is a subversive sequel to Eden in another, more optimistic sense. Her narrative calls into question any claim that God's subordination of wom-an in Genesis 3 was fixed and enduring. God's pronouncement, "Your desire is to your husband and he shall rule over you," at first proves to be true for Sarah, as she silently submits to, and God tacitly supports, Abraham's exclusion of her. But by the story's end, we see a great deal of forward motion. As the prime mover toward change, God has instructed man and encouraged woman. In response, Sarah slow-ly gains confidence, first hearing more actively and then speaking more clearly than ever before. And in a resounding reversal of the admonishment given to Adam who had regrettably heeded woman's voice, the resistant Abraham is commanded by God: "Regarding all that Sarah tells you, heed her voice."

As we turn to the next round of sequels, we await further signs of change in God, woman, and man. We will look closely to see if in ensuing stories, God will communicate with woman more directly, modeling, rather than merely instructing, her inclusion. In addition, we will search for indications that man follows God's lead in embracing change. Of special interest will be woman's own actions. Will she assume more of an initiative, seeking solutions to her own problems rather than waiting for God and man to come to her aid? In sum, we look to the biblical sequel to consider the possibility that, with concerted efforts on the part of God, woman, and man, the male-female relationship might more fully recover its initial equality and harmony.

Sarah's narrative and its subsequent sequels all pivot on woman's fertility, an emotionally charged issue that has potential to produce both positive and negative developments. If the barren woman attaches exclusive significance to her reproductive success, she risks undervaluing her potential as *Ha-adam* and *Ishah*, and of being under-esteemed by those around her. But infertility, as a focus of discontent, is also a potential catalyst for positive change. It may motivate woman to seek God's help and man's partnership, thereby advancing her growth and promoting her expanded presence in God's covenantal narrative.

Once fertility is attained, the challenge remains for both woman and man to appreciate the deeper connection between offspring and godliness. The first commandment of *peru u-rvu,* be fruitful and increase, is not a goal in itself. It is one means to spiritual fulfillment and covenantal continuity. Procreation offers parents the opportunity to educate future generations in God's ways of justice and righteousness, as God said concerning Abraham:

> For I have singled him out, that he may instruct his children and his posterity to guard the path [*sh-m-r derekh*] of the LORD by doing what is just and right ... (Gen. 18:17–19)

In Eden, the word combination of *sh-m-r derekh* referred to the ever-turning swords that *guard the path* to the tree of life, ensuring that no one could approach it.[51] In God's charge to Abraham, God offers the same words as keys to unlocking the blockade. If Abraham—and we may add, his covenantal partner Sarah—will produce children who will *guard* the *path, sh-m-r derekh,* of the LORD, they will pave the way back toward Eden's elusive, coveted tree of life.

---

51. The two verses, Genesis 3:24 and 18:19, are the only two verses in the Bible in which the terms *sh-m-r* and *derekh* are conjoined.

Chapter 6

The Tent, the Field, and the Battlefield:
Rebekah and Other Mothers

It is the eye of ignorance that assigns a fixed and unchangeable color to every object.
—Paul Gauguin

The Bible's first two matriarchs, Sarah and Rebekah, have a great deal in common. Both women are barren, and at critical moments both stand aside as their husbands appeal to God for a solution. Both are ultimately redeemed by God and are able to produce children. Yet even after they give birth, both women continue to struggle in matters relating to the covenantal destiny of the children. In each narrative the patriarch claims that the matriarch is his sister, not his wife.

These and other similarities bid us to compare the stories of the two women. Once we do so, we note some stark contrasts between them, signaling the presence of the subversive sequel. For example, Sarah's husband takes a second wife; Rebekah's does not. Isaac prays for Rebekah's fertility, while Abraham never prays for Sarah's. Perhaps most significantly, Sarah remains silent before God, while Rebekah seeks and receives divine answers.

Taken together, these stories will reveal movement toward a deepening of the male-female relationship and toward an empowerment of the female figure before man and God. Moreover, they will recall the tripartite woman of God's initial creation, in many ways replaying her challenges and triumphs. Ultimately, the pairing of Rebekah's story with Sarah's will point to woman's vast potential for change and will remind us that the road to her fulfillment is long and circuitous.

But to reach a much deeper appreciation of the text's presentation of biblical woman, we must reach beyond the binary model of the subversive sequel. As we closely examine the stories of an increasing number of female protagonists, we note that the Bible's internal conversation takes place not only in narrative pairs, but sometimes in triplets or in longer chains. Thus in the coming chapter, in addition to comparing Rebecca with Sarah, we will focus on the stories of three other extraordinary women: Deborah, the unnamed "wife of Manoah," and Hannah, whose stories are narrated in the books of Judges and Samuel. In the artful mosaic that is the biblical text, their stories will play upon one another, on the tropes of both Sarah's and Rebekah's narratives, and on literary and thematic elements from the story of the Bible's first woman.

We begin our exegetical journey with an analysis of Rebekah, the second matriarch of Genesis.

Rebekah as "Patriarch"

Even before we meet her, we know that Rebekah will have to be remarkable. In order to be chosen as Isaac's wife, she will have to live up to the strict criteria of two very discriminating men, Abraham and his senior, most trusted servant.[1] When Abraham sends his servant, he commands him as follows:

> "Put your hand under my thigh and I will make you swear by the Lord, the God of heaven and the God of the earth, that you will not take a wife for my son from the daughters of the Canaanites among whom I dwell, but will go to the land of my birth and get a wife for my son Isaac." And the servant said to him, "What if the woman does not consent to follow me to this land, shall I then take your son back to the land from which you came?" Abraham answered him, "On no account must you take my son back there!" (Gen. 24:3–6)

Abraham is set on three requirements. First, the woman must not be from the Canaanites, a nation considered to engage in morally depraved practices.[2] In addition, she must come from Abraham's own homeland. Finally, she must be willing to leave her home to come to Canaan and marry Isaac.

---

1. The midrash (Gen. Rabbah 59:9) identifies the servant as Eliezer, although he is never mentioned by name in the entire episode. This is a reasonable conjecture, based on Gen. 15:2, in which Abraham refers to Eliezer as the man in charge of his household.
2. See Leviticus 18 for an elaboration and a warning to the Israelites not to emulate the behavior of the Canaanites.

These criteria reflect Abraham's thoughts as he senses his death approaching. He worries about the moral character of his descendants, which he expresses by forbidding intermarriage with a Canaanite woman. In addition, he is concerned about broader ideological continuity. It would not be enough to keep out negative influences. He must find a way to retain the positive spirit that initially moved him to respond to God's command of *lekh lekha*. Where would Abraham find a successor who would possess his own pioneering spark? Abraham's son Isaac, a devoted follower, would not innovate. He would reinforce, and at times reenact, many of Abraham's deeds, thereby sending an encouraging signal to the world that his father's legacy would endure long beyond his lifetime.[3] If Abraham were to pass on to posterity the innovative, self-sacrificing spirit that first moved him, he would need to look elsewhere: to the wife his servant would find for Isaac.

Isaac's spouse would have to demonstrate her likeness to Abraham by retracing his trailblazing steps, beginning in Abraham's homeland, Haran, and culminating in God's chosen land, Canaan. And indeed, like Abraham, Rebekah comes from Haran, and agrees to "go" away from all that is known toward a mysterious, yet spiritually promising future in Canaan. In response to her family's inquiry as to whether she would leave them in order to follow Abraham's servant, Rebekah utters the succinct and very resonant, *"elekh*, I will go" (Gen. 24:58), in a sense reenacting Abraham's eager responsiveness to the divine call of *lekh lekha*.

Further support for an Abraham-Rebekah nexus comes in the blessing that Rebekah's family bestows upon her before she leaves them, which is almost identical to God's blessing to Abraham after the binding of Isaac:

> And they blessed Rebekah and said to her, "O sister! May you become thousands of myriads; may your **descendants seize the gates of their foes.**"[4] (Gen. 24:60)

At the conclusion of the binding of Isaac, God's angel says to Abraham:

> I will bestow my blessing upon you and make your descendants as numerous as the stars of the heaven and the sands on the seashore; and your **descendants** shall **seize the gates of their foes.** (Gen. 22:17)

---

3. For a series of Isaac's reenactments of Abraham's actions, see Genesis 26.
4. Author's translation.

As a result of her willingness to go forth to unfamiliar divinely-chosen territory, Rebekah, like Abraham, receives a promise that her descendants will be both multitudinous and mighty. Rebekah's blessings further echo those of Abraham with their use of the unusual imperative form of the verb "to be."[5] Rebekah's family says "*hayi le-alfei revavah,* may you *become* thousands of myriads," much as God, at the beginning of Abraham's journey, says "*heyeh berakha, be* a blessing" (Gen. 12:2). Both Abraham and Rebekah were moved to "go" in order to "become" truer, more blessed versions of themselves.

In seeking a suitable mate for Isaac, Abraham chooses a female variant of himself, the visionary who will leave everything behind in order to pursue a promise of greater spiritual meaning. Perhaps at long last internalizing God's messages of woman's essential role within the *berit,* God's covenant, Abraham is able to look to a woman as his son's full partner in ensuring the continuity of his mission. The text's language strongly suggests that his wishes are fulfilled in the servant's choice of Rebekah.

In fact, the chosen wife may be even more similar to Abraham than he initially imagined, thanks to the servant. After receiving Abraham's carefully specified orders, the servant sets additional criteria for choosing Isaac's future wife:

> And he said, "O Lord, God of my master Abraham, grant me good fortune this day, and deal graciously with my master Abraham: Here I stand by the spring as the daughters of the townsmen come out to draw water; let the maiden to whom I say, 'Please, lower your jar that I may drink,' and who replies, 'Drink, and I will also water your camels'—let her be the one whom You have decreed for your servant Isaac. Thereby shall I know that You have dealt graciously with my master." (Gen. 24:12–14)

Suddenly, and without explanation, the servant shifts the focus of the search from geography to character. Perhaps the servant perceives that something of critical importance has been omitted from his master's criteria. At the chapter's opening, the text lays the literary foundation for the servant's unique suitability to understand, and at times to anticipate, Abraham's needs:

> Abraham was now **old** [*z-k-n*] advanced in years, and the Lord had blessed Abraham in **all** things [*ba-kol*]. And Abraham said to the senior servant

---

5. The imperative form of the verb *h-y-h* is used in the masculine singular only five times in the Pentateuch, twice in reference to Abraham (Gen. 12:2 and 17:1); it is used in the feminine singular only this once.

of—literally "the **elder** of [*z-k-n*]"—his household, who had charge of **all** [*be-khol*] that he owned ..." (Gen. 24:1–2)

The trusted servant, who has grown **old** with his master and who, together with him, rules over his household with **all** its many blessings, now knows even more about choosing a wife for Isaac than the master himself. While it is important for the woman to share Abraham's innovative spirit, there must be a great deal more. She must possess his abundant capacity for giving, his *hesed*, as well.

In her caring for others, Rebekah exemplifies one of Abraham's defining features. We recall that when three strange men arrive at Abraham's tent in the heat of the day, Abraham acts tirelessly on their behalf, highlighting the priority he places on bountiful hospitality:

> Looking up, he saw three men standing near him. As soon as he saw them he **ran** [*r-v-tz*] from the entrance to the tent to greet them ... Abraham **hastened** [*m-h-r*] into the tent to Sarah, and said, "**Quick** [*m-h-r*] three seahs of choice flour! Knead and make cakes! Then Abraham **ran** [*r-v-tz*] to the herd, took a calf, tender and choice, and gave it to a servant-boy who **hastened** [*m-h-r*] to prepare it. (Gen. 18:2,6–8)

In his zeal to meet every need of these unknown visitors to his tent, Abraham runs, *r-v-tz*, twice. In addition, the word "hasten" (or quick), *m-h-r* recurs three times: twice to describe Abraham's own actions, and once as he encourages those around him to rush to the aid of his guests. Abraham's servant, who has been with him throughout his life, knows how essential hospitality is to his master, and understands that the woman who will continue Abraham's line must share his values as well as his ideological passion. As a result, he adds this element to his master's list of criteria, seeking a mate for Isaac who possesses Abraham's capacity for *hesed*. And, in fact, the test he prepares is successful beyond his greatest hopes. Rebekah, like Abraham, **runs,** *r-v-tz*, and **hastens,** *m-h-r*, to tend to the needs of others:[6]

> The servant ran toward her and said, "Please, let me sip a little water from your jar." "Drink, my Lord," she said, and she **quickly** [*m-h-r*] lowered her

---

6. The root *r-v-tz* appears a third time, in Gen. 24:17, in reference to the servant, not Rebekah. Perhaps the servant's emulation of his master's style reinforces his likeness to Abraham. He understands the need for Abraham-like *hesed* because he himself possesses it.

jar upon her hand and let him drink. When she had let him drink his fill, she said, "I will also draw for your camels, until they finish drinking." **Quickly** [*m-h-r*] emptying her jar into he trough, she **ran** [*r-v-tz*] back to the well to draw, and she drew for all his camels ... The maiden **ran** [*r-v-tz*] and told all this to her mother's household. (Gen. 24: 17–20,28)

The servant is amazed by Rebekah's extraordinary likeness to his master. She, and no other, will be the appropriate choice to carry on Abraham's legacy.

As similar as Rebekah is to Abraham, her story represents a radical departure from that of her predecessor, Sarah. While Sarah is "taken" by Abraham in their move toward godly territory (Gen. 12:5), Rebekah makes the choice to go on her own. And while Sarah follows her husband's orders in providing food to needy travelers (18:6), Rebekah discerns and tends to the needs of passing strangers on her own (24:15–20). In practical concerns and in matters of the spirit, it seems that Rebekah is more like a patriarch than a traditional matriarch.

A Return to Matriarchy

Of all the matriarchs in the Book of Genesis, only Rebekah is introduced as a full-fledged character outside the context of her relationship with her husband. Her bold, authoritative actions evoke the autonomous woman of Genesis 1, the female half of the masterful *Ha-adam*. But as Isaac enters the narrative, there are hints that in the presence of a bonafide patriarch, Rebekah will be recast in more traditional terms, as tent-dwelling wife and mother. In a narrative sequence that is similar to the complex portrayal of primordial woman, we now meet a second Rebekah. This matriarch behaves in ways that are similar to the *Ishah* of Genesis 2. Like her, Rebekah will be greatly valued by her husband. Yet at the same time she will be overshadowed by him, as he becomes God's—and the text's—primary focus. Note the changes in Rebekah as she meets Isaac for the first time:

And Isaac went out to meditate[7] in the field toward evening, and, raising his eyes, he saw camels approaching. Raising her eyes, Rebekah saw Isaac. She

---

7. The Hebrew word *lasuah*, translated here as "to meditate," is a *hapax legomenon:* it appears in this exact form only once in the entire biblical canon, and so it is difficult to define. Its root is most likely *s-v-h,* to speak. But since no other person is present, it seems reasonable to conclude that Isaac is engaged in some form of silent meditation. Rashi (24:63, s.v. *lasuah*), basing his comments on *Berakhot* 26b and Gen. Rabbah 60:14, interprets Isaac's actions as prayer before God.

fell down from the camel and said to the servant, "Who is that man walking
in the field toward us?" And the servant said, "That is my master." So she
took her veil and covered herself. The servant told Isaac all the things that he
had done. Isaac then brought her into the tent of his mother Sarah, and he
took Rebekah as his wife. Isaac loved her, and thus found comfort after his
mother's death.[8] (Gen. 24: 63–67)

In Rebekah's initial encounter with Isaac he has "gone out, *y-tz-'*," to the *sadeh*,
the field. In "going out" to the field, Isaac follows the patriarchal model set down by
Abraham who stood at the doorway to his tent, waiting to engage with the world
around him. Previously, it was Rebekah who "went out" to meet others (Gen. 24:15,45).
But now, upon meeting Isaac, she is "brought in" to the more circumscribed—and
traditionally matriarchal—environment, the tent (24:67).

Paradoxically, the field can represent a private, as well as a public, space. In
Genesis the field is an open, yet isolated place where beasts roam (Gen. 2:19,20)
and which is devoid of human habitation (4:8). Thus its occasional occupants may
feel impervious to outside influence and pressure and may feel free to unselfcon-
sciously express themselves. Significantly, Isaac chooses this place to enter into a
state of deep meditation, or perhaps prayer.[9] Isaac's presence in the field indicates
his innate capability to communicate with God, which will become more apparent
as his story unfolds.

In going out to the field, Isaac assumes two traditionally patriarchal roles:
engaging with the outside world and with God. It appears that as Isaac asserts
himself as patriarch, Rebekah grows more matriarchal. Not only will Rebekah
physically move from the public domain to the interior spaces of the tent, we
will soon discover that she will assume a background position in matters of the
spirit as well.

We may detect subtle literary hints of Rebekah's changing stature in a close
reading of her first encounter with Isaac. Whereas Rebekah first "arose" to mount her
camel (Gen. 24: 61), now, in meeting Isaac, she "falls down" from her camel (24: 64).
Perhaps there is special significance in her ascent to, and fall from, this particular animal. In her first appearance, Rebekah's patriarchal qualities are demonstrated by her
alacrity and determination in attending to the servant's camels. Now, upon meeting

---

8. Author's translation.

9. See note 7.

Isaac, Rebekah can no longer maintain her bearings atop the camel. Her fall symbol-izes a shift away from the bold independence of her early narrative.[10]

Rebekah's veil may present yet another symbol of her changing status.[11] Until now, Rebekah has been a visible and vocal presence in her family and in the public sphere. Now, upon learning Isaac's identity, Rebekah covers herself with a veil. Like Sarah, who was frequently unseen (Gen. 18:9) and unheard (12:13–14) by her hus-band and by others, Rebekah now engages in a symbolic act of self-effacement in the presence of the patriarch.[12]

With time, as Rebekah inhabits her mother-in-law's tent, she will come to re-semble her more and more. Like Sarah, Rebekah (Gen. 24:67) will be barren. And like Sarah, she will defer to her husband when it becomes necessary to appeal to God:

> Isaac was forty years old when he took to wife Rebekah, daughter of Bethuel
> the Aramean of Paddan-aram, sister of Laban the Aramean. Isaac pleaded
> with the LORD opposite his wife,[13] because she was barren; and the LORD re-
> sponded to his plea, and his wife Rebekah conceived. (Gen. 25:20–21)

In this passage, a new word for the patriarch's prayer appears: *va-ye'etar*. This word is then echoed in God's response, *va-ye'ater,* from the same root *'-t-r.* The verb repetition suggests a common language and natural communication between God and His male prophet, in which Isaac alone pleads with God and he alone is answered. These verses mark the continuation of early patterns, in which biblical woman is silent while communication with the divine is carried out exclusively by the patriarch.

Yet despite Rebekah's retreat to the more limited role of the traditional matriarch, she enjoys greater devotion from her husband than we have previously seen. Unlike Abraham who never prayed for Sarah, Isaac uses his status as mediator between God and

---

10. See *Ha-amek Davar* on 24:64, s.v. *va-tissa Rivka.* Netziv views Rebekah's fall as symbolic of her faltering status in relation to her husband.

11. Ibid.

12. This reading is borne out by a comparison with the only other verse in the Bible that contains the combination of the root *kh-s-h*, to cover, and the noun *tza'if*, veil. In Gen. 38:14, Tamar covers herself with a veil in order to hide her identity.

13. Author's translation. Both Rashbam (25:21 s.v. *le-nokhah*) and NJPS translate *le-nokhah ishto* as "on behalf of his wife." Rashi claims that both Isaac and Rebekah prayed, each in one corner of the room. Closer to the plain sense of the text is that Isaac alone prayed "opposite" his wife, a reading that is borne out by the only other verses in the Bible in which the term *le-nokhah* appears: Gen. 30:30 and Prov. 4:25. I am grateful to Shmuel Klitsner for directing me to these verses.

woman in an inclusive way, in this case praying for a child in Rebekah's presence (Gen. 25:21). In addition, Rebekah is twice called "his wife," *ishto*, suggesting Isaac's exclusive attachment to her. Of all three patriarchs, only Isaac is monogamous, despite the couple's twenty infertile years together (25:19, 26). Isaac's commitment is accompanied by the first biblical statement of affection by a man for a woman: Isaac "loves" Rebekah (24:67).

In this context, we may revisit Isaac's escorting Rebekah into Sarah's tent, an act that in some ways signals a constricting of Rebekah's role. In addition to connoting limitation, this act suggests a deepening of the emotional bond between husband and wife. When Isaac ushers Rebekah into Sarah's tent he finds "comfort after his mother's death" (Gen. 24:67). By replacing Sarah with Rebekah as the primary woman in his life, Isaac enacts the promise of Genesis 2. "Hence a man leaves his father and mother and clings to his wife, so that they become one flesh" (2:24). Seen this way, Rebekah's entry into the tent is an expression of intimacy between her and Isaac.

It is noteworthy that Rebekah's trajectory parallels that of the Bible's first woman. In Rebekah's first appearance, she is capable and authoritative, like *Ha-adam* in Genesis 1. But then Rebekah begins to resemble the *Ishah* of Genesis 2. Like the *Ishah*, Rebekah is dependent on her husband for communication with God. Yet like her forebear in the Garden of Eden, Rebekah is appreciated by her husband in profound ways.

Perhaps encouraged by Isaac's love and by his inclusion of her in his prayers, Rebekah initiates an encounter with God that breaks the mold of godly exclusion cast by both Sarah and the *Ishah* of the Garden of Eden. When her twin sons struggle within her womb, a distraught Rebekah goes to "inquire[14] of the LORD" (Gen. 25:22–23). In an even more astonishing development, "the LORD answered her."[15] For the first and only time in the annals of Genesis, God delivers a verbal response to a woman in need.

Rebekah's remarkable encounter with God provides the foundation for the stories of later, even more spiritually enabled biblical heroines. But Rebekah's prophetic

---

14. The verb *d-r-sh* can mean "to inquire" or the more emphatic "to demand."

15. It is surprising that many commentators conclude that God's words were delivered through an intermediary. See Rashi (based on Genesis Rabbah 63:7), Rashbam, and Ibn Ezra. In explaining Rashi's view, the super-commentary *Siftei Hahamim* (no. 50, referring to Rashi vs. 23, s.v. *va-yomer Adonai lah*) provides a rationale for this reading: the verse's anomalous word order (this syntactic construction appears only four times in all of the Bible). Instead of the more common *"va-yomer lah Adonai,"* the verse says *"va-yomer Adonai lah."* Despite these efforts, the plain sense of the text is that God spoke to Rebekah.

interlude proves to be an isolated experience for her. Following this encounter, she will not meet God again. Thus, this portion of Rebekah's story is only a temporary digression from a growing move toward greater marginalization. Her narrative will not only inspire later feminine advancement; it will demonstrate the need for redress in the form of subversive sequels.

Why Do I Exist?

In her move toward more familiar matriarchal functioning, Rebekah begins to pour her considerable energies into the challenge of childbearing. Like Sarah, Rebekah will feel desperate and inchoate when faced with fertility problems. Sarah had urgently pleaded with Abraham to produce a child with Hagar in the hopes that she would be "built up" through the surrogate birth (Gen. 16:2). When Rebekah's pregnancy becomes difficult, she indulges in a much more elaborate form of self-doubt, questioning her very right to be: "If this is so, why do I exist?" (25:22). Like Sarah, Rebekah fears disintegration if her hopes for motherhood are unfulfilled.

Rebekah's sense of existential fragility will continue even after her children are born; she will promote the future of her son Jacob as if her own life depended on it. At one point, she will risk her own "blessed" life (Gen. 24:60) by offering to take on any curses Jacob might incur—"Your curse, my son, be upon me!" (27:13). Later, Rebekah will question her existence for a second time, in this instance wondering what point her life has if her son Jacob will marry an inappropriate woman (27:46).

Like Sarah, Rebekah will grow more distant from her husband as her children develop distinct personalities and directions (Gen. 21:9–10; 25:27–28). In Rebekah's narrative, the first signs of divergence from her husband are already detectable at the birth and naming of their twin sons:

> The first one emerged red, like a hairy mantle all over; so they named him Esau. Then his brother emerged, holding on to the heel of Esau; so he[16] named him Jacob. Isaac was sixty years old when they were born. When the boys grew up, Esau became a skillful hunter, a man of the field, but Jacob was a mild man who dwelled in tents. Isaac loved Esau because he had a taste for game; but Rebekah loved Jacob.[17] (Gen. 25:26–28)

---

16. Author's translation. The NJPS translation, "they named him," makes the text flow more naturally, but does not reflect the text's shift from a plural to singular pronoun.
17. Author's translation.

Each parent loves a different son. Perhaps their preferences are based on the perceived similarities between parent and child. Esau, like Isaac, is a man of the *field*, while Jacob inhabits the traditionally matriarchal *tent*. It appears that Isaac and Rebekah, each with a chosen son in tow, grow apart from each other as they retreat to the confines of familiar territory.

We might detect further hints of the growing chasm between husband and wife in the naming of the two sons. Isaac and Rebekah act in tandem to name Esau, "*They* called his name Esau" (Gen. 25:25). Yet when it comes to naming their second son, Rebekah's favorite, the matriarch suddenly vanishes. Only Isaac names this son.[18] He alone attaches the pejorative label of "follower"[19] or "usurper"[20] that will define Jacob for a good deal of his life.

By his lone, unilateral act of naming, Isaac asserts his control not only over his son, but arguably over his wife as well. Despite their conflicting opinions of Jacob's nature and destiny, Isaac's act of naming is exclusive and final. In her state of vulnerability, Rebekah yields, at least overtly, to Isaac's authority. Instead of confronting her husband directly, Rebekah resorts to eavesdropping. She "listened as Isaac spoke to his son Esau" (Gen. 27:5), preparing him to receive the blessings of the first-born son. Her act of stealth recalls Sarah's listening "at the doorway to the tent" when the divine messengers brought word of her impending pregnancy (18:10).

In her exclusion from Isaac's covenantal plans for their sons, Rebekah speaks her mind only to her beloved son, Jacob. Twice, with great urgency, she orders him: "Now, my son, *heed my voice [shema be-koli]*"[21] (Gen. 27:43). Rebekah's words carry tragic irony, reversing Sarah's earlier gains for biblical woman. After a long, mostly silent struggle for her husband's recognition of her essential place in God's covenant, Sarah finally managed to overturn God's declaration at Eden, "Because *you heeded the voice* of your wife ... cursed is the ground"[22] (3:17). Upholding Sarah's superior grasp of His wishes and her position as covenantal partner to Abraham, God instructed Abraham, "Whatever Sarah tells you, *heed her voice*"[23] (21:12). Yet now, despite Rebekah's many

18. See Rashi on 25: 26 s.v. *va-yikra shemo Ya'acov.* Although Rashi brings this as a second possible interpretation (after claiming that God called the child Jacob), the plain sense of the text is that Isaac alone named Jacob.
19. This is the original meaning of the term; since Jacob is born holding Esau's heel, he becomes the "holder of the heel," or the follower.
20. This meaning is consistent with Esau's accusation in Gen. 27:36.
21. Author's translation.
22. Ibid.
23. Ibid.

advances in relation to people and God, her voice is silenced, even more so than that of her reticent predecessor. To Rebekah's mind, Isaac, who holds firm to his own interpretation of his children's destinies, will not heed her voice. Her only chance to be heard is through her son.[24]

Rebekah instructs her son to deceive his father in order to receive the blessings she feels are rightfully his. On one level, Rebekah's subterfuge is successful, as her chosen son in fact receives the coveted blessings (Gen. 27:33). But on a larger plane, she fails in achieving her overall goals. As the narrative unfolds, we find that her triumph comes at an enormous cost, as it sends Abraham's ideological enterprise into a tailspin. In her second command to her son, Rebekah orders him to flee: "Now, my son, **heed my voice.** Flee now [*berah lekha*] to Haran, to my brother Laban"[25] (v. 43).

Abraham began his journey by heeding God's call of *lekh lekha,* go forth. Rebekah's *elekh* (Gen. 24:58) reinforced Abraham's courageous decision and expanded on it by choosing God's path even without a divine command, retracing his steps from Haran toward the promised land of Canaan. Now this same Rebekah orders her child to reverse the process by going *from* Canaan back *toward* Haran, as *lekh lekha* (lit. "go for yourself") is replaced by *berah lekha* (lit. "flee for yourself").[26] As a result of Rebekah's actions and the resulting negative effects within her household, she writes the subversive sequel to an essential part of her own story. By sending her son back to Haran, she sets in motion a plan that will require her son temporarily to abandon the path of two generations.

Rebekah's actions cause further damage as Esau, the wronged brother, has thoughts of killing his brother. As we have seen, to protect Jacob, Rebekah orders him to flee. But again she does not dare reveal her true thoughts to her husband. Instead she says the following:

> I am disgusted with my life because of the Hittite women. If Jacob marries a Hittite woman like these, from among the native women, what good will life be to me? (Gen. 27:46)

---

24. Perhaps Jacob's response to his mother's "heed my voice" supports the comparison to the Garden of Eden narrative. Jacob says: "If my father touches me, I shall appear to him as a trickster and bring upon myself *a curse,* not a blessing (Gen. 27:12)." In this case, listening to the matriarch may again bring a curse upon man. I am grateful to Shmuel Klitsner for this insight.

25. Author's translation.

26. I am grateful to Daniel Shapiro for this insight.

Drawing on a known fear of Isaac's[27] (Gen. 26:34), Rebekah refashions the danger that she herself has created. Intermarriage, not fratricide, should concern Isaac, and so he must now urgently lend his blessing to Jacob's flight. To make her point, Rebekah resorts to familiar language, the dramatic questioning of her existence (see 25:22). In her final recorded speech, Rebekah's words are infused with deception and self-doubt, a far cry from her early succinct truths and determined actions.

Rebekah: Reversal and Continuity

In many notable ways, Rebekah's story reverses the story of Sarah. To begin with, Rebekah's early autonomous behavior overturns Sarah's position of dependence on her husband. In addition, the emotional bond that first characterizes Rebekah's relationship with Isaac bridges the distance that so often separated Sarah and Abraham. Rebekah makes great strides in relation to God, as well. Her "inquiring of the LORD" replaces Sarah's silence before God in matters of fertility.[28] In this part of Rebekah's chronicle, God and the male prophet are more inclusive of woman, and woman herself is more assertive. *Ha-adam* merges with the best part of *Ishah*, as woman is loved, valued, and spiritually enabled.

But despite these advances, Rebekah's narrative also complements and continues the stories of her predecessors, as she faces marginalization by God and man. As a result of her exclusion, Rebekah invests virtually all her energies in her chosen son Jacob. At the end of her story, Rebekah comes to resemble *Havvah*, a woman who on the one hand finds legitimacy and redemption in her role as mother, but on the other hand risks losing her sense of self with her exclusive focus.

Childbirth or "Death": Sarah, Rebekah, Rachel

The motif of woman defined narrowly as progenitor poignantly finds its way into the generation after Rebekah—with Jacob's beloved wife, Rachel. In presenting her character, the text returns to many of the themes established by

---

27. Rebekah draws on a rare moment of unity between herself and her husband as well. Both were bitter about Esau's choice of a Hittite wife, as the Hittites are a branch of the Canaanites (Gen. 26:34).

28. Rebekah stands out among all the matriarchs of Genesis as the only one personally to receive God's word as prophecy, rather than as a rebuke. God spoke to Sarah only to reprimand her for laughing, and He never once addressed Rachel or Leah. Moreover, Rebekah is unique among the matriarchs in her ability to speak to God.

the previous matriarchs. Like her mother-in-law Rebekah (Gen. 24:67), Rachel is loved by her husband (29:30). Like Sarah (16:3–4), Rachel has a second, more fecund rival for her husband's affections (29:31). Rachel, like Sarah, is silent before God, yet God makes the effort to "hear" and "remember" her (30:22), much as He "took note" of Sarah (21:1). Like Sarah (16:5), Rachel engages in an angry confrontation with her husband due to her inability to conceive (30:1–2). In her frustration, Rachel, like Rebekah (25:22), questions her very existence. But Rachel takes her existential reflections to new dramatic heights with her cry to Jacob: "Give me children, for if not I shall die" (30:1).[29] Rachel's anguished words underscore the frustration and despair frequently experienced by the matriarchs of Genesis. If woman is defined solely on the basis of motherhood, infertility renders her life irrelevant.

The comments of the 15th-century Spanish exegete Isaac Arama[30] address the tragic error in Rachel's thinking:

> The two names *"Ishah"* and *"Havvah"* indicate two purposes. The first teaches that woman was taken from man, emphasizing that, like him, she was capable of understanding and advancing intellectually and morally, as were the matriarchs and many righteous women and prophetesses, and as is indicated by the literal meaning of Proverbs 31 about the "woman of worth" (*eshet hayil*). The second alludes to the power of childbearing and rearing children, as is indicated by the name *Havvah*, the mother of all the living. A woman deprived of the power of childbearing will be deprived of the secondary purpose and be left with the ability to do evil or good, like the man who is sterile ... Jacob was therefore angry with Rachel when she said, "give me children or if not I shall die." [By exhibiting anger he sought to] reprimand her and make her understand this all-important principle: her childlessness did not render her a dead person as far as their joint purpose in life was concerned, just the same as it would be [i.e. he would not have been considered as dead] had he been childless.[31]

---

29. Author's translation.
30. Arama's philosophical commentary to the Pentateuch is called *"Akedat Yitzhak."* I first learned of this excerpt—as did many of my peers—from Nechama Leibowitz's frequent references to it in her classes about Rachel's barrenness. This excerpt was translated by Aryeh Newman in Leibowitz's *Bereishit*, 334. I have made some minor changes to Newman's translation.
31. *Akedat Yitzhak* on *Parashat* Bereishit, ninth *sha'ar*.

Arama identifies two, rather than three dimensions of biblical woman,[32] and argues for their full integration. In his interpretation of Jacob's rebuke he uncovers a message that is strikingly similar to what we have seen thus far. Reducing woman to a single dimension—the life-giving *Havvah*—is not only an affront to woman. It also undermines God's plan for a multi-faceted creation, which He deemed "very good" (Gen. 1:31).

The Book of Genesis leaves us with the echoes of women who feel diminished and dependent. Although man and God take strides toward woman's greater inclusion and expansion, we have not yet arrived at the truly subversive sequel that will offer a more comprehensive reversal of negative patterns and a return to more encouraging ones. But the theme of infertility, so central in measuring woman's status before God and man, is absent throughout the rest of the Pentateuch. To pick up the thematic and literary trails set down by the women of the Book of Genesis, we must turn to the books of the Prophets.

The Book of Judges: Radical Satire

Our search for the subversive sequel to the early matriarchal narratives takes us first to what seems to be an unlikely destination. The story of Deborah, religious and martial leader of Israel, makes no mention of infertility, spousal conflict, childbirth, or a struggle for succession. In place of the vulnerable, narrowly defined wife and mother, we are met with an intrepid commander and prophetess:

> Deborah, woman of Lappidoth, was a prophetess; she led Israel in that time. She used to sit under the Palm of Deborah, between Ramah and Bethel in the hill country of Ephraim, and the Israelites would come to her for decisions.
>
> She summoned Barak son of Abinoam, of Kedesh in Naphtali, and said to him, "The Lord, the God of Israel, has commanded: Go [*lekh*] march up to Mount Tabor, and take with you ten thousand men of Nahptali and Zebulun. And I will draw Sisera, Jabin's army commander with his chariots and his troops, toward you up to the Wadi Kishon; and I will deliver him into your hands." (Judg. 4:4–7)

---

32. While we have pointed to three dimensions of woman: *Ha-adam, Ishah,* and *Havvah,* Arama suggests only two, collapsing the first two into the name *"Ishah."* Although Arama ignores the relational side of woman, as manifest by *Ishah* in Gen. 2, his analysis brings him quite close to our analysis of woman in these chapters.

The narrative introduces two radiant figures: Deborah, a woman of *Lappidoth* (literally, torches)[33] and Barak, whose name means lightning.[34] Their combined luminescence would extinguish the mighty Sisera, who had "oppressed Israel ruthlessly for twenty years" (Judg. 4:3). But sparks of irony find their way into the story as one of the flames is reluctant to shine:

> But Barak said to her, "If you will go with me, I will go; if not, I will not go." "Very well, I will go with you," she answered. "However, there will be no glory for you in the course you are taking, for then the LORD will deliver Sisera into the hands of a woman." So Deborah went with Barak to Kedesh. Barak then mustered Zebulun and Naphtali at Kedesh; ten thousand men marched up after him; and Deborah also went up with him. (Judg. 4:8–10)

Unlike Abraham and Rebekah, who felt moved to bravely "go" toward God, Barak equivocates when God's messenger, Deborah, tells him to "go" into battle. He will go, but only if Deborah comes with him. Otherwise, his response is the definitive "*lo elekh*, I will not go." In this tale of reversals, a satiric tone takes hold of the narrative. Not only are the spiritual positions of man and woman completely transposed; man will not even take steps toward fulfilling God's word without a reassuring feminine buffer. Man is unsure of himself, while woman is a confident oracle, general, and judge. Although Deborah agrees to Barak's terms, she gives voice to the unprecedented nature of their situation, winking at the reader in recognition of the ironic state of affairs. She will hold his hand in battle, but he must know that his reputation will pay the price, the merciless ridicule of society.

Another story in the Book of Judges gives voice to society's scorn for those who seem overly reliant on women. In this passage, the evil Abimelech, son of Gideon goes to battle:

> Abimelech proceeded to Thebez; he encamped at Thebez and occupied it. Within the town was a fortified tower; and all the citizens of the town, men

---

33. While the construction *"eshet x"* generally means "wife of," it can also be a description of the woman ("woman of"), as in *"eshet hayil,"* a woman of valor (Prov. 31:10). Ehrlich, in *Mikra Kifshuto* p. 51, claims Lappidoth is not the name of Deborah's husband; if so, his lineage would have been listed. *"Eshet lappidot"* is then a description of Deborah as a woman of flames, parallel to Barak, man of lightning.

34. For a confluence of these two terms, see Nahum 2:5. In addition, both *"berakim"* and *"lapidim"* appear in the Exodus account of the God's giving the Torah (19:16; 20:15). The terms seem to be used interchangeably to refer to lightning.

and women, took refuge there. They shut themselves in and went up on the roof of the tower. Abimelech pressed forward to the tower and attacked it. He approached the door of the tower to set it on fire. But a woman dropped an upper millstone on Abimelech's head and cracked his skull. He immediately cried out to his attendant, his arms-bearer, "Draw your dagger and finish me off, that they not may say of me, 'A woman killed him!'" So his attendant stabbed him, and he died. (Judg. 9:50–54)

Fully aware of prevailing attitudes, Deborah's words mock the mockers. Society and its general are fully dependent on a woman for their salvation. Yet, if acknowledged, such dependence would be considered a source of unspeakable shame.

It is not by chance that the character who articulates society's misogynous perspective is named Abimelech. This was the name of Genesis's kings of Gerar, who were twice involved in wife-sister imbroglios,[35] once with Sarah and once with Rebekah. Abimelech may be seen as a symbol of patriarchal attitudes, in which husbands and kings vie for possession of silently suffering matriarchs. Many of these sexist tendencies continue into the Book of Judges, yet suddenly a sardonic, countervailing voice presents itself, the voice of Deborah. Her comments to Barak intimate: let the hypocritical public continue to belittle the worth of women out of one side of its mouth while pleading for their help out of the other.

With a combination of Deborah's strategic guidance and her moral support, the war is won. Continuing its wry tone, the text depicts this woman's military triumph in the most bombastic terms possible, invoking the defeat of the Egyptians at the Sea of Reeds. In both narratives, heavy emphasis is placed on "chariots," "pursuing," and "fleeing." In both "the LORD threw [the enemy] into a panic [*va-yahom*]" (Exod. 14:24; Judg. 4:15).[36] Both stories reach the same triumphant claim, in which "not one [of the enemy] remained" (Exod. 14:28; Judg. 4:16).[37] With unabashed hyperbolic flourish, this text casts Deborah as Moses, the prophet who brought the world's greatest empire to its knees. Lest the allusion be overlooked, Deborah, like Moses, sings an elaborate song of praise to God. Like him she opens her song with the momentous term

---

35. It is likely that Abimelech is not a proper name, but a title, like Pharaoh. Thus the Abimelech of Genesis 26 need not be the Abimelech of Genesis 20.

36. The root *h-m-m* is used in this form in these two verses, and never again in all of the Bible.

37. Author's translation. The Hebrew in Exodus and Judges is nearly identical. In Exodus the verse reads *lo nishar bahem ad ehad*, and in Judges, *to nishar ad ehad*.

"*Ashirah*, I will sing" (Judg. 5:3; Exod. 15:1). The Book of Judges is not satisfied with merely positing new, women-centered narratives. It insists on rewriting familiar stories, literarily transplanting women into the most exalted male roles.

The battle is won, but woman's work is not yet complete. With the evil Sisera still at large, a new heroine ascends the stage: Jael, wife of Heber the Kenite.

> Jael came out to greet Sisera and said to him, "Come in, my Lord, come in here, do not be afraid." So he entered her tent, and she covered him with a blanket. He said to her, "Please let me have some water; I am thirsty." She opened a skin of milk and gave him some to drink and she covered him again. He said to her, "Stand at the entrance of the tent. If anybody comes and asks you if there is anybody here, say 'No.' Then Jael wife of Heber took a tent pin and grasped the mallet. When he was fast asleep from exhaustion, she approached him stealthily and drove the pin through his temple [*be-rakato*] till it went down to the ground. Thus he died. (Judg. 4:18–21)

Jael's story takes place in the tent, formerly the protected, interior space of the biblical matriarch. Sarah cooked her meals there; Abraham viewed it as woman's natural dwelling place. Upon her betrothal to Isaac, Rebekah too entered the tent. She then developed a preference for the one of her two children who was created in the matriarchal image, the tent-dwelling Jacob.

The Book of Judges, in its continued efforts to overhaul our assumptions about biblical woman, now takes aim at the primary symbol of woman's narrow definition, the tent. Jael, like Sarah and Rebekah, is in her tent. At first, that is all the unsuspecting Sisera sees. He does not note Jael's unorthodox behavior as she comes out to meet him, and, in patriarchal language, urges him to deter from his path, *sura*, and enter her domain (Gen. 18:1–3; 19:1–3). Oblivious to her deviation from established etiquette, Sisera addresses Jael as biblical men have traditionally spoken to their women: "Please let me drink a little water [*hashkini na me'at mayyim*]" (Gen. 24:43). But again, rather than conforming to the stage directions of a familiar script, Jael writes a new one. Instead of merely quenching Sisera's thirst with "a little water," she prepares him for sleep, giving him milk and blankets.

Perhaps responding instinctively to Jael's managerial behavior, Sisera, like Jael, breaks with convention. He asks her to leave the confines of the tent and move to its opening, *petah ha-ohel*, a position previously associated with Abraham

(Judg. 4:20; Gen. 18:1). At Sisera's suggestion, Jael moves from matriarchal to patriarchal position so that she can ward off unwanted visitors.[38]

In a brazen rejection of earlier role delineations, the text now presents a woman who is undercover agent, sentry, and assassin. Jael redraws established feminine models by providing man with liquid not to sustain or revive him (as in Gen. 21:7–8; 24:17–18), but to prepare him for his death. Next, she grabs hold of the tent's very foundations, the tent pin. By using it as a weapon, Jael strikes not only at Sisera's temple, but at our own sense of the tent-oriented structure of matriarchal society.[39] With her action, she delivers a crushing blow both to the mighty general and to our stereotypes regarding biblical woman.

Barak, who has been chasing Sisera, is now met with a surprise:

> Now Barak appeared in pursuit of Sisera. Jael went out to greet him and said, "Go and I will show you [lekh ve-areka] the man you are looking for." He went inside with her, and there Sisera was lying dead, with the pin in his temple [be-rakato].[40] (Judg. 4:22)

Earlier, Barak agreed to "go" into God's war only under Deborah's protective wing. Jael now promises him that the victory will be complete if he will follow her instruction and "go" one more time.[41] Jael's words, "Go and I will show you," recall God's initial charge to Abraham, "*Go* forth from your land … to the land that *I will show you*" (Gen. 12:1). In fact, these are the only two verses in the entire Bible in which the words *lekh*, go, and *areka*, I will show you, appear together. Jael coopts God's words for ironic purpose. Instead of instructing Barak, as God instructed Abraham, to go out into the world and achieve greatness on his own, Jael summons Barak to follow her on the short distance to the inside of her tent. There he would discover that his job has already been done; the mighty Sisera has been felled by a woman. With this literary parallel, the text again points out the absurdity of a sexist society. On the one hand, its leaders display a near-total dependence on women.

---

38. The text's unorthodox grammar supports Sisera's shift to patriarchal language. When he tells Jael to stand at the tent's opening, he uses the masculine imperative *amod* instead of the feminine form of the verb.

39. The verb used to depict Jael's striking of Sisera, *t-k-*, plays ironically on the verb for pitching a tent, *t-k-*. Jael destroys the tent with the same verb that is normally used to erect it.

40. Author's translation.

41. The word *lekh*, "go," is anomalous here. Jael should have beckoned him to "come," in order to follow her back into the tent. To smooth over this irregularity, NJPS translates *lekh* as "come."

On the other hand, their dependence must be hidden so that the image of the conquering masculine hero can be maintained.

To hammer home the message even more strongly, Jael strikes the tent pin into Sisera's temple, *be-rakato,* a pun on the name of the ineffectual male would-be savior, *Barak.* When Jael strikes Sisera, she effectively strikes Barak as well, a general who chases shadows while two women defy society's assumptions and preconceptions by winning his battles. Together, Deborah and Jael, aware of the novelty and ironic humor in the situation, expose the truth, a new and seemingly limitless gamut of women's capabilities.

This new perspective rings out in Deborah's song of triumph:

> In the days of Shamgar son of Anath,
> In the days of Jael pathways [of caravans] ceased, [*hadelu orahot*]
> And wayfarers went
> By roundabout paths.
> Deliverance ceased,
> Ceased in Israel,
> Till I Deborah arose
> Until I arose, a mother in Israel![42] (Judg. 5:6–7)

An oblique reference to Sarah, the woman of the tent, infuses Deborah's poem with ironically seditious intent. The Hebrew words *h-d-l orah,* which literally mean a pathway that stops, occur in only two verses in the Bible: in Deborah's poem and in reference to Sarah's infertility. When Sarah overheard the prediction of her pregnancy, the text informs us that "Abraham and Sarah were old, advanced in years; Sarah had stopped the menstrual periods, literally 'the pathway,' of women, *hadal lihyot le-Sarah orah kanashim*" (Gen. 18:11). As a result, Sarah had scoffed at her own value with the words, "after I am withered, am I to have enjoyment?" (Gen. 18:12). Deborah uses the language of Sarah's hopeless infertility, *h-d-l orah,* in an ironic manner, to refer to the Israelites, for whom traditional avenues of salvation have ceased. With her choice of words Deborah strongly hints that even when traditional "pathways" are closed off to both the Israelites and to women, there are new paths—unorthodox, unexpected, and previously unimagined—to pursue.

---

42. Author's translation.

In the story of Deborah and Jael, the female protagonists do not merely speak of new paths; they embark on them as well. Despite the absence of children in the biblical record of her life, Deborah calls herself a "mother in Israel" (Judg. 5:7). She nurtures her people by prophesying, judging, and leading them to military victory. Jael, too, is a mother of sorts, using her tent to tend to the physical needs of others. But, like Deborah, she breaks all maternal molds, as Jael kills a man in order to save many others. These are women who, in a defiant rejoinder to Rachel's desperate cry, do not consider themselves "dead" without children in their narrative. On the contrary, each embraces life to the fullest as an *eshet hayil,* a woman of worth.

These two groundbreaking "mothers" are contrasted with a third mother in the poem, the nameless mother of Sisera.

> Through the window peered Sisera's mother,
> Behind the lattice she whined:
> "Why is his chariot so late in coming?
> Why so late the clatter of his wheels?" (Judg. 5:28)

Like Abimelech in Genesis (26:8), Sisera's mother "peers, *sh-k-p,* out the window." The view from her window is similar to that of Abimelech and the patriarchal structure in which he functioned. Women—wives and mothers—are at the mercy of their men, silently complying, often silently waiting for their return. This type of waiting, wailing mother contrasts starkly with the new model that Deborah presents, a mother who "rises up" to confront her own foes. Deborah's vocabulary emphasizes the contrast between her and Sisera's passively helpless mother. Deborah uses the word *k-v-m,* "to rise" twice and the word *'-v-r,* "to awaken" four times in reference to herself.

In Deborah's song, Sisera's mother is comforted by her wise female advisor, who assures her that her son is safe:

> The wisest of her ladies gives answer;
> She too, replies to herself:
> "They must be dividing the spoil they have found:
> A damsel or two [lit. "a womb or two"] for each man [lit. "for the head of man"],
> Spoil of dyed cloth for Sisera,
> Spoil of embroidered cloths,
> A couple of embroidered cloths
> Round every neck as spoil." (Judg. 5:29–30)

On the plainest level, Sisera's delay can be attributed to his gathering the rewards of his victory. In this case, "a womb or two for the head of man" alludes to the sexual favors he would garner from a woman or two. But Deborah places stinging double entendres into the mouth of the female advisor, hinting at the dubious payment Sisera actually received. The two women—"wombs" in the poem's graphic language—who greet him are Deborah and Jael, neither of whom is known for the productivity of her womb. These two women combine their efforts "for the head of man." But rather than gratifying the sexual appetite of Sisera the conquering hero, these women *remove* his head.

Deborah's vivid wordplay continues as she alludes to the colors around Sisera's neck. These could be the colored cloths given a conquering general, or the crimson-colored blood that quite literally encircles Sisera's head as Jael strikes it. No subject is too sacred for Deborah's song. She mocks men and women alike in their persistent underestimation of women. She laughs at the gruesome death her enemy has incurred, and finally she derides conventional motherhood as embodied by the woeful mother of Sisera.

In this satirically subversive sequel to the early matriarchal stories, with their focus on tents and on childbearing, Deborah and Jael define motherhood in radically new ways. Mothers can be warriors or oracles, strategists or poets. Different as they are from the tent-dwelling mothers, they too are blessed. Moreover, in the words of Deborah the prophetess:

> Most blessed of women be Jael, wife of Heber the Kenite, more blessed than women in tents [*minashim ba-ohel tevorakh*].[43] (Judg. 5:24)

In the new philosophy expounded by this chapter, a great blessing befalls those women who dare to pass the tent's threshold on their way to the outside world. They are blessed *even more* than are the women of the tent.

Manoah's Wife: From the Tent to the Field

With its irreverent perspective and satiric eye, the story of Deborah introduces the possibility of profound reversals of traditional gender roles. Earlier in the

---

43. I prefer this translation to that of NJPS: "Most blessed of women in tents." Support for reading the *mem* as an indication of comparison—*a* more than *b*—may be found in Deut. 7:14: "*barukh tihyeh mi-kol ha-ammim*," which NJPS renders "you shall be blessed *above* all other peoples." I am grateful to Daniel Schwartz for suggesting this proof text.

story of Rebekah, woman lost her balance, falling off her camel when meeting man. In this version of her story, she remains confidently and securely poised, ready to lead all followers.

With these extraordinary developments as background, we are prepared for the possibility of a radically new version of the story of the redemption of the barren woman. The Deborah/Jael story serves as a forewarning that the familiar tale might be severely tampered with. We sense that we are unlikely to encounter a hapless woman, dependent on her spiritually empowered husband to pray to God to help her conceive. And in fact the thirteenth chapter of the Book of Judges lives up to, and then and exceeds, expectations. This passage will first draw on the language and themes of the Genesis narratives, thereby affirming its place on the continuum of the developing relations between biblical matriarchs and patriarchs. But it will then manipulate the earlier stories to such an extent that it will go beyond subversive sequel and into the realm of parody.

The story begins with the introduction of a man and his barren wife, a script with which we are now most familiar:

> There was a certain man from Zorah, of the stock of Dan, whose name was Manoah. His wife was barren and had borne no children. (Judg. 13:2)

Like Sarah, this woman's infertility interrupts numerous generations of unimpeded reproduction,[44] and like Sarah, her condition is expressed in double language to reflect the novelty her situation represents. But almost immediately, these similarities give way to an unexpected new course:

> An angel of the Lord appeared to the woman and said to her, "You are barren and have borne no children; but you shall conceive and bear a son. Now be careful not to drink wine or other intoxicant, or to eat anything unclean. For you are going to conceive and bear a son; let no razor touch his head, for the boy is to be a nazirite[45] to God from the womb on. He shall be the first to deliver Israel from the Philistines." (Judg. 13:3–5)

---

44. In fact, this is the first barren woman on record since the matriarchs of Genesis.
45. A nazirite is one who is "set apart for the LORD" (see Num. 6:1-21), and who must maintain a higher level of purity by abstaining from all intoxicants, by refraining from cutting the hair, and from coming into contact with dead bodies.

In a rare departure from accepted biblical protocols, "an angel of God appeared to *the woman*."[46] This unadorned phrase resounds and startles. To begin with,
it is highly unusual for God to send a messenger directly to a woman. But in an even
more surprising twist, God sends the angel to a woman who has expressed no dis-
tress regarding her barren state and who has not asked her husband to intercede
with God on her behalf. The angel simply appears, *va-yera:* unbidden, unheralded,
and in relation to woman, most uncommon.

It seems that the woman is unprepared for this event. Rather than engaging the visitor in established modes of prophetic discourse, her first reaction is
to seek out her husband, whom she deems to be the more natural recipient of
divine revelation:

> The woman went and told her husband, "A man of God came to me; he looked
> like an angel of God, very frightening. I did not ask him where he was from, nor
> did he tell me his name. He said to me, 'You are going to conceive and bear a son.
> Drink no wine or other intoxicant, and eat nothing unclean, for the boy is to be
> a nazirite to God from the womb to the day of his death!'" (Judg. 13:6–7)

Despite her unfamiliarity and discomfort with receiving God's word, the
woman's account to her husband reveals an intuitive understanding of the norms of
human-divine interaction: one must recognize the bearer of the miraculous news as
an angel, while refraining from asking his name. The biblical text introduced these
norms in Genesis, in the story of Jacob wrestling with a godly being. There the text
recounts Jacob's awareness of the divine nature of his interlocutor (Gen. 32:31), as
well as his error in asking the visitor's name. In response to Jacob's misguided query,
the man of God sharply admonishes, "Why do you ask my name!" (Gen. 32:30–31).
In contrast, Manoah's wife is quick to grasp the godly essence of her caller and she
knows better than to ask him his name. Yet it seems from her repeated, dutiful relaying of all divine communication to her husband that she is slow to grasp the basic
fact that *she* is the intended recipient of God's messages.

Unlike his wife, Manoah will consistently misread divine cues. He *will* ask the
angel his name (Judg. 13:17), thereby eliciting the identical rebuke that was delivered

---

46. While the appearance of an angel to a woman is not unprecedented (see Gen. 16:7–13; 21:17–18), the
phrase "an angel of God appeared to the woman" is. When angels appear to Hagar, the conventional
term for God's deliberate visitation to a human being, *"va-yera,"* is missing. Instead, one angel "finds
her," *"va-yimtza'a"* (Gen. 16:7) and another "calls" to her, *"va-yikra"* (21:17).

to Jacob in Genesis (v. 18). Moreover, despite the mounting evidence, he will *not* recognize the visitor as an angel (v. 16).[47]

Manoah and his wife both err in assuming that he, and not she, is the primary target of the angel's words. After hearing the details of his wife's encounter, Manoah responds with an entreaty:

> Manoah pleaded with the LORD. "Oh, my LORD!" he said, "please let the man of God that You sent come to us again, and let him instruct us how to act with the child that is to be born." (Judg. 13:8)

With these words, Manoah beseeches God to restore order in divine-human relations. He, the man, should be included in all future communications regarding his wife's pregnancy. Perhaps Manoah fears a demotion to the role of the traditional matriarch, in which he, like Sarah, would have to resort to overhearing messages related to the upcoming birth. In presenting Manoah's request, the text indulges in an ironic twist on recognized patriarchal language. Like Isaac, "Manoah pleaded, *va-ye'etar*, with the LORD" (Gen. 25:21). But whereas Isaac was duly answered, *va-ye'ater*, by God (Gen. 25:21), no such response awaits Manoah, as the satiric tale continues.

> God heeded Manoah's plea, and the angel of God came to the woman again. She was sitting in the field and her husband Manoah was not with her. (Judg. 13:9)

Technically, God grants Manoah's wish by resending the angel. But adding to his insult, the angel appears again to *the woman*. If that were not sufficiently humiliating, the text adds: "She was sitting in the field" (Judg. 13:9). In this tale of reversals, the woman inhabits the former patriarchal space. Rather than remaining inside her tent, waiting to receive a mediated account of God's word, she is now in the field, where human beings can potentially communicate directly with God (Gen. 24:63). For added emphasis as to her exclusive suitability to receive God's word, the text assures us, "And Manoah her husband was not with her."

While we as readers are increasingly convinced of Manoah's irrelevance to this divine interaction, his wife continues to behave as though God's word were directed primarily toward him. Even more deferential than before, the woman now

---

47. Although as we will see in the coming verses, Manoah understands that in some sense the visitor is a "man of God" (Judg. 13:6), the text informs us that Manoah does not recognize him as an angel (v. 16).

hurries to fetch her husband while the visitor is still present, so that Manoah will be assured of hearing God's prophecy directly.

> The woman ran in haste to tell her husband. She said to him, "The man who came to me before has just appeared to me." Manoah promptly followed his wife. He came to the man and asked him: "Are you the man who spoke to my wife?" "Yes," he answered. Then Manoah said, "May your words soon come true! What rules shall be observed for the boy?" The angel of the Lord said to Manoah, "The woman must abstain from all the things against which I warned her. She must not eat anything that comes from the grapevine, or drink wine or other intoxicant, or eat anything unclean. She must observe all that I commanded her." (Judg. 13:10–14)

When at last Manoah comes face to face with the man of God, he asks for identification, in a further attempt to assert his position as master of the proceedings. Then, assuming that the protocols have been set straight and that he has taken over as family spokesman, Manoah asks, "What rules shall be observed for the boy?" But his ego suffers yet another blow as the angel responds, "*The woman* must abstain from all the things against which I warned *her*."[48] He goes on to repeat the woman's basic restrictions, ending with the reprise, "She must observe all that I commanded *her*." In short, the necessary information has already reached its appropriate recipient, the woman.

At this point, the story takes a farcical turn, with its exaggerated description of Manoah's obtuseness in recognizing the true nature of God's messenger.

> Manoah said to the angel of the Lord, "Let us detain you and prepare a kid for you." But the angel of the Lord said to Manoah, "If you detain me, I shall not eat your food; and if you present a burnt offering, offer it to the Lord."— For Manoah did not know that he was an angel of the Lord. So Manoah said to the angel of the Lord, "What is your name? We should like to honor you

---

48. According to the plain sense of the text, the pronouns are all in third person feminine and refer to the woman. There is, however, room for an intriguing grammatical ambiguity, in which the pronouns could be understood to be in the second person masculine. In this case they would refer to Manoah. (I am grateful to Martin Lockshin for pointing out the ambiguity.) Perhaps the ambiguous pronouns highlight the chasm between reality and Manoah's expectations. Although the angel speaks of the woman as the parent responsible for the child's spiritual welfare, Manoah continues to hear his words as if they applied to him.

when your words come true." The angel said to him, "You must not ask for my name; it is unknowable!"

Manoah took the kid and the meal offering and offered them up on the rock to the Lord; and a marvelous thing happened while Manoah and his wife looked on. As the flames leaped up from the altar toward the sky, the angel of the Lord ascended in the flames of the altar, while Manoah and his wife looked on; and they flung themselves on their faces to the ground.—The angel of the Lord never appeared again to Manoah and his wife.—Manoah then realized that it had been an angel of the Lord. (Judg. 13:19–21)

In his exchange with the angel, Manoah makes every possible mistake. First, he offers to feed the guest "for Manoah did not know that he was an angel of the LORD" (Judg. 13:16).[49] Next, as we have seen, unlike his wife, who knows when to keep silent, Manoah asks the visitor his name. Despite the angel's refusal to answer and the accompanying reproach he delivers, Manoah still fails to grasp his identity. The ensuing description of events borders on the preposterous. The angel "ascended in the flames of the altar while Manoah and his wife looked on" (v. 19), yet still Manoah remains unconvinced of its divine nature. It is only when the angel fails to return, that "Manoah *then* realized that it had been an angel of the LORD" (v. 21).

Although he has at long last discovered the nature of the visitor, the farce continues as Manoah is still perplexed about the purpose and consequences of his visit:

And Manoah said to his wife, "We shall surely die, for we have seen a divine being." But his wife said to him, "Had the Lord meant to take our lives, He would not have accepted a burnt offering and meal offering from us, nor let us see all these things; and He would not have made such an announcement to us." (Judg. 13:22–23)

With what is perhaps strained patience, Manoah's wife explains to her husband that the purpose of the divine visit was information, not annihilation. Her

---

49. Manoah's obtuseness offers another intriguing similarity between this story and the story of Rebekah. He offers a kid, *gedi izim*, and bread (Judg. 13:15,16,19), the same items Rebekah prepared in the deception of her husband, Isaac (Gen. 27:9,17). In their exclusion from God's messages, both Rebekah and Manoah make mistakes with these two foodstuffs.

words are obvious to every reader, but they must be explicitly articulated to the master of the house. Playful throughout, the story ends with a mischievous flourish: "The woman bore a son and named him Samson. The boy grew up, and the LORD blessed him" (Judg. 13:24).

Unlike all other formerly infertile women who "conceive" before they give birth (Gen. 21:2; 25:21; 29:32; 30:23), there is no hint of a husband in this child's formation. The text goes to almost absurd extremes in highlighting the woman while expunging Manoah from the record of Samson's birth, denying him credit even for his act of fertilization. To complete the picture, the woman names her son with no participation of her husband.

It seems incongruous that despite her obvious prophetic advantage, the hero of the story, "Manoah's wife," is left nameless. This is especially troubling given the significance of names in the biblical chronicle, as we have seen in chapter 2 of this volume. Perhaps her anonymity compels the reader to notice time and again the remarkable novelty inherent in the tale. The events described, previously the sole province of man, now regularly befall a character simply called "the woman."[50] The angel too rejects all labeling, as seen by his reprimand to Manoah, "You must not ask for my name ...!" (Judg. 13:18). The angel's namelessness requires the text to repeatedly refer to him simply as "the angel of God." By leaving both of its main characters nameless, the reader is compelled to come face to face with the extraordinary reality this narrative presents, the meeting of God's angel and a woman.

In addition to highlighting her gender, the repetition of "the woman," *ha-ishah* in Hebrew, has further ironic overtones, as it draws us back to the Garden of Eden and the second manifestation of primordial woman. The *Ishah* of the Garden was dependent on her husband to deliver God's words to her, including God's prohibition of eating from the forbidden tree. In contrast, in this story it is the *Ishah* who serves as man's conduit to the divine, delivering a message to *him*

---

50. There are numerous biblical narratives in which women are not named. (See especially 2 Kings, for the story of the unnamed heroine, "the *Shunamit.*") I do not mean to suggest that each time this happens the text seeks to upgrade the status of woman. I suggest that here, in this story of reversals, this familiar style is used in an ironic way. In general, the absence of women's names is highly disturbing and flies on the face of Buber's contention that "only a person of name can 'have dealings with *Elohim.*'" See chapter 2, p. 47 and note 35. Surely the absence of names in relation to women who communicate with God is a textual phenomenon in need of the type of *tikkun* afforded by the subversive sequel.

about forbidden consumption, in this case wine and other intoxicants for the mother of the nazirite child.[51]

At every stage of the story, Manoah's wife draws the correct conclusion, while her husband misses the mark. Yet despite her superior comprehension of events, her prophecy seems accidental. She receives it without fully grasping the fact that it is intended for her ears. She never initiates contact with the angel, nor does she respond to his messages. With dutiful regularity she informs her husband of developments and waits for his responses. Perhaps she sees her prophetic abilities as similar to Rebekah's, as a one-time phenomenon. Yet despite her hesitance, the narrative voice of the text is unequivocal in its endorsement of this woman as God's chosen vessel.

All in all, this story combines with the narrative of Deborah to posit an extravagantly overstated alternative to the patterns set down by the Book of Genesis. There is no pretense of evenhandedness or of an equitable solution to the imbalance in male-female relations. Instead, the stories present a parodic counter-weight to the prevailing biblical norm of male privilege. Taking the stories of Deborah and Manoah's wife as a unit, man is presented as ineffectual and as spiritually and physically dependent on woman. To return to the image of Rebekah's fall from her camel upon meeting Isaac: in these stories, if one figure falters in the male-female encounter, it is the man.

As these stories entertain, they also dramatically expand the spectrum of possibilities for biblical woman. But they raise concerns as well. For instance, why, in correcting the early imbalances between man and woman, must the Bible overreach? Must male-female relations always be a zero-sum game, with God privileging one at the expense of the other? As we continue to explore female-centered texts, we look for signs of repair. We seek a narrative that contains a better balance, one that might combine the best elements of primordial woman: equality before God, harmony and intimacy between spouses, and woman's fulfillment as "mother of all the living."

Hannah, Woman of Words

In numerous ways, the story of Hannah functions as sequel to all the stories we have studied so far. Hannah's narrative begins the Book of Samuel, the next prophetic book after the Book of Judges. The story begins in a conventional way.

---

51. I am grateful to Shmuel Klitsner for drawing the connection between the two texts in relation to forbidden consumption.

There was a man from Ramathaim of the Zuphites, in the hill country of Ephraim whose name was Elkanah son of Joroham son of Elihu son of Tohu son of Zuph, an Ephraimite. He had two wives, one named Hannah and the other Peninnah; Peninnah had children, but Hannah was childless. This man used to go up from his town every year to worship and to offer sacrifice to the Lord of Hosts at Shiloh.—Hofni and Phinehas, the two sons of Eli, were priests of the Lord there.

One such day, Elkanah offered a sacrifice. He used to give portions to his wife Peninnah and to all her sons and daughters, but to Hannah he would give a double portion because he loved Hannah—for the Lord had closed her womb. Moreover, her rival, to make her miserable, would taunt her that the Lord had closed her womb. This happened year after year: Every time she went up to the House of the Lord, the other would taunt her, so that she wept and would not eat.[52] (1 Sam. 1:1–7)

At first, Hannah comes across as a composite of all the barren matriarchs of Genesis. Like Sarah, Hannah silently suffers as another woman produces children for her husband. Both Sarah and Hannah must stand aside as their fertile rivals challenge their position as "wife" (Gen. 16: 3; 1 Sam. 1: 4). Like all the matriarchs of Genesis, Hannah's infertility is ordained by God. But here, for the first time, this causality is stated in categorical terms. Instead of simply asserting that the female protagonist "was barren" (Gen. 11:30, 25:21; 29:31), the text unequivocally proclaims that "God had closed her womb" (1 Sam. 1: 5).[53] Like Sarah and Rachel, Hannah is ultimately redeemed by God: He "takes note," p-k-d (Gen. 21: 1; 1 Sam. 2: 21) and "remembers," z-kh-r her (Gen. 30: 22; 1 Sam. 1: 19).

But Hannah's story does not draw only on the anguished, often marginalized matriarchs of Genesis. In many ways it is modeled on the stories of the more empowered female figures we have seen such as Deborah, the intrepid "woman of torches" and Manoah's wife, God's chosen prophet. Like the early Rebekah and the heroines of the Book of Judges, Hannah will exhibit abilities more commonly associated with the patriarchs than with the matriarchs.

---

52. Author's translation.

53. Although the causality is not explicitly stated in the tales of the matriarchs of Genesis, it is strongly indicated at in the statement: He (God) "opened her womb" (Gen. 29:31; 30:22).

Assessing her situation, Hannah notes that it is God who has closed her womb; therefore only He can open it. Her husband, woman's traditional conduit to God, has resigned himself to her barrenness and will not plead her case for her:

> Her husband Elkanah said to her, "Hannah, why are you crying and why aren't you eating? Why are you so sad? Am I not more devoted to you than ten sons?" (1 Sam. 1:8)

While Elkanah is wonderfully sympathetic and loves his wife (1 Sam 1:5), we will see that his words do nothing to relieve Hannah's "wretchedness" (v. 10). Already the father of children, Elkanah expects Hannah to deem his love for her as compensation for her childlessness. With his rhetorical question, "Am I not more devoted to you than ten sons?" (v. 8) he implies that his love should be enough to complete her.

But Hannah yearns for more. Elkanah had intended to soothe Hannah into accepting her situation, but his words have the opposite effect, instead spurring her to action. Hannah now realizes that no one, not even her husband, will come to her aid. She has no choice but to look inward, to her own reserves of strength, and upward, to God.

Embarking on a previously uncharted path for biblical woman, Hannah formulates a proposition that will result in her bearing a child. Hannah seeks no mediation between herself and God. Instead she addresses Him directly.

> After they had eaten and drunk at Shiloh, Hannah rose.—The priest Eli was sitting on the seat near the doorpost of the temple of the LORD.—In her wretchedness, she prayed to the LORD, weeping all the while. And she made this vow: "O LORD of Hosts, if You will look upon the suffering of Your maidservant and will remember me and not forget Your maidservant, and if You will grant Your maidservant a male child, I will dedicate him to the Lord all the days of his life, and no razor shall ever touch his head." (1 Sam 1:9–11)

The early matriarchs remained largely silent before God in response to their barrenness. But Hannah's misery leads her directly to an outpouring of words. Although, as we will see in the coming verses, her words are inaudible to others, they are plentiful and rich.[54] In one verse alone, no fewer than five words

---

54. See *Berakhot* 31a-b, in which every aspect of Hannah's prayer is held up as a rabbinic standard of what prayer should be.

refer to Hannah's speech: *"va-titpallel, u-vakho tivke, va-tidor neder, va-tomar,* she **prayed,** she **cried** (with double language used), she **made a vow,"** and "she **said."** The first word used for her prayer, *va-titpallel,* is especially noteworthy. Throughout the trials of the matriarchs and the patriarchs, this term is used in only one context, when Abraham prays for the alleviation of infertility: *"va-yitpallel Avraham el ha-Elohim,* Abraham prayed to God" (Gen. 20: 17). But as we have seen, he does not offer his prayer for his own barren wife. He pleads only for the infertile court of Abimelech, King of Gerar. Now, in contrast with Sarah, who waited in vain for her husband's help, Hannah assumes responsibility for her own situation, undertaking a traditionally patriarchal action. For the very first time, a biblical woman calls out to God in order to conceive.

Perhaps because her actions are unprecedented, Eli, the High Priest does not recognize them as an act of prayer:

> As she kept on praying before the Lord, Eli watched her mouth. Now Hannah was praying in her heart; only her lips moved, but her voice could not be heard. So Eli thought she was drunk. Eli said to her, "How long will you make a drunken spectacle of yourself? Sober up!" And Hannah replied, "Oh no, my lord! I am a very unhappy woman. I have drunk no wine or other strong drink, but I have been pouring out my heart to the Lord. Do not take your maidservant for a worthless woman; I have only been speaking all this time out of my great anguish and distress." "Then go in peace," said Eli, "and may the God of Israel grant you what you have asked of Him." She answered, "You are most kind to your handmaid." So the woman left, and she ate, and was no longer downcast. Early next morning they bowed low before the Lord, and they went back home to Ramah. (1 Sam. 1:12–19)

In responding to Eli's suspicions, Hannah invokes yet another patriarchal term for speech, as she refers to her silent entreaty as *sihi,* from the root *s-v-h* (1 Sam. 1:16). This term recalls Isaac's meditative "speaking, *s-v-h*" to God in the field (Gen. 24:63), just prior to his first meeting with Rebekah. With her use of this word, Hannah continues in the tradition of Manoah's wife who occupied Isaac's *place* of prayer, the field. Now Hannah adopts the verb used for Isaac's *act* of prayer. Between them, these two women perform a matriarchal reenactment of Isaac's patriarchal deed.

Although in some ways the story of Hannah and that of Manoah's wife act in tandem to undermine the Genesis tales, the two narratives do not always complement one another. In fact, in one notable respect, the story of Hannah reverses the narrative of Manoah and his wife. In the story of Manoah and his wife, God approached a barren woman and offered her redemption by means of a trade: conception in exchange for the child's eternal devotion to God, as an ascetic nazirite. In Hannah's narrative, the results of her deal with God are very similar, as she too will overcome her barrenness by giving birth to a nazirite child. Yet the dynamics of the interaction with God are inverted. In this story, Hannah, and not God, initiates both the human-divine communication and the conditions of the bargain.

At long last, the greatly anticipated child is conceived and born.

> Elkanah knew his wife Hannah and the LORD remembered her. Hannah conceived, and at the turn of the year bore a son. She named him Samuel, meaning, "I asked the LORD for him." And when the man Elkanah and all his household were going up to offer to the LORD the annual sacrifice and his votive sacrifice, Hannah did not go up. She said to her husband, "When the child is weaned, I will bring him. For when he has appeared before the LORD, he must remain there for good." Her husband Elkanah said to her, "Do as you think best. Stay home until you have weaned him. May the LORD fulfill His word." So the woman stayed home and nursed her son until she weaned him. (1 Sam. 1:19–23)

In significant ways, Hannah's story acts as subversive sequel to many of the biblical narratives we have examined. To begin with, Hannah and Elkanah overturn the negative relationship of Adam and *Havvah* by replacing competitive struggle with cooperation. Like Adam, Elkanah "knew his wife" (Gen. 4:1). Like *Havvah*, Hannah names her child in triumph. But here the similarity ends and the reversal begins. Adam and *Havvah* had their child in the context of God's statement, "To your husband is your desire and he shall rule over you." We have seen that *Havvah* perpetuates the adversarial relationship between herself and her husband by attempting to counter-dominate. She names her child *Kayin*, from the Hebrew root *k-n-h*, "to acquire," suggesting her ownership of her husband and perhaps by extension, of her newborn son. In contrast to *Havvah*, Hannah eschews possession, suggesting that the child is not hers at all. Rather he is on loan from God (1 Sam. 1:27–28). Moreover, Elkanah's name—from the same *k-n-h* root—literally means "God has acquired." This story substitutes woman's ownership of man with God's, thereby further underscoring its message that human beings, who belong only to God, cannot acquire one another. The male protagonist Elkanah respects the newly cooperative status quo between husband and wife, deferring to Hannah in all matters related to their child. His words, "Do as you think best," (v. 23) recall God's instruction to Abraham, "Whatever Sarah tells you, heed her voice" (Gen. 21:12). But in this version of events, man does not wait for God to order him to heed his wife. Instead, he independently embraces the truth and wisdom of her views.

God too has embarked on a series of reversals since the Garden of Eden. Perhaps we will never know why, in the Bible's earliest chronicles, God excludes woman from His discourse. But as we have seen in the dramatic unfolding of the Bible's subversive sequels, God gradually draws her in from the periphery to the center of His conversation. We recall that God acts to include Sarah by speaking *of* her to Abraham. He then speaks directly *to* Rebekah, albeit in a one-time digression from His ongoing dialogue with the male prophet, Isaac. Later, God turns to two women, Deborah and Manoah's wife, as the preferred recipients of His messages. The story of Hannah extends woman's role even farther. The female protagonist no longer waits for signs of her election. Instead she becomes her own self-appointed pleader. In this point in the chain that makes up biblical woman's story, woman takes her own fearless first steps toward correcting her situation. But this time, man need not stumble in order for woman to maintain her balance. In this narrative, with God's guidance and support, both man and woman stride confidently and harmoniously in His direction.

Conclusion

Throughout the stories we have examined, the quest for fertility has acted as a catalyst for woman's development and as a traceable measure of her successes and failures in relation to God, herself, and the world around her. Childbirth lies at the core of woman's story, presenting not only her greatest challenge, but her greatest gift. To be "the mother of all the living" is to achieve a measure of eternity and of divine grandeur.

Yet in these narratives, biblical woman has taken many forms. She has been dependent and despondent; at times, in her impotence, she has flirted with a death wish. She has dwelled in the *ohel*, straining to overhear prophetic words that will determine her own future. Yet at other times, she has assumed patriarchal dimensions, exiting her tent and inhabiting the *sadeh*, the formerly patriarchal field. Overcoming a myriad of handicaps and vulnerabilities, biblical woman at times emerges a pragmatic and spiritual leader who exhibits authority and initiative, and who acts as conduit of God's messages to others.

While it may seem that achieving the status of patriarch is the greatest measure of woman's success, these narratives, when taken together, suggest that her primary journey is toward fulfillment as *matriarch*. In fact, we have found that many of the actions and positions traditionally associated with the patriarchy are deemed by the Bible to be authentically matriarchal as well. As the first chapters of Genesis attest, womanhood is expressed not only by living as mother and wife, but also by conquering and creating, by achieving unmediated access to God, and by living in full equality with man.

In addition to warning against too narrow a characterization of woman, these stories also insist that we not define motherhood too strictly. First, motherhood must not be viewed in a vacuum, as an end in itself to woman's search for meaning. If woman looks at motherhood as an act of acquisition designed to fill existential voids, she will never realize God's more encompassing plan for her development.

In a further caution against restrictive definitions, these narratives warn against defining motherhood exclusively as the biological act of childbearing. They demonstrate motherhood's larger parameters by including on their spectrum such women as Deborah the prophetess, who "mothers" her nation by tending to its spiritual and security needs. Later, the Book of Isaiah expands the boundaries of motherhood even more by instructing that the childless, too, are parents of sorts, achieving their slice of eternity by taking part in God's covenant: "I will give them, in My house and within My walls, a monument and a name better than sons or daughters. I will give them an everlasting name which shall not perish" (Isa. 56: 5).[55]

While expanding our definitions, a more comprehensive view of biblical woman warns against simplistic classifications and stereotype. In the sampling of stories we have perused, we have witnessed a transformation of the female character from a position of silent spiritual dependency to one of bold, verbal initiative. Although her story still contains disturbing elements, it signals a remarkable narrative undercurrent of re-examination and repair.[56]

The subversive sequel is a useful narrative model for the unfolding story of feminine achievement. As the Bible repeatedly sets up its paradigms and then takes

---

55. This passage is cited by Arama in his comments to the creation story in Genesis. See note 31.

56. Despite Hannah's great advances, it is noteworthy that God never directly addresses her. Moreover, Hannah speaks of her redemption as arriving with the birth of a "male child" (1 Sam. 1:11,20). These details suggest that this story too is incomplete and that the search for subversive sequels should continue.

artful aim at them, woman's story is constantly under review. In fact, no biblical woman may be labeled the definitive "biblical woman." In the expansive gamut of her occupations and preoccupations, biblical woman is righteous and she is wicked; she is martial leader and she is chattel; she is a victim of rape and violence and she is the perpetrator of sexual harassment and violence. Woman is prophet and prostitute; midwife and murderer; maidservant and monarch; litigant and judge; poet, songstress ... and blessedly, the mother of all the living.

Afterword

Throughout this book, I have sought to draw out the vibrant conversation taking place within the biblical canon rather than to view the Bible as a series of declarations. If texts *declare*, the results may be cogent, complex, and inspiring, but ultimately they may also be static, one-directional, and circumscribed. If, however, texts *converse*, the result is an invitation to creative engagement and to a perpetual reconsideration of assumptions and conclusions.

In the relatively fixed world of the medieval era, the canon was seen as primarily declarative. It was expertly mined for harmonious resolutions of textual difficulties and for the extraction of clear messages. With their meticulous attention to syntax, grammar, and context, the early commentators afforded readers access to the intricacies of the text and to a deeper understanding of the biblical medium and message.

But to allow the Bible to "speak in every language and in every age," an additional approach to Bible study is needed, one that meets the needs of our current age, in which assumptions and models are subject to a dizzying pace of review and revision. I have suggested a model of study in which the biblical canon itself is engaged in a process of self-scrutiny and reassessment. In this book, I have drawn on the intertextual model often used by the ancient midrashic exegetes. When deployed to its fullest, this approach allows us not only to read the Bible but to *hear* it, as a vibrant, at times discordant, and often vociferous discourse.

In this view, the Bible is oriented much more toward process than toward conclusions. As the Bible revisits vital issues and situations again and again, we, as readers, are called upon to be alert to its changes, and to search for signs of development from one narrative to the next. We learn to take note as characters, relationships, and moral challenges follow the path of a particular stream. Then further down their often turbulent course, they are suspended, re-examined, and rerouted toward new directions. In this mode of interpretation, texts are regularly filtered through changing sensibilities, circumstances, and experiences, revealing new layers of meaning. This process is reminiscent of the dynamic nature of the Oral Law.

The rabbis of the Talmud conducted a skilled negotiation between the Bible's words and the pragmatic and moral concerns presented by changing historical circumstances. The result often appears to be a subversive reframing of the law from its initial plain meaning. Paradoxically, the frequently innovative readings that characterize the Oral Law were often employed to ensure the enduring relevance of a fixed, sacred text. It was only through subversive reinterpretation that biblical law sustained its applicability in a dynamic reality. Thus, time and again, innovation preserves tradition.

I have suggested in this volume that as devoted students of the Bible we expect no less from its narratives than we do from its laws. By exploring the dynamically subversive nature of the intra-biblical discourse, we become privy to a constant negotiation and renegotiation, a distilling and often a refinement of ethical positions. As with the Oral Law, these reworkings help to ensure, rather than undermine, the sacred and enduring stature of the text.

My role in exposing the conversation among texts has been twofold. First, I have acted as moderator, pitting certain passages against others and letting them converse. In addition, I have inevitably brought my own perspective to these conversations, that of a 21st-century reader who is both profoundly influenced by tradition and deeply affected by a modern feminist and universal ethos. Some might question the authenticity of reading the ancient text through an unabashedly modern prism. According to this thinking, exegetical efforts would be more wisely expended in an effort at faithful recovery of the elusive original intent of an ancient document. But the vibrant discourse begun by the text suggests that the conversation is meant to continue. If we are truly to search for original intent, perhaps the closest we might get is to be true to the text's own dynamic nature. Thus, following the Bible's own model, we continue to interpret in line with a changing reality even after the canon has been closed.

In reexamining textual attitudes from a modern perspective, I have focused on issues I consider to be in most urgent need of renegotiation. In this volume I have addressed concerns such as gender relations, Jewish attitudes toward non-Jews, relationship to self and to community. My studies have been guided by a deep belief in the Bible's profundity, dynamism, and enduring relevance. These convictions are so strong as to render impossible the notion that any modern issue can leave the Bible behind.

To return to the analogy with the Oral Law, the great 20th-century Jewish philosopher Eliezer Berkovits has defined authentic *halakhah*, Jewish law, in a way that resonates with this volume's subversive sequels. He notes that two primary functions of Jewish law are to "render the Torah ethically significant and spiritually meaningful ... in a given historic situation."[1] Berkovits supports his conclusion by citing a talmudic discussion about the verse in Psalms, "I shall walk before the Lord in the lands of the living." Of this verse, Rabbi Yehudah remarked: "The lands of the living? These are the market places" (*Yoma* 71a). Berkovits views this remark as no less than a philosophy of Judaism:

> What is authentic Judaism? It is the application of Torah to the "market plac-es" of our existence, to the historic reality and uniqueness of our contempo-rary situation. This is the very essence of the *Halakhah*. There is no other way to walk before God in the lands of the living.[2]

The Bible is not only our primary source of Jewish law. It is the foundational text of Jewish philosophy, ethics, history, and myth. As such, it must set the stan-dard for enduring relevance. In order to retain its beauty throughout the changing landscape of history, the Bible must be constantly and vigorously interpreted in line with an ever-dynamic reality. In Heschel's words, "The Bible is a seed, God is the sun, but we are the soil. Every generation is expected to bring forth new under-standing and new realization."[3]

1. Berkovits, "Authentic Judaism," 72.
2. Ibid., 76.
3. Heschel, *God in Search of Man,* 274.

Bibliography

Alter, Robert. *The Art of Biblical Narrative*. New York: Basic Books, 1981.

———. *Genesis, Translation and Commentary*. New York: W.W. Norton and Company, 1996.

———. "Introduction to the Old Testament." In *The Literary Guide to the Bible*, edited by Robert Alter and Frank Kermode, 11–35. Cambridge: Harvard University Press, 1987.

Anisfeld, Rachel. "The Generation of Bavel: A Misguided Unity." *Bikkurim: Midreshet Lindenbaum Torah Journal* (May 1990): 7–17.

Arnow, David. "Reflections on Jonah and Yom Kippur," *Conservative Judaism* 54, no. 4, (summer 2002): 33–48.

Bal, Mieke. *Lethal Love*. Bloomington: Indiana Press, 1987.

Berkovits, Eliezer. "Authentic Judaism and Halakhah." *Judaism* 19, no. 1 (Winter 1970): 66–76.

Berlin, Adele, and Brettler, Marc Zvi. *The Jewish Study Bible*. New York: Oxford University Press, 2004.

Besdin, Abraham R. *Reflections of the Rav*. Jerusalem: Alpha Press, 1979.

Breuer, Mordechai. *Pirkei Beresheit*. Alon Shvut: Tevunot, 1999.

Brown, Francis, Driver, S.R., and Briggs, Charles A. *A Hebrew and English Lexicon of the Old Testament*. Oxford: Oxford University Press, 1906.

Bruns, Gerald. "Midrash and Allegory: The Beginnings of Scriptural Interpretation." In *The Literary Guide to the Bible*, edited by Robert Alter and Frank Kermode, 625–46. Cambridge: Harvard University Press, 1987.

Buber, Martin. "Abraham the Seer." In *On the Bible*, edited by Nahum N. Glatzer, 22–43. New York: Schocken Books, 1968.

Buber, Martin, and Franz Rosenzweig. "Leitwort Style in the Pentateuch." In *Scripture and Translation*, translated by Lawrence Rosenwald and Everett Fox. Bloomington: Indiana University Press, 1994.

———."The Question to the Single One." In *The Writings of Martin Buber*, edited by Will Herberg, 63–88. New York: Meridian Books, 1956.

Cassuto, Umberto. *Commentary to the Book of Genesis.* Jerusalem: Magnes Press, 1978 (in Hebrew).

———. *Commentary on Exodus.* Jerusalem: Magnes Press, 1967.

Ehrlich, Arnold. *Mikra Kifshuto.* Berlin: Poppelauer, 1900; Jerusalem, 1969.

Fokkelman, J.P. *Narrative Art in Genesis.* Oregon: Wipf and Stock Publishers, 1992.

Fromm, Eric. *Escape from Freedom.* New York: Avon, 1969.

———. *To Have or to Be?* New York: Bantam Books, 1976.

Fox, Everett. *The Five Books of Moses.* New York: Schocken Books, 1995.

Heschel, Abraham Joshua. *God in Search of Man.* New York: Harper and Row Publishers, 1995.

Idel, Moshe. *Kabbalah, New Perspectives.* New Haven: Yale University Press, 1988.

Klitsner, Judy. "From the Earth's Hollow Spaces to the Stars." In *The Torah of the Mothers,* edited by Ora Wiskind Elper and Susan Handelman, 262–88. Jerusalem: Urim Publishers, 2000.

Klitsner, Shmuel. *Wrestling Jacob: Deception, Identity, and Freudian Slips in Genesis.* Jerusalem: Urim Publishers, 2006.

Korn, Eugene. "Tradition Meets Modernity: On Liberty—and Halakah." *Tradition: A Journal of Orthodox Jewish Thought* 25, no. 4 (Summer 1991): 30–47.

Leibowitz, Nehama. *New Studies in Shemot.* Jerusalem: The World Zionist Organization, 1981.

———. *The Study of Bible Commentators and Methods of Teaching Them: Genesis.* Jerusalem: The World Zionist Organization, 1975 (in Hebrew).

Leibowitz, Yeshayahu. *Judaism, the Jewish Nation, and the State of Israel.* Jerusalem: Schocken Books, 1975 (in Hebrew).

Lockshin, Martin. *Rabbi Samuel ben Meir's Commentary on Genesis.* Queenston: Edwin Mellon Press, 1989.

———. "A Bible Commentary for the 21st Century?" *The Canadian Jewish News,* February 15, 2007, 9.

Marx, Karl. "Alienated Labor." In *Karl Marx Early Writings,* edited and translated by T.B. Bottomore, 120–134. New York: McGraw Hill Book Company, 1964.

Muffs, Yohanan. *The Personhood of God.* Vermont: Jewish Lights Publishing, 2005.

Orwell, George. *1984.* New York: Penguin Books, 1950.

Pardes, Ilana. *Countertraditions in the Bible, a Feminist Approach.* Cambridge: Harvard University Press, 1992.

Reiner, Yitshak. *Mo'adei Nehama.* Jerusalem: The Jewish Agency for Israel, 2005.

Sarna, Nahum. *Exploring Exodus.* New York: Schocken Books, 1986.

———. *Understanding Genesis*. New York: Schocken Books, 1966.

———. *The JPS Torah Commentary, Exodus*. Philadelphia: The Jewish Publication Society, 1991.

———. *The JPS Torah Commentary, Genesis*. Philadelphia: The Jewish Publication Society, 1989.

Shapiro, David S. *Studies in the Jewish Thought*. New York; Yeshiva University Press, 1975.

Simon, Uriel. *Mikra le-Yisrael: Jonah and Obadiah*. Tel Aviv: Am Oved, 1992.

Skinner, John. *The International Critical Commentary on Genesis*. Edinburgh: T. & T. Clark, 1930.

Soloveitchik, Joseph. "The Lonely Man of Faith." *Tradition* 7, no. 2 (Summer 1965): 5–67.

Trible, Phyllis. *God and the Rhetoric of Sexuality*. Philadelphia: Fortress Press, 1978.

———. "Depatriarchalizing in Biblical Interpretation." In *The Jewish Woman: New Perspectives*, edited by Elizabeth Kolton, 217–36. New York: Schocken Books, 1976.

Wolosky, Shira. "The Lonely Woman of Faith." *Judaism* 52, nos. 1–2 (Winter-Spring 2003): 3–18.

Zakovich, Yair. *Through the Looking Glass: Reflection Stories in the Bible*. Tel Aviv: Hakibbutz Hameuchad Publishing House, 1995 (in Hebrew).

Classical Jewish Sources

Abravanel, Don Isaac (1437–1508), Portugal, Spain. Expelled from Spain in 1492, Abravanel was a philosopher, statesman, and biblical exegete. In his commentary, he cites many Christian sources.

Akedat Yitzhak Commentary to the Pentateuch of Isaac Arama (1420–1494), Spain. Arama wrote his philosophic commentary to the Pentateuch at the time of the expulsion from Spain.

Babylonian Talmud (BT) A fundamental Jewish text that is an interpretation and elaboration of the Mishnah, prepared by the teachers (*amoraim*) in the great academies of Babylon. The Talmud, which is customarily dated between the 3rd and 5th centuries C.E., contains both legal sections (*halakhah*) and homiletic sections (*aggadah*).

Ha-amek Davar Commentary to the Pentateuch of Naftali Zvi Yehuda Berlin, known by the acronym, Netziv. A talmudic scholar, Netziv (1817–1893), headed the illustrious yeshiva in Volozhin (today, part of Belarus), where he introduced regular Bible study. He sought to harmonize the talmudic interpretation of the Bible text with its plain meaning and often added psychological layers to his interpretations of the behavior of biblical characters.

Ibn Ezra, Abraham (1089–1164), Spain. A poet, philologist, grammarian, astronomer, mathematician, philosopher, and exegete, Ibn Ezra's style is concise and often enigmatic; he places great emphasis on the importance of rational thought in biblical interpretation.

Jerusalem Talmud Compiled in the Land of Israel approximately a century before the Babylonian Talmud. Although there are many important differences between the two, both Talmuds are essentially the results of amoraic discussion and elaboration of the Mishnah.

Kaspi, Joseph (1279–1340), France. A philosopher, biblical commentator, grammarian, and prolific writer, Kaspi admired Rambam's methods of synthesizing religion and reason.

Kimhe, R. David, known by his acronym Radak (1160–1235), France. The most famous member of a family of exegetes, Kimhe concentrated on philology, syntax, and the order of passages, while making strict distinctions between *peshat* (the plain meaning of the verse) and *derash* (homiletic readings of the text).

Malbim An acronym of Meir Loeb ben Jehilel Michel (1809–1880), Russia. Malbim's exegesis is based on strong linguistic principles, the most central of which is his belief that no two biblical words have identical meanings. A staunch opponent of reform, Malbim sought to prove the fundamental centrality of the Oral Law.

Midrash A genre of extremely varied rabbinic literature compiled from the 5th through the 12th centuries c.e. Midrash can be *aggadic* or *halakhic* in nature. *Aggadic* midrash may offer expansions on biblical verses based on sermons given by the early rabbis; it can be exegetical as well. *Halakhic* midrash deals primarily with laws derived from the Bible. Exact dating of individual midrashim is difficult and is often derived from noting a source's citation of earlier midrashic works.

In this volume, we have drawn from the following midrashim:

Mekhilta of R. Ishmael—a tannaitic midrash (from the rabbis of the Mishnah, 1st to 2nd century c.e.) on Exodus, containing *halakhic* and *aggadic* interpretation.

Midrash Eliyyahu Rabbah—an *aggadic* work from approximately the 8th century c.e.

Midrash Genesis Rabbah—one of the earliest midrashim, compiled in approximately the 5th century c.e.

Midrash Ha-Gadol—midrash to the Pentateuch and Scrolls, from ancient tannaitic sources, compiled in the 13th century c.e.

Midrash Petirat Moshe—*aggadic* work compiled approximately in 7th to 8th century c.e.

Midrash Pirkei de-Rabbi Eliezer—*aggadic* work compiled approximately in 750 C.E.

Midrash Song of Songs Rabbah—homiletic midrash compiled approximately in the 6th to 7th century C.E.

Midrash Tanhuma—compilation of homiletic midrashim containing many sayings attributed to Rabbi Tanhuma (4th century C.E.), who was a prolific *aggadist.*

Yalkut Shimoni—midrashic anthology compiled in the 12th century C.E.

Meshekh Hokhma, R. Meir Simha Ha-Cohen of Dvinsk (1843–1926), Russia. In his biblical commentary, R. Meir Simha combines his vast talmudic knowledge with a philosophic approach to basic principles in Judaism.

Mishnah This foundational Jewish text from the tannaitic era lays out the Oral Law, a multivalent interpretation, expansion, and companion to the Written Law of the Bible. The Mishnah is divided into six sections called "orders," which are subdivided into 63 tractates. The Mishnah was codified and redacted at the beginning of the 3rd century C.E. by R. Judah Ha-Nasi.

Or Ha-hayyim Commentary on the Pentateuch of Hayyim ibn Attar (1696–1743), Morocco. He was a noted kabbalist and talmudist who led a migration of his disciples to the Land of Israel.

Rambam, R. Moses ben Maimon (1135–1204), Spain. The most influential figure in post-talmudic Jewish history, Rambam was a philosopher, codifier, explicator of Jewish law, and a biblical exegete. He was a leader of Egyptian Jewry and a renowned physician.

Ramban, R. Moses ben Nahman (1194–1274), Spain. Ramban's commentary to the Bible includes Jewish thought and Jewish law; it incorporates *peshat* and *derash* and includes mystical interpretation. Ramban often cites interpretations of his predecessors—most frequently Rashi and Ibn Ezra—then takes issue and presents his own perspectives. Ramban's commentary displays a literary sensitivity and a profound psychological understanding of textual characters.

Rashbam, R. Shemuel Ben Meir (1080–1160), France. The grandson of Rashi, Rashbam was a talmudist and biblical exegete. In his commentary on the Bible, Rashbam sought the "deep" *peshat* of the text, a plain reading that was more independent of rabbinic homilies than was that of his grandfather.

Rashi, R. Shelomo Yitzhaki (1040–1105), France. Rashi remains the pre-eminent medieval exegete of the Bible and Talmud. His Bible commentary combines an encyclopedic knowledge of the Bible with an ability to succinctly instruct on matters related to the *peshat*, or plain sense of the biblical text. In his frequent use of midrashim, he carefully selects those that help interpret the text over those that provide educational or moral homilies.

Seforno, Obadiah (1470–1550), Italy. Seforno was a doctor, philosopher, philologist, and mathematician. Although his commentary tends toward the plain sense of the text and frequently excludes aggadic interpretation, it includes midrashic comments that relate to moral behavior.

Siftei HaKhamim Super-commentary to Rashi of Shabbetai ben Joseph Bass (1641–1718), Poland. The well-traveled, multi-faceted Bass was a singer and the first Jewish bibliographer.

Torah Shelema An encyclopedic midrashic compilation and commentary written by Mehahem Kasher (1895–1983). This work cites verse-by-verse comments to the Pentateuch that are collected from the Oral Law. Kasher includes source material previously accessible only in manuscript form and adds his own notes, expositions, and supplements.

Tosefta A collection of tannaitic material not included in the Mishnah. The Tosefta is arranged according to the order of the Mishnah and, for the most part, runs parallel to it.

Zohar First published in 13th century Spain, the Zohar is the principal tract of the mystical discipline of Kabbalah. It is attributed to, and purported to record many of the sayings of, the Tanna R. Shimon B. Yohai.

Index of Subjects

L

laughter
    of Abraham, 124
    of Sarah, 125–127, 129
leaders
    burdens of, 86–87
    characteristics of, 4–5, 7, 52, 64, 75, 80, 83–
        84, 91, 153, 168
leadership models, 78
lefanai, 16
lehem, 85
leitwort, xixn6, 34, 61n79
lekh lekha, 41, 65, 66, 73, 78, 120, 137, 146
Lemekh, 4
levadekha, 86, 87, 89
leveinim, 35, 49
literary approach to Bible study, xvii
lo, 54, 56
lo tov, 86, 87, 88
Lockshin, Martin, xxx, 117n18, 118n20, 160n48
Lot, 67

M

m-g-n
    root used by God, 74
    root used by Melchizedek, 85n35
m-h-r
    in Abraham narrative, 139
    in Rebekah narrative, 139–140
ma'aseh merkavah, xviii
mah zot
    in Abraham-Sarah narrative, 119, 120
    in Garden of Eden narrative, 119
Maimonides, 44
Makhpelah, Cave of, 132
man
    creation of, 97–98
    loneliness of, 98–100
    mortality of, 108
Manoah
    asking angel's name, 46–47
    obtuseness of, 160, 161n49
    seeking divine message, 159–161
Manoah, wife of

    infertility of, 157
    receiving divine message, 158–160, 163
meditation, 140–141
Melchizedek
    and Covenant between the Pieces, 73–75, 77
    as non-Jewish priest, 63
    characteristics of, 75
    influence on Abraham, 70–71, 74–77, 91
    meaning of name, 69
    moral nature of, 69, 71
mem (letter)
    as conjunction, 156
    as preposition, 53
men
    listening to wives, 131
    relying on women, 150, 153–154, 168
messengers
    announcing Sarah's pregnancy, 124–125
    non-Jewish, of God, 17, 93–94
Messianic era, 109
mi-lifnei, 16
midwives, in Exodus narrative, 56–62
Moses
    appointing judges, 86–87
    dying outside of Canaan, 83, 89–90
    flight to Midian, 80–81
    individuality of, 80, 82–83, 90
    interceding on behalf of Israel, 6
    joining society, 84–87
    rescue of by women, 61–62, 78–79
    rescuing women at well, 84
    striking Egyptian, 80–83
    striking rock, 89–90
mot tamut
    in Abimelech narrative, 128
    in Garden of Eden story, 128
Mt. Sinai, covenant at, literary elements of, 77
Muffs, Yochanan, xxivn20, xxvn23, xxivn

N

n-h-m
    in Jonah narrative, 10–11
    in Noah narrative, 4, 10
Nabal, 47

Index of Biblical and Rabbinic Sources

LaVergne, TN USA
26 July 2010
190972LV00005B/1/P